An Introduction to

The Law of Trusts

GW00726135

An Introduction to

The Law of Trusts

Paul Todd, MA, BCL

of the Faculty of Law, University College, Cardiff

Financial Training

First published in Great Britain 1986 by Financial Training Publications
Limited, Avenue House, 131 Holland Park Avenue, London W11 4UT.

©Paul Todd, 1986

ISBN: 1 85185 021 X

Typeset by Kerrypress Ltd, Luton, Beds
Printed by Dotesios Printers Ltd, Bradford-upon-Avon, Wilts

All rights reserved. No part of this book may be reproduced or transmitted in any
form or by any means, electronic or mechanical, including photocopying,
recording, or any information storage or retrieval system without prior
permission from the publisher.

Contents

Preface

This is intended as an introductory book, aimed primarily at law students in their second or third year of study. The aim has been to state the law as shortly and clearly as possible, without (I hope) sacrificing clarity of exposition in the more complex areas.

Concentration is on principle rather than detail, because it is easy to allow obsession with detail to obscure the main principles. I have confined detailed coverage to those areas which are commonly covered in trusts courses at university level, rather than attempting to encompass, for example, the entire law of trusts and equity. This is partly because most undergraduate courses themselves concentrate on trusts, and partly because general equitable concepts are somewhat miscellaneous, and are usually covered on other courses (e.g., land law, contract and the English legal system).

A common difficulty with the law of trusts is that it seems to (some!) students to be further removed from the everyday world than other subjects, a major (but by no means the only) role of the trust being a device to enable the wealthy to hang on to their wealth. Sometimes, in particular, students are confused by the terminology, especially in the cases; sometimes they cannot see the point of certain types of transaction. I have tried to explain these. Some of the legal concepts are also fairly abstract, and I have tried to explain such concepts as fully as possible.

Where controversy as to the law exists, I have usually stated that it does, and then given either the orthodox view or my own view. These may not be the only views that can be held, but students who wish to pursue the controversy further will find the main cases and articles referred to in the relevant section.

Finally, a great many trustees and beneficiaries today are women. This was not the case until a hundred years or so ago, but is especially so now that many matrimonial homes, and homes of unmarried cohabitees, are in joint names, or where at least wives and female cohabitees contribute to the purchase money of their home. The use of 'he or she' can lead to clumsy sentences, however, quite apart from greatly lengthening the book. So I have used 'he' throughout as shorthand, and not because of any assumption that those about whom I am talking are, or should be, male.

I should like to thank my wife, Dr Pauline Todd, who teaches trusts at University College, Cardiff, for the very substantial assistance she has given me in writing this book, especially in the later chapters. Without her assistance, the book could not have been written on time, if at all, and would probably have appeared full of errors. I should also like to thank those of my colleagues whom I have badgered into reading and commenting on individual chapters and sections, especially Philip Wylie, who made helpful suggestions about chapter 13. Finally, I found the comments of Roy Heywood, of Wildy and Sons (Law Booksellers), London, on the likely market for an introductory trusts book very helpful.

I have frequently ignored the advice of my wife and other colleagues, so all errors and omissions are down to me. The law is stated as at 20 February 1986.

Table of Cases

Table of Statutes

1

History and Outline of Equitable Jurisdiction

1.1 DIVISION OF OWNERSHIP INTO LEGAL AND EQUITABLE ELEMENTS

A surprising feature of English law, and one that is peculiar to it, is that it has two completely different concepts of ownership of property. Even more surprising is that both types of ownership can arise simultaneously. In other words, a single item can be owned, and frequently is, at the same time, by more than one person in more than one way.

Most personal property (i.e., goods) is owned by one person absolutely, and in that case the ownership of the item is not split up. It will be, however, where a person (or persons) holds property on trust for another (or others). In the simplest variety of trust, there will be two people simultaneously owning the property, though the relationship of each to it will be quite different. There is a legal owner, who is called a trustee. He has essentially a management role, and is subject to quite stringent duties. There is also an equitable owner, who is called a cestui que trust, or beneficiary. It is the beneficiary who is entitled to enjoy the property, and whose position is therefore closest to being what a layman might consider to be an owner. It is to the beneficiary that the trustee's duties are owed, and he can enforce them against the trustee.

Figure 1.1 is a diagrammatic representation of this division of ownership.

Figure 1.1

	A is absolute owner	A holds on trust for B
Legal title	A	A (Trustee)
Equitable title	A	B (Beneficiary or cestui que trust)

Everything that is capable of being owned is capable of being held in trust. This includes not only goods, and freehold and leasehold estates in land, but also lesser interests. For example, it is possible to own a right of way over the land of another (this is an example of an easement), and rights of way can be held in trust. It is even possible for the beneficiary's equitable ownership itself to be held in trust, in which case a subtrust is created.

1.1.1   Terminological difficulties over land

The purpose of this section is simply to clarify terms which are used later on. All the above applies to land, as well as goods, money, shares, etc. However, for technical reasons, which for the most part do not affect the law of trusts (in so far as they do they are summarised in section 1.2.7 below), it is not possible to own land. This may also come as a surprise to students who are unfamiliar with land law. The technical position is that one can have title to an estate in land. The term title, for the purposes of this book, can be taken to mean the same as ownership; i.e., the differences between title and ownership are irrelevant to the law of trusts. The title is not to the land itself, however, but to an estate in land. Title to an estate can be divided, by means of a trust, into separate legal and equitable elements.

An estate in land can be regarded as a right to possess land for a period of time. Leasehold estates, for example, are often for a fixed number of weeks, months or years. The period of time can be infinite, as with the usual freehold estate, which is called the fee simple absolute in possession—this is the estate most people buy when purchasing freehold property. But there are also lesser freehold estates. For example, a settlement of land, intended to keep the land in the family, may be in the form of a life estate to the surviving widow, followed by a fee simple in favour of the eldest son. Both the widow and eldest son have estates immediately, even though the son has no right to possess the land yet. All settlements must inevitably contain an estate which does not give an immediate right to possession. It is also possible to have entailed estates, which pass automatically on death, usually to a male heir, and which cannot therefore be left by will.

Subject to the provisions of the 1925 property legislation, which is discussed in section 1.6, it is possible for estates in land to be held in trust, thereby splitting legal and equitable title. The real point of this section, however, is to explain the terms that will be used when talking about trusts involving land, and why I shall not refer to ownership of land, except on occasions as a convenient shorthand.

1.2   EARLY HISTORY OF EQUITY

This book is about trusts, not about equity in general. Yet the concept of the trust is derived from equitable principles; it is indeed equity's central concept, and it is therefore necessary to understand equity at least in general terms.

In effect the English legal system divides into common law and equity: two different systems and until recently two separate jurisdictions. Equity and trusts are found exclusively in England and in other non-Roman legal systems, and neither has any place, for example, on the Continent. That a legal system should develop two separate concepts of ownership, both of which can apply simultaneously to the same property, and effectively two separate legal systems, is by no means self-evident. The reason lies in historical differences between England and Continental countries, dating from the feudal era, and in particular the Norman Conquest.

1.2.1 Feudalism and the Norman Conquest

Though equity is English in origin, and though it developed as an incidental result of feudalism, feudalism was by no means an exclusively English phenomenon. Indeed, although feudalism existed even before 1066 in England, it was probably more developed on the Continent at this time, and it was a modified form of European feudalism that was imposed on England by the Norman Conquest.

Furthermore, true feudalism in England did not last very long after 1066; in its original form it was inefficient, and so had pretty well died out by around 1150, long before the conception of equity. It is nonetheless important in the development of equity, because of its indirect consequences, especially regarding methods of holding land. These resulted, for example, in transfers of land at common law becoming very difficult, and hence to the impetus for the growth of a new and separate system, of equity, the principles of which remain today. Other indirect consequences, such as the development of the doctrine of estates, and leasehold title, are mainly of interest of land lawyers.

In pre-feudal times land was owned absolutely. The essence of the feudal system was that, in relatively lawless times, landowners collectively and for their mutual protection bound themselves to an overlord, who was often a military expert, offering service (often of a military nature) or produce in exchange for protection. Eventually the land became held on condition that services or produce was provided, and tenure of land became the exclusive bond between overlord and tenant. The system probably developed faster in Europe than in England because of a greater degree of anarchy overseas at that time.

Feudal structures were initially developed well before 1066, possibly by the smallholders themselves, rather than externally imposed upon them. Though feudalism became universal, it was not centralised; each great estate or manor had its own overlord and its own law and customs. It is true that the Crown in Europe granted some of its own land to lords in exchange for money or military services, so the Crown became supreme lord of some, but not all, of the land. But the system was essentially *ad hoc*, and indeed came into being *because of* the lawlessness resulting from the lack of a strong central government.

The peculiarity of English feudalism after 1066 came about because the chief landowners forcibly resisted the attempt of William I to assert supremacy over them. William therefore confiscated all land following his successful conquest, and subsequently allowed it to be held (or often redeemed) only from the Crown (directly by overlords) in exchange for money or services. So *all* land came to be held from the Crown in exchange for money or services. It is still technically so held, though the services have usually not been collected for so long that they are barred by limitation (i.e., time-barred). Thus in England alone feudal land tenure became centralised, and was imposed from above with the Crown as supreme landlord.

The large landowners or overlords, holding directly (or immediately) from the Crown, allowed others to hold from them, also as tenants in exchange for personal services. These tenants thus held *immediately* from their lords, and *mediately* from the Crown. They allowed yet others to hold some of their land from them on similar bases, and so on, so large tenurial chains developed. Figure 1.2 is a simplified diagrammatic representation.

Figure 1.2

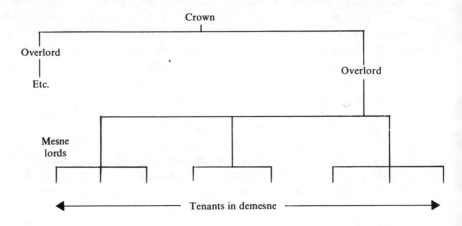

As can be seen from the diagram, those who held from other lords, and were not themselves in occupation, were called 'mesne lords'. It is likely that many of those at the bottom of these chains ('tenants in demesne') had been holding the same land, from the same immediate lords, before the Conquest; though some evidence of dispossessions has recently come to light, a large-scale movement of people would surely have achieved little. So for many the effect of the Conquest was merely to add the Crown to the top of the chain.

1.2.2 *Quia Emptores* 1290

The creation of subtenancies in this way was called 'subinfeudation', whereas an out-and-out transfer of a tenancy (which was not originally allowed) was called 'substitution'. Eventually the system became so complex that it created problems for the overlords in collecting their feudal dues, and subinfeudation was therefore abolished (except for the Crown) by the statute *Quia Emptores* 1290. This statute is still in force, having survived an attempt to repeal it in 1967, and is often regarded as being a pillar of the law of real property. After 1290, therefore, no new freehold subtenancies could be created; those existing remained (a few still remain in rural areas where manorial lords remained active) but as the feudal dues became less valuable many of the intermediate lords did not bother to collect them, and eventually were time-barred. The result is that today nearly all land is held directly from the Crown.

1.2.3 Demise of feudalism

The original services were personal in nature; tenure was therefore for life only, and was inalienable. It soon became clear, however, that it was more efficient to allow families to remain in possession of land over successive generations if they so wished, or if they did not to allow them to alienate (e.g., sell) the land and to convert the services into money payments, with which equivalent services could be hired in the general market. Certainly this was a better way, for example, of raising armies, because it mattered that the best soldiers were recruited, and they were not necessarily, after the first generation, holding land on military tenures. Unfortunately (for the lords at any rate), as soon as services became converted into money payments, they quickly lost their value through inflation; it is for this reason that most feudal dues had lost their economic value by about 1150, and were not collected for so long that they became time-barred. Many remaining dues were eventually abolished by the Tenures Abolition Act 1660, after the Civil War. The Crown was the main beneficiary by then, as supreme landlord, of the remaining feudal incidents; they were abolished because they effectively constituted extra-parliamentary revenue for the Crown, and military tenures promoted the creation of private armies.

1.2.4 The remaining feudal dues

Nevertheless, though the value of the services themselves diminished, important feudal incidents remained long after 1150. For example, the lord was entitled to payment on succession of land to an heir, and to the right of escheat if a tenant died without an heir, which meant that the land reverted to him. He was also entitled to various rights when the land was held by a minor. As long as any feudal dues remained valuable the lords desired to protect them, and rules about title to land at common law were developed to aid this process. Many of the rights arose on the death of a tenant, especially if there was no heir or the heir was a minor, and could have been avoided by conveying the land to younger adult members of the family, or leaving the land by will. For this reason taxes were imposed upon conveyances, and until 1540 freehold estates could not be left by will. It was also important to be able to ascertain who held the land, so until at least 1535 transfers of land at common law had to be open and notorious, whereas many people preferred secret transfers. For similar reasons it was necessary for all conveyances to take immediate effect, so future interests (and therefore settlements) could not be created at common law until 1540.

1.2.5 Discretion of the medieval Chancellor, and early equity

The rigidity of many legal systems is mitigated by discretionary executive power. In England and Wales today, for example, there is a great deal of executive discretion in both prosecution and sentencing under a criminal law which, if rigidly enforced, could be very burdensome, even for relatively law-abiding individuals. The medieval Chancellor (who was usually an ecclesiastic) performed an analogous function in relation to the rigidity of the common law at the time; he had the power to issue the royal writs, and this function came to be exercised in a discretionary manner, based on notions of conscience and justice. He also had powers to act against individuals, and to enforce his orders against them by imprisonment. This discretionary use of power was the foundation of equity. Eventually, probably during the 15th century, the Chancellor's office took on many of the features of a court, and the Court of Chancery was born.

Equity originally developed to avoid the restrictions placed on transfers by the common law, and to avoid feudal dues. Its character in this regard has not altered significantly to this day; equitable doctrines still develop where common law doctrines are regarded as inflexible. For example, a new equitable interest in land, the restrictive covenant, was created in 1848 (*Tulk* v *Moxhay* (1848) 2 Ph 774), partly because the common law easement, though well-suited to rural economies, was insufficiently flexible to deal with the growth of urban residential land. More recently, though equity no longer retains the full extent of its original flexibility, the promissory estoppel doctrine has been used to mitigate the supposed rigidity of common law consideration in contract. There are also current developments in land law, whose eventual outcome is still uncertain, in an attempt to avoid the rigours of common law privity of contract: the contractual and estoppel licence and possibly a new variety of the constructive trust. It should also not be forgotten that the trust has always been, and is, essentially a tax avoidance device (see chapter 13), just as early equitable intervention was used as a device to avoid feudal dues.

The Chancellor's power could theoretically be exercised without altering the substance of the common law, though in practice his jurisdiction significantly affected the exercise of common law rights. For example, he might refuse to issue a writ to a claimant at common law, or compel a common law owner to convey his property to someone else. One might have thought that conflict between the two systems was therefore inevitable, but it should be remembered that in these early days the common law was not itself a very well-defined system, and it was not thought odd that the King, through the Chancellor, should exercise a residual discretion. Conflicts between common law and equity did eventually arise, but not until some centuries later.

1.2.6 Uses

One of the most important early developments was the use, which was the predecessor of the modern trust. In fact, even before the Conquest, land was sometimes held by one person on behalf of another for a particular purpose or use. General uses originated probably around or before 1230: land was conveyed to X to the use of Y, where, for example, Y was a community of Franciscan friars which at that time was not allowed to hold property. Later uses became more common, generally as conveyancing devices, often specifically to avoid the common law restrictions. The difficulty was that X had legal title; the common law did not recognise the use. Clearly, however, Y was intended to enjoy the property. From about 1400 the Chancellor ensured, by acting on the conscience of X, that X held the land for the benefit of Y. X, who became known as the 'feoffee to uses', therefore retained legal title, and indeed the common law was theoretically unaffected, but Y, the 'cestui que use', came to be regarded as equitable owner. Hence the division of ownership (or title), and hence the development of two separate legal systems.

The device was used to avoid the feudal dues described above; the legal estate could be vested in a number of feoffees to uses as joint tenants. Jointly held estates pass automatically to the survivors on the death of a joint tenant, so it was possible to avoid the dues on death and ensure that a minor never had title at common law, while allowing equitable title to pass from (say) father to son on the father's death. Legal estates also rarely needed to be transferred, because the joint tenants at law held the land merely in a nominal, or managerial role, the right to enjoy the property taking effect behind the use. It was also possible to devise the equitable estate, and to create settlements by means of future interests.

Figure 1.3 is a diagrammatic representation of legal and equitable titles during a possible transfer over four generations. Ideally, legal title should not have needed to be transferred at all.

1.2.7 Equity follows the law

One of the consequences of the early feudal tenurial system was that no one could be said to own land. The lord was not in possession, and owed obligations to the

Figure 1.3

Legal title
(managerial in nature—rarely changes)

Feoffees to uses as joint tenants

Grandfather ⟶ Father ⟶ Son ⟶ Grandson ⟶ Etc.

Equitable title
(beneficial in nature—often changes)

tenant. Tenure, on the other hand, was subject to obligations to the lord. An appropriate analogy today might be the tenure of a High Court judge in office— however secure the post may be, it cannot sensibly be said that anyone owns it, either employer or employee, and this would continue to be so even in the unlikely event that such posts became inheritable. So far as early landholding was concerned the very concept of ownership was meaningless, and certainly no such concept was protected by the common law. Some of the consequences of this, which still remain, are of greater interest to students of land law than trusts, for example that title to land is to this day a relative concept. But the impossibility of owning land also influenced the development of uses and later trusts. In particular, as land became marketable, and some concept similar to ownership was therefore required, the doctrine of estates developed. An estate, as we have seen, is the right to hold tenure for a period of time, and many estates can exist in the same land simultaneously. The concept, which for these historical reasons is peculiar to common law, as opposed to Roman law systems, is very useful in its own right.

When the Chancellor created the use it was necessary to decide which equitable estates would be protected. One meaning of the maxim 'equity follows the law' (on equitable maxims, see section 1.4.1) is that equity recognises all the estates (and other interests in land) recognised by the common law. In fact, for a greater part of equity's history, and today, equity has also recognised estates and interests which are not recognised at common law; today, however, this is mainly because limits have been placed on the number of possible legal estates in land by the 1925 property legislation (see section 1.6.1).

1.3   STATUTE OF USES 1535

It is clear from the above that one of the functions of the use was to enable feudal dues to be avoided, and soon a great proportion of land was held to uses. Obviously this affected the Crown most adversely, as supreme landlord. Henry VIII therefore decided to counter the device, and the effect of the Statute of Uses 1535 was to execute many uses, that is to say, to convey the legal estate to the cestui que use. Henry was unable to get his way entirely, and the Act was a compromise. It was not of universal application, as it did not apply to leaseholds or to situations where the feoffees to uses had active duties to perform. Where it applied, however, the advantages of the device were negated, because the feoffees to uses disappeared. Figure 1.4 illustrates this, and it can also be seen that the number of transfers of the legal estate is necessarily increased to achieve the same result.

Figure 1.4

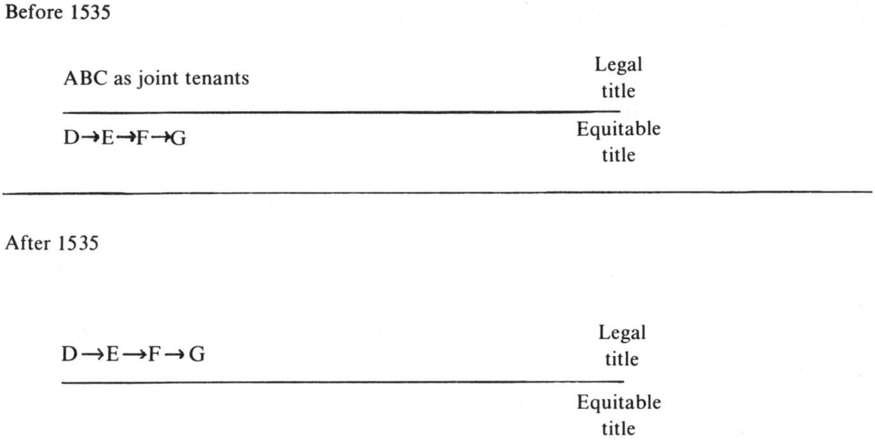

Before 1535

ABC as joint tenants	Legal title
$D \rightarrow E \rightarrow F \rightarrow G$	Equitable title

After 1535

$D \rightarrow E \rightarrow F \rightarrow G$	Legal title
	Equitable title

The eventual solution, which seems to have been reached by around 1700, was to employ a second use, called a trust. An example might be a conveyance 'to X unto the use of Y and his heirs in trust for Z and his heirs'. Though the first use was executed the second (trust) was not. Hence Y held the legal estate in trust for Z, who became equitable owner. In later conveyances X would have been omitted completely. The effect of the statute in this regard, therefore, was to do little more than change the name of the use to trust and to add a few words to conveyances. The terminology has also changed. The legal owner has become the trustee: the equitable owner the cestui que trust, or beneficiary.

The legal history of, and even the legal basis for the subversion of a properly enacted statute by the Court of Chancery is obscure. Certainly by 1700 the political situation had completely changed, with the abolition of many feudal dues in 1660 and a more satisfactory parliamentary basis for royal finances.

The statute had incidental effects which were longer lasting, but mainly of interest to land law students. Because the uses were executed, the common law was faced with the problem of dealing with the future interests in land which had been developed in equity, and in fact they came in general to be recognised by the common law. They are not any more, however, because of the 1925 property legislation (discussed in section 1.6). Creation of perpetuities in equity was possible before 1535, but after the statute the same problem also faced the common law. Soon after, the modern rule against perpetuities developed. This is discussed in outline in section 3.7 and in detail in textbooks on land law.

1.4   AN OUTLINE OF MODERN EQUITABLE PRINCIPLES

In its early days equitable jurisdiction was exercised on an *ad hoc* basis, and its transformation into a modern system did not come until after around 1700, by which time Chancellors tended to be lawyers rather than ecclesiasts and a system of precedent was beginning to develop. Yet many features of the early use remain in the modern trust. Indeed it was necessary for equity to retain many of its early features to avoid conflict with the common law (a major problem in the 17th century). It should be noted, however, that today's trust applies to goods, as well as land.

It may be that the development of principles some 200 years ago, followed by increased rigidity in the law more recently, has had undesirable consequences. The 18th century was, after all, before modern banking practices and limited liability companies (as presently constituted) existed. Most trusts tended to be of the family settlement variety. Yet the principles that were well-suited to such settlements also apply in essence today. We shall see in chapter 3 how assumptions based on family-type trusts impeded until very recently the development of the law relating to certainties, and it may also be that trustees' duties are too onerous for similar reasons. The nub of the problem is that family trusts are not in their nature intended as risky ventures, and a significant difficulty is in guarding against fraud of the trustees. To apply similar principles to professional trustees, who may well be expected to take business risks, is arguably inappropriate.

1.4.1   The equitable maxims

As equity shook off its *ad hoc* origins, certain principles developed which became embodied in the form of equitable maxims. These are not rules to be construed like statutes, but rather a general basis around which much of the law of equity was formed. They frequently appear as part of the reasoning in judgments. All have relevance to the law of trusts—the first was a rationalisation of the basis of the jurisdiction exercised originally by the medieval Chancellor, and the second we have already come across. Many of the rest will appear in later sections and chapters, so for convenience all of the 12 usually quoted are listed below, though their full explanations will be found at the appropriate part of the book.

(a)   Equity will not suffer a wrong without a remedy.
(b)   Equity follows the law.
(c)   Where there is equal equity, the law shall prevail.
(d)   Where the equities are equal, the first in time shall prevail.
(e)   He who seeks equity must do equity.
(f)   He who comes to equity must come with clean hands.
(g)   Delay defeats equities.
(h)   Equality is equity.
(i)   Equity looks to the intent rather than the form.
(j)   Equity looks on that as done which ought to be done.
(k)   Equity imputes an intention to fulfil an obligation.
(l)   Equity acts *in personam*.

Though only the above 12 are usually regarded as the definitive equitable maxims, equity has developed additional principles which may be treated to all intents and purposes as if they were among the maxims. The following may not be an exhaustive list, but all these principles will appear again in the book:

(m)   Equity will not assist a volunteer (see chapter 4).
(n)   Equity will not perfect an imperfect gift (see chapter 4).
(o)   Equity will not construe a valid power out of an invalid trust (see sections 2.5 and 3.1.4).
(p)   Equity will not permit the provisions of a statute intended to prevent fraud to be used as an instrument for fraud (see chapter 6, and sections 3.5 and 7.6).
(q)   Equity will not permit a trust to fail for want of a trustee.

The exact language of these maxims and principles appears to vary slightly between different authorities.

1.4.2   Equity acts *in personam*

One feature of equitable jurisdiction has always been that it is exercised against specific persons—equity acts *in personam*. This is also an important maxim of equity. In the case of the use the remedy was personal against the feoffee to uses, who held the legal estate in the land. Also in a modern trust the action is against the owner of the legal estate in land, or the legal owner of money or goods.

Consequently it does not matter, for example, if the land, money or goods are themselves situated abroad, so long as the legal owner or trustee can be found.

1.4.3 Nature of legal and equitable ownership

To return again to the use, it is clear that it was the equitable ownership which was enjoyed; the feoffee to uses merely managed the property on behalf of the cestui que use. The same position obtains with the modern trust. Legal ownership, or trusteeship, is a management function. So far from being desirable, a trustee is liable to onerous duties (on which, see chapters 9 and 10) and is often paid for undertaking trusteeship. (Banks, for example, are paid to act as trustees, and so are solicitors—for conditions attaching to payment, see section 9.5.) The equitable owner, or beneficiary, on the other hand, is entitled to enjoy the property. Of course, where no trust is imposed, the same person will be both legal and equitable owner, as is the case with the majority of ordinary possessions owned absolutely by one person (refer back to figure 1.1). In this event legal ownership is by no means a burden, because there is nobody to whom any duties are owed, and most owners of goods would be surprised if it were otherwise. Here also, though, the correct analysis is probably that it is the equitable title, which is also enjoyed by the absolute owner, which gives rise to the enjoyment right.

1.4.4 Other equitable interests

The equitable principles discussed in this section do not apply only to full equitable ownership of chattels or estates in land arising out of the type of transactions already considered. Equity also recognises other interests in property which are less than full ownership, and some of the following cases and examples are about equitable interests rather than full equitable ownership.

For example, suppose A has freehold legal title to land and contracts to lease the land to B for seven years. Under the contract B is entitled to possession and enjoyment of the land for that period. The contract is enforceable at common law, just like any other contract, and if a lease is not executed or B is denied possession or enjoyment of the land, he can claim damages. The common law does not recognise B as actually being lessee, however, until the lease is executed in the prescribed formal manner. But, unlike many contracts, this arrangement is also enforceable in equity, allowing B to claim the equitable remedies of specific performance, which forces A to execute the lease, and injunction, which stops A acting in a manner inconsistent with the grant of the lease. Furthermore, 'Equity looks on that as done which ought to be done' (see section 1.4.1) and B is treated as if he were *already* a lessee in equity, even if no formal lease has yet been executed (*Walsh* v *Lonsdale* (1882) 20 ChD 9). So a contract for a lease can create an immediate equitable interest in land, called an estate contract (a lease being an estate in land), to which the equitable principles discussed below apply.

The same applies to contracts for lesser legal rights in land. A contract to create a legal easement (e.g., a right of way—a right much less extensive than legal ownership) can give rise to an equitable easement, which is another equitable interest less than full ownership. Additionally, there are some interests in land which exist only in equity, for example, restrictive covenants, which are a narrowly defined specialist type of contract between landowners. The principles discussed in this section apply to these interests also.

Furthermore, some other contracts concerning property are enforceable both at common law and in equity. It does not necessarily follow that all these contracts create equitable interests in the property, however. They may create 'mere equities'. Probably contractual licences to occupy land fall into this category—so far as the equitable remedies are concerned the principles discussed in section 1.4.5 apply to them, but not all the principles applicable to full equitable interests apply: in particular, as they are purely personal rights, those discussed in section 1.4.6 do not.

Terminologically, so far as land is concerned, an 'estate', whether legal or equitable, connotes an interest akin to ownership; an 'interest in·land' can include an estate, but also includes rights that are much less extensive than ownership.

1.4.5 Equitable remedies

Originally equity developed its own remedies, which were not available to the common law. Nor did equity administer common law remedies. This position was to some extent altered by the Common Law Procedure Act 1854, which gave the common law courts some jurisdiction to give equitable remedies, and the Chancery Amendment Act 1858, which allowed the Court of Chancery to award the common-law-derived remedy of damages, but only in addition to, or in substitution for, an equitable remedy. In 1873–5 the courts were fused (see section 1.5) but the principles governing the grant of equitable remedies were not changed by that legislation and are still applicable to actions to protect equitable interests or estates and other rights having an equitable origin. Thus, it is still necessary to consider the equitable remedies separately from the common law remedies.

The main equitable remedies are the injunction, specific performance and remedy of account. Damages could not originally be awarded, and can be now only on the basis of the 1858 Act. In any event the quantum of equitable damages may differ from that appropriate in a common law action.

A major difference between the two systems is that whereas common law remedies are available as of right, equitable remedies retain the discretionary nature of early equitable jurisdiction. The onset over the last two centuries or so of defined systems of precedent and law reporting has curtailed somewhat the early discretion to create wholly new equitable rights and principles but remedies are nevertheless still discretionary, though that discretion is now exercised in accordance with fairly clear and even rigid principles. It should be noted that if an equitable estate or interest depends on the award of an equitable remedy, the refusal to grant the remedy destroys the interest.

1.4.5.1 Exercise of the discretion

A common ground for refusal of a remedy is the behaviour of the party claiming the equitable remedy: 'He who comes into equity must come with clean hands'— see section 1.4.1. For example, in *Coatsworth* v *Johnson* (1886) 54 LT 520, CA, the plaintiff was in possession of land under a contract for a lease, where no lease that would be recognised at common law had been executed. The landlord in fact turned the plaintiff out and the plaintiff sued for trespass. He would have won the action had he been regarded as a lessee, either at common law or in equity. As we saw above, equity in principle enforces contracts for leases and would normally regard the plaintiff as being an equitable lessee. In the particular case he was in breach of various covenants under the agreement, however. In these circumstances, the Court of Appeal held, the equitable remedy would have been refused *and the plaintiff therefore lost his interest*. Thus he was thrown back on his common law rights and, of course, he had no lease at common law. So he lost. Not only is this case a good example of the discretionary nature of equitable remedies but it also emphasises the need to treat common law and equitable rights and remedies separately and additionally. Also, the entire interest was lost because the remedy was refused.

Figure 1.5

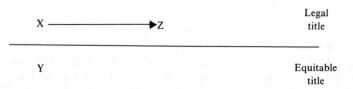

Another example, which students of the law of contract may remember, is the Court of Appeal decision in *D & C Builders Ltd* v *Rees* [1966] 2 QB 617. While two of the judges applied conventional common law consideration reasoning, Lord Denning MR was in principle attracted by the equitable doctrine of promissory estoppel, in the development of which he had played a major role. He refused to apply it in favour of the defendant because of his sharp practice, however. Thus, even in the opinion of the Master of the Rolls the defendant was forced back on to his common law position and lost.

The behaviour of the party claiming the remedy is not the only factor. Innocent plaintiffs can also lose their remedies. For example, a remedy might also be refused if to grant it would put the other party in breach of a contract with a third party (*Warmington* v *Miller* [1973] QB 877).

1.4.6   Bona fide purchasers for value without notice

One difficulty that can arise is illustrated in figure 1.5: property is conveyed to X on trust for Y. X disposes of the legal estate in the property to Z. The common law in this situation recognises only Z's rights, but equity imposes obligations on him as well as on X, or anyone else who comes to hold the legal estate, except a bona fide purchaser of the legal estate for value without notice. The basis of the action against Z is the same as that of the action against X; equity imposes on the conscience of the third party. This explains also the exception, the bona fide purchaser etc. He is regarded as being innocent, so equity has no reason to impose on his conscience. The bona fide purchaser rule applies not only to full equitable ownership or title but also to any lesser form of equitable interest in property. It does not apply, however, to mere equities, which are only enforceable by and against the original contracting parties.

Suppose that A has an estate contract enforceable against B and B sells the land to C. A, as owner of an equitable interest, is in a much better position than he would have been if he had only his common law contractual action against B. Contracts at common law are not enforceable against third parties. Of course, he still has a common law action against B, but it is of little use if B has gone bankrupt, or disappeared or spent the purchase money. In any event A does not want the common law damages; he wants the land at the agreed price. Equity allows this, so long as C does not fall within the bona fide purchaser exception. It can be seen, therefore, that the creation of equitable interests, or trusts, can be used as a device to avoid the privity of contract doctrine; in chapter 6 we shall see how the constructive trust is being developed today for precisely that purpose.

1.4.6.1   Importance of the rule
The bona fide purchaser doctrine is theoretically, therefore, of great importance in equity. A major difference between common law and equitable ownership is that common law ownership can be enforced against anyone at all (subject, in the

case of sale of goods, to the exceptions contained in the Factors Act 1889, ss. 2, 8 and 9, and the Sale of Goods Act 1979, ss. 21 to 26. These are discussed in detail in textbooks on that subject). Equitable ownership, on the other hand, can be lost to a bona fide purchaser of the legal estate for value without notice. In reality, though it is still true that equitable ownership can be lost whereas common law ownership cannot, the doctrine has today lost much of its importance.

The doctrine theoretically applies to chattels (i.e., goods) as well as land, and there have indeed been a few cases where it has been so applied. In practice, however, buyers of chattels nearly always fall within the exception as they generally have no reason to suspect that the seller, if he has legal title, does not also have equitable title. In the first place, the vast majority of chattels are not held in trust. Also, transfers of goods do not normally involve the degree of investigation and documentation that would be appropriate in the case of land, so an assumption of absolute ownership is normally reasonable.

If the seller does not have legal title, such title can nevertheless pass to the buyer in certain circumstances (under the Factors Act and Sale of Goods Act sections mentioned above), but these circumstances are so drawn up that it is almost inconceivable that a buyer who acquires title in this way would be acting in bad faith, or have any notice of an equitable interest. On the other hand, if the seller has no title, and the buyer also acquires no title, because the Factors Act etc. provisions do not apply in his favour, he will necessarily be bound by any prior equitable interests. This will be so whether or not he acts in good faith, and whether or not he has notice, because he does not acquire any legal title.

It is possible to conclude, in the case of goods, that in practice the determining factor will be whether the buyer acquires legal title to the goods rather than the presence or absence of good faith or notice.

With land, however, the doctrine still occasionally applies, but even there its importance has been much reduced by the 1925 property legislation (see section 1.6.2).

1.4.6.2   Working of the rule
Subject to those provisos, where the doctrine nonetheless applies, the purchaser, to take free of (or in other words take priority over) prior equitable interests, must acquire a *legal* estate or title: 'Where there is equal equity, the law shall prevail' (see section 1.4.1). In this situation the equities are equal because each party can be regarded as being equally innocent.

A purchaser of an *equitable* estate or interest will not generally, therefore, take priority over a prior equitable interest. Yet another maxim applies: 'Where the equities are equal, the first in time shall prevail'. In other words, priorities of equitable interests generally rank according to the order of time in which they have been created (there is an exception—for a mortgage of personalty, the rule in *Dearle* v *Hall* (1823) 3 Russ 1 applies—this is outside the scope of this book, but refer to any land law textbook).

The general position is illustrated by Figure 1.6.

Figure 1.6

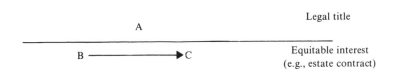

It is assumed in the diagram that B and C have both entered estate contracts with A to purchase his legal estate in land. As we have seen, estate contracts are equitable interests in land. Clearly A cannot sell the same land to both of them, so B's estate contract will prevail in equity. C can still sue A for damages for breach of contract at common law, of course.

The purchase must be for value. Value includes not only consideration recognised at common law but also equitable consideration. Thus, for example, as well as value in terms of money or money's worth (which are recognised as consideration by both systems) equity also recognises a future marriage as consideration, and so it constitutes value for the purposes of the bona fide purchaser rule. On the other hand, the common law allows contracts under seal to be enforced even in the absence of consideration; equity does not take the same view and such contracts do not provide value for the purposes of this rule (nor incidentally can such contracts be enforced using equitable remedies). Where the value is money, the purchaser must pay all the money before receiving notice of the equitable interest.

Notice itself includes not only actual, but also constructive notice. For dealings in land this means that the purchaser must inquire about equitable interests with no less diligence than he would inquire of legal interests, and these standards are determined by ordinary conveyancing practice. Thus a careless purchaser is not protected, nor one who could have discovered the existence of an interest by inspecting the land. Additionally, knowledge of an agent (e.g., solicitor) is imputed so that the purchaser is treated as having any knowledge that his agent acquires. But we are really trespassing on land law and the whole of this subject is given a much more detailed airing in land law textbooks.

1.5   JUDICATURE ACTS 1873-5

Whereas until 1873 common law and equity had been administered in different courts, equity being administered only in the Court of Chancery, the legislation of 1873-5 provided that subsequently the High Court, though divided for convenience into divisions, would administer both systems. Section 25 of the 1873 Act, now replaced by the Supreme Court Act 1981, s. 49, provided that in a case of conflict the rules of equity were to prevail: this was effectively the position also before 1873.

No doubt a major motivation for the legislation was that the Court of Chancery had become overworked and exceptionally slow (*Bleak House* was not a work of pure fiction). The 1873-5 Acts were almost certainly intended to be procedural only—in fact they constituted the final stage of a legislative process which began in 1854. Procedural change was probably their only effect—the generally held view is that they did not alter the substantive law.

There are those who argue, however, that as a result of the procedural fusion of the two systems equity's freedom to develop has been fettered by virtue of its closer association with the common law. It is probably true that its original flexibility and rapid development have been largely curtailed and that it is now almost as rigid and rule-bound as the common law. Of course, it still continues to develop: see, for example section 5.5 and chapter 6 for developments in the application of resulting and constructive trusts to new situations. The doctrine of promissory estoppel has also already been mentioned. The nature of equitable development and its pace, however, are frankly similar to those of the common law, which also adapts to changed social circumstances.

At least three observations can be made in reply to this argument. First, it is probable that legislation, whose role and extent have increased greatly since 1875, today takes on many of the functions once taken on by equity; where the law appears rigid and unjust, legislation is now a possible and realistic answer. It may well be better suited to modern democratic conditions than the exercise of discretionary power by a court. Megaw LJ, for example, expressed this view in *Western Fish Products Ltd* v *Penwith District Council* [1981] 2 All ER 204, 218. Additionally, the nature of case law makes it inevitably uncertain as a method of law reform. Sometimes, on the other hand, legislation responds rapidly to newsworthy events, often for a short-term political payoff, but without sufficient regard for general principle.

The second observation is that the curtailment of equitable discretion is explicable as a simple consequence of the development of effective law reporting, inevitably leading to precedents coming to be regarded as binding. Probably it has nothing to do with the 1873-5 legislation. The third observation is that unfettered judicial discretion may nowadays be a bad thing; it is arguably better to promote certainty in a society in which expectations are relied upon, than discretion. Not only is the latter quality inherently unpredictable but if administered by a court is also retroactive. Its exercise can therefore cause considerable injustices, especially where commercial and property transactions are concerned.

It has been suggested by Lord Diplock in *United Scientific Holdings Ltd* v *Burnley Borough Council* [1978] AC 904 that since 1875 law and equity should themselves be considered as being fused, and that it is no longer meaningful to speak as though rules of equity still retain a separate identity. Whether or not this is correct (and it is difficult to see it as being more than a semantic argument), there are practical reasons for continuing to treat the two systems separately. Rights which owe their derivation to equitable principles differ, as we saw in section 1.4, from those which derive from the common law. Both types of right can exist simultaneously in a given situation, and it is without doubt more convenient to continue to subject them to a separate analysis.

Suppose, for example, A has freehold title to a house, and makes a contract with B allowing B to go into possession for three years. Suppose also that, for technical land law reasons (with which we need not be concerned), B's right is to be as licensee not as lessee. In addition to giving consideration under this contract, B also relies to his detriment on A's promise that he can stay, perhaps by improving the property. B now has the benefit of both a common law contractual and equitable estoppel licence. Here then, both common law and equitable rights exist simultaneously, and since 1875 have been administered in the same court. It may well be asked, then, why it is necessary or convenient to continue to recognise their separate existences. It is because the common law and equitable consequences may be very different.

Thus, the common law rights, if A breaks the contract, are to damages alone; they can be obtained as of right, and can be used as a cause of action and a defence against A. If A sells the house to C the orthodox view is that they are not available against C, because of the doctrine of privity of contract. On the other hand, as we have seen, the remedies available on the basis of the estoppel licence are discretionary, and almost certainly do not include damages. The estoppel can be used to defend a possession action by A, if B is in possession, but arguably (views differ) does not give rise to a cause of action in its own right. C may in certain circumstances be bound by the estoppel, whereas he would not be by the contract.

The conclusion that I would draw is that it is still sensible to consider common law and equity separately, even 110 years after both doctrines have been administered in the same court.

1.6 THE 1925 PROPERTY LEGISLATION

The 1925 property legislation comprised the Law of Property Act, Settled Land Act, Land Registration Act and Land Charges Act, the last of which was amended and re-enacted in 1972. They are mainly of interest to land law students, but their effect on trusts and equitable doctrines was also quite considerable.

Perhaps the main purpose of the 1925 property legislation was to make it easier for people to sell or otherwise alienate land. The ability to alienate land easily had become increasingly necessary following the social upheavals brought about by the First World War and much of the legislation was directed towards improving the conveyancing process.

The effect on equity and trusts of this legislation was threefold. In the first place, many estates in land can now exist only in equity. Secondly, the bona fide purchaser doctrine (see section 1.4.6) was severely curtailed. Thirdly, the trust for sale, which was used as a conveyancing device before 1925, was substantially enhanced in importance.

1.6.1 Reduction in number of legal estates

Many estates in land can now exist only in equity (i.e., as beneficial interests under a trust) because of the reduction in 1925 (in order to aid conveyancing) in the number of possible legal estates. We have seen that though before 1535 the number of legal estates that could exist in land was very limited, and no future interests could be created at common law, this changed with the Statute of Uses, because on the execution of uses the common law came to recognise most of the wider range of equitable estates. This in turn led to difficulties for purchasers, who might have a great number of legal titles to investigate, in addition to equitable estates and interests. For example, if land was settled in order to keep it in a family, the present tenant's life estate and the future tenant's entailed estate could both be legal estates.

Even greater complexity could arise where there were concurrent interests in the same land (i.e., where land was shared but not divided, as, for example, where a matrimonial home was held jointly by husband and wife). Though for reasons that have already been explained in section 1.1.1, the terms 'owner', and therefore 'co-owner', are not strictly accurate, it is convenient in this context to use 'co-owner' as shorthand. In this situation each co-owner often had a separate legal estate. Furthermore, each of these estates could be further split, and frequently would be where land was held by large partnerships or settled equally among sons and grandsons over several generations. Thus, a prospective purchaser would have to investigate, and buy, large numbers of legal estates before investigation of equitable title had even begun. Effectively, this could render shared land unsaleable.

The Law of Property Act 1925, s. 1, reduced the number of possible legal estates in land to two, those that are now commonly known as freehold (fee simple absolute in possession), which must take immediate effect, and leasehold (term of years absolute). Future freehold interests and life interests, as are commonly found in settlements, can only exist in equity, and concurrent interests in land only take effect behind a trust for sale (i.e., in equity: see further sections

1.6.3 and 2.7). In this respect, therefore, the 1925 legislation increased the contribution of equity to the law of real property.

1.6.2 Bona fide purchaser doctrine

So far as the equitable estates and interests themselves were concerned, the bona fide purchaser doctrine (described in section 1.4.6) was not altogether satisfactory. Innocent owners of equitable interests could lose them to a bona fide purchaser for value without notice through no fault of their own; there was no way of being sure that they would be brought to his notice, and if they were not he would take free (i.e., without being bound by those interests). Purchasers, on the other hand, were put to great expense to discover the existence of all possible equitable interests, in case they should find themselves bound. The system was lucrative for lawyers, but not conducive to safe and rapid alienation of land.

Broadly speaking, the 1925 legislation distinguishes between equitable estates in land (i.e., akin to full ownership) and interests less than ownership. For most equitable interests, but not estates, the 1925 legislation replaced the bona fide purchaser doctrine with registration provisions; such interests today can be and have to be registered for protection against purchasers. The idea is that if the interest is registered the purchaser has notice; if it is not registered, however, the purchaser is not bound whether or not he has notice in fact, and whether or not he even acts in good faith (see, e.g., *Midland Bank Trust Co. Ltd* v *Green* [1981] AC 513, where a purchaser in bad faith took free from a prior equitable interest, under certain provisions of the Land Charges Act). There are in fact two systems of registration in operation currently, depending on the geographical location of the land.

The details of the registration systems, provided for by the Land Charges and Land Registration Acts, are dealt with in land law textbooks. Trusts lawyers need to be aware of them in so far as they reduce the importance of the bona fide purchaser doctrine.

The bona fide purchaser doctrine has not in fact been completely abolished for dealings involving land. It still exists at the margins. Indeed, the courts have been unhappy with the logic of *Midland Bank Trust Co. Ltd* v *Green*, and have been at some pains to bring back good faith requirements where they can. For example, in those areas of the country where the Land Charges Act is in operation, not all equitable interests are expressly covered by the statute. For those that are omitted the old rules apply, and the courts have been unenthusiastic about extending the legislation to cover them by implication (see, e.g., *E.R. Ives Investments Ltd* v *High* [1967] 2 QB 379; *Shiloh Spinners Ltd* v *Harding* [1973] AC 691).

In areas where the Land Registration Act is in operation, a similar trend is apparent, and there are authorities importing a good faith requirement into the statute. This may lead to a return to a doctrine similar to that of the bona fide purchaser (see, e.g., *Peffer* v *Rigg* [1977] 1 WLR 285; *Lyus* v *Prowsa Developments Ltd* [1982] 1 WLR 1044). If so, then the net effect of the registration provisions will be greatly reduced where, though an interest has not been entered on the appropriate register, the purchaser nevertheless knows about it.

Equity has also developed new interests since 1925, which not surprisingly were not covered by legislation. To these also, of course, the bona fide purchaser doctrine applies. Thus new developments in constructive trusts (see chapter 6) are subject to the old doctrine, and so (arguably) are estoppel licences.

1.6.3   Trusts for sale: overreaching

Full equitable estates in land are treated differently by the 1925 legislation. In the case of land held concurrently (i.e., shared), the Law of Property Act 1925 requires that it be held on a statutory trust for sale, and the interests of the co-owners thus become beneficial interests under a trust for sale. Trusts for sale are described in detail in section 2.7 but it should be noted that their purpose in this context is simply as a conveyancing device; in other words, the theoretical intention to sell is a legal fiction.

The main effect is that on sale the interests of the co-owners cease to be interests in land, and become interests in the purchase money only. Indeed, as we shall see in the next chapter, for some purposes their interests become interests in the money only even before the sale takes place. A purchaser is thus enabled to 'overreach' them. This means that he is relieved from having to inquire of them so long as he pays the purchase money to at least two trustees, because they take effect as interests in the purchase money only, rather than in the land itself. Thus the beneficiaries are protected by being able to take a share of the purchase money, and the purchaser is not concerned with their interests. A large proportion of matrimonial and cohabited property is now held in this manner, and it goes without saying, of course, that the bona fide purchaser doctrine is no longer relevant to this situation.

1.6.4   Settled land

The Settled Land Act 1925 was also directed towards easier alienability of land, but a more specific aspect of the problem. It dealt with the difficulties encountered when (as commonly used to be the case) land was settled for generations in families, and continued the policy of the earlier Settled Land Acts 1882 to 1890.

The nub of the problem was that large rural aristocratic estates were tied up in such a way that nobody could sell them or develop them. There was some sense in this up to the 1832 Reform Act, because the political power of a family depended partly upon its continued ownership of such estates. During the 19th century, however, the practice of settling estates in this way became a nuisance. It became more profitable in many cases to develop the land industrially, whereas, on the other hand, agricultural prices became depressed. The families themselves suffered, as did workers and their families living on their land, because estates that could be neither sold nor developed became impoverished and were allowed to decay. The general community also suffered while land continued to be inextricably tied to outmoded purposes.

Though there is hardly any settled land left today, there are aspects of the legislation which are important:

(a) The 1882–90 legislation gave extensive powers, including sale, to the tenant for life in possession, whatever the provisions of the settlement might say. In other words, since 1882 it has been impossible to tie up land in this way. If the land was sold, all interests in it (i.e., future interests and the life interest of the tenant for life himself) were overreached by purchasers, in much the same way as with concurrent interests described above, so long as the purchase money was paid to trustees of the settlement. One method by which the purchase money might be split would be to allow the life tenant to take the interest on it for his life, the capital sum being retained to compensate for the sale of the future interests.

(b) The 1925 legislation continues the policy of that of 1882–90, but also gives the legal fee simple to the life tenant in possession. This is a device to ease conveyancing. It also ensures that somebody has the legal estate, because in most pre-1925 settlements nobody had the fee simple absolute in possession; usually there was a life interest followed by an entail. In accord with the policy of the 1925 legislation, these estates can now exist only in equity. So somebody had to be given the fee simple absolute in possession, otherwise nobody could have a legal estate in the land at all!

(c) Most people wishing to tie up land today use (ironically) an express trust for sale (described in section 2.7) because they are exempt from the provisions of the 1925 Settled Land Act. This is another use, therefore, to which trusts for sale can be put.

(d) Settled land is another area, then, where the bona fide purchaser doctrine no longer has any application.

2

Nature and Classification of Trusts

2.1 REASONS FOR CREATING TRUSTS

Trusts arise in many everyday situations, which cover widely differing social circumstances. It is perhaps unfortunate, therefore, that similar (but, as we shall see, not identical) principles are applicable to each variety of trust.

2.1.1 Family settlements

The purpose of many express trusts (i.e., those which are deliberately created by a settlor) is the retention of wealth by the wealthy. Probably the majority of trusts we shall meet in this book have this purpose as their main aim. They are often family settlements, which tie up wealth within the family, and are also drafted to minimise liability to taxation (on which see chapter 13). Sometimes they are made by will, but it can be advantageous from a taxation viewpoint for them to be constituted during the life of the settlor (i.e., *inter vivos*). Though they were more important historically than they are today, family settlements are still common, and frequently give rise to litigation. It is not, of course, the function of this book to comment on the desirability or otherwise of these schemes. This is a political question, upon which views may validly differ. Only the legal consequences are appropriate for discussion in this book.

The trustees may be members of the family, and in the early days of such settlements often were. They may be solicitors who are familiar with the family business. Neither of these appointments is considered by the courts to be very desirable, however, because of the likelihood of conflicts of interest where the trustee is too closely connected to, or involved with, the beneficiaries. There is even a possibility of fraud, especially where family members are constituted trustees. So in the rare cases where the court has to appoint trustees (say, where the existing trustees fail to carry out their duties—see further chapters 3 and 9), such people are unlikely candidates. Further, it is probably because the modern law of trusts largely developed at a time when this sort of trust was exceedingly common, and when the trustees were normally family members, that the nature of trustees' duties (on which, see chapters 9 and 10) is so stringent.

Family trusts may also be administered by the trustee and executor departments of banks. Proper professional administration can be of the greatest importance if tax benefits are to be maximised. Banks charge quite heavily for taking on these duties, by way of a charging clause that they insist on putting into the trust instrument. The charges are therefore usually fixed at the outset, and do not depend on how the trust is administered. This, as we shall see, is very important when we come to consider conflicts of interest in section 9.5.

The terminology relating to settlements will arise again throughout the book. All settlements involve the creation of successions of interests, and the simplest form would be where A leaves property to B for life and thereafter for C. B is the *life tenant*, and is usually entitled to the immediate income on the property. He is sometimes referred to as an income beneficiary. C is entitled in remainder. He is the *remainderman*, sometimes referred to as a capital beneficiary.

In this case the extent of C's interest is known at the outset, and so it is a *vested* interest. Suppose on the other hand the gift is to B for life and then to the first of C, D and E to marry. It is unknown yet which will marry first, and the interests of C, D and E are said to be 'contingent'. More is made of this distinction in section 3.7.

In citations of cases 'ST' indicates a settlement trust and 'WT' a will trust.

2.1.2 Shares

Shares are often owned out and out by the shareholder, but they may be held by nominees, this practice being more common in holdings of shares in public, rather than private companies. The nominee is often a bank. In this case the legal estate is held by the nominee in trust for the shareholder. One reason for this might be if it is intended that the trustee should manage the portfolio, as would be the case, for example, with a unit trust. Pension funds may only be held by trust corporations.

2.1.3 Charities, trade unions and unincorporated associations

Trusts can also be used to enable property to be held for the benefit of people who for some reason cannot hold it themselves. Interestingly, some of the earliest uses for Franciscan friars had this as their main purpose. Incorporated bodies, such as companies, which are incorporated under the Companies Acts, and universities, which are incorporated by charter, have legal personality, and can therefore hold property themselves. So there is no need, for example, for treasurers or directors to hold the property on their behalf as trustees, and normally they do not do so. As we shall see in section 9.5, however, they may owe fiduciary duties, which are akin to those of trustees.

Charities (on which, see chapter 8) can also be incorporated, in which case they too may hold property in their own right. If they do so, the courts are undecided whether they hold absolutely, subject to the articles of association under the Companies Acts, or whether they are held on trust for charitable purposes. We will come upon purpose trusts again in chapter 3, and we shall see that they are rather unusual in that there are no true beneficiaries.

Not all charities are incorporated, however. Unincorporated bodies have no legal personality, and cannot hold property themselves. In the case of unincorporated charities, the property is held by trustees, who are often individuals, for the purposes of the charity. Donations to charity therefore commonly give rise to trusts.

A trust can also be, in theory, a method of enabling property to be held by members' clubs, which are also unincorporated. Nominated trustees (who would usually be officers of the club) could hold the property on trust for the members. This gives rise to no difficulties so long as the membership is fixed, or the club is of short duration (e.g., a club which is geared to a specific, one-off event). Most clubs have a fluctuating membership, however, and in this case, as we shall see, the trust solution can give rise to perpetuity problems, because the interests of future members may not vest until outside the perpetuity period (on which, see further sections 3.3 and 3.7). This is not a problem that arises in the case of charities, because they are exempt from the perpetuity rules.

The usual analysis for members' clubs is not based on the trust, therefore. It is more likely that the present members hold the club property absolutely, subject to their *contractual* rights and duties arising from membership. These may, for example, prevent them taking their share of the club property for themselves on resignation, or at any other time. They may allow the officers to decide how the property is to be used. If property is held by officers, they will hold it as agents of the members, not as trustees.

Trade unions are in a peculiar (and unique) position, being regarded as unincorporated for most purposes, though sharing some of the features of corporate bodies. Section 2 of the Trade Union and Labour Relations Act 1974 (re-enacting earlier legislation) prevents them from being corporate entities, but also provides that the trustees of a union hold on trust for *the union itself*, not for the members. So a union, unlike other unincorporated bodies, can be an equitable owner, though not a legal owner of property. Another feature of unions is that the trustees are nominal owners of the property only, and have no significant discretion, because rule books nearly always provide that they act under the directions of the executive.

2.1.4 Trusts arising from marriage or cohabitation

Unlike express trusts, resulting and constructive trusts, as we shall see, can arise in quite different circumstances from those described above. Resulting trusts (and some argue also constructive trusts—see section 5.5) often arise from informal family arrangements. A common variety is where a wife or female cohabitee (X) provides money towards the purchase of a home, which though intended to be jointly occupied, is conveyed into the name of the man alone (Y).

Y holds X's interest in the home on resulting trust, so that both parties share equitable title. Furthermore, as we have seen, a statutory trust for sale arises in this situation under the provisions of the Law of Property Act 1925. A statutory trust for sale also arises where the home is originally conveyed to X and Y jointly, and we may suppose that these are among the commonest trusts in existence today.

2.1.5   Reason for distinguishing similar concepts

Trusts, then, are used in widely differing social situations, of which the above examples are by no means exhaustive. Sometimes, however, wholly different concepts are applicable, instead, in similar situations. We have already seen, for example, that members' clubs are normally constituted on a contractual and agency basis, whereas the property of charities which are unincorporated is held by trustees. Banks may be trustees if they are specifically constituted as such, but ordinary accounts create only a debtor-creditor relationship. Company directors are not usually trustees, but share many of the trustees' duties. As will be shown in chapter 6, constructive trusts have been held to arise in similar situations to an estoppel licence, but the legal consequences are very different.

It is necessary, then, not only to describe the nature of the trust, but also to distinguish it from other concepts that can arise in similar situations.

2.2   NATURE OF TRUSTS

As we saw in chapter 1, a trust involves a division of the ownership of property. An example of a typical express trust is as follows. The settlor is the original owner of property, and creates a trust by conveying it to one or more trustees, and manifesting an intention that it is to be held on trust for one or more beneficiaries. The trustees become owners at common law, and are given control of the property. No trust is created, whatever intention the settlor has manifested, unless legal title is vested in (i.e., given to) the trustee (see further on this chapter 4). This is called 'constituting' the trust. The trustees come under an equitable obligation enforceable by the beneficiaries.

Though this example describes the essence of a trust, there are several possible variations and qualifications:

(a)   It is not necessary for settlors, trustees and beneficiaries to be different people. A settlor can validly constitute a trust by declaring *himself* trustee of his own property, on behalf of one or more beneficiaries. An example is *Paul* v *Constance* [1977] 1 WLR 527, CA, where though a man opened a bank account, in which to deposit a single lump sum, in his sole name, the court was able to find from the circumstances that it was only put into his sole name to save embarrassment, and that he intended to hold the money in the account on trust for himself and his mistress equally. He had died, and had the decision been otherwise, the money would have been regarded as his, and his wife would have been entitled to succeed to it as part of her husband's estate.

The intention must be irrevocable, because trusts are of their nature irrevocable, and it must be an intention to create a trust, rather than some other transaction (e.g., an outright gift). For example, in *Jones* v *Lock* (1865) LR 1 Ch App 25, the father of a baby boy handed a cheque to his nine-month-old son, uttering words which made it clear that he meant the child to have the sum represented by the cheque, although he immediately removed the cheque from the baby for safe-keeping. He died some days later, without having endorsed the cheque, which would have been necessary to pass title in it to the child. The court refused to construe his actions as amounting to a declaration of trust, with himself as trustee, in favour of the child. Lord Cranworth LC did not think that an irrevocable intention to part with the property had been manifested. There was an intention to make an outright gift, but no gift had actually been made. It was not therefore a declaration of trust. It should also be noted that whereas an intention to make an outright gift is common, and will easily be inferred, the intention to declare oneself a trustee, and so to take on the onerous duties of trusteeship, is much less common, and is not readily inferred.

The settlor may be a beneficiary, and will always be in the case of a resulting trust (see chapter 5). A trustee may be the beneficiary, or one of a number of beneficiaries. Settlors can even be trustees *and* beneficiaries, and this is normal in the case of statutory trusts for sale (see section 2.7).

(b)   The property settled can include an equitable, and not only a legal, interest. In other words a beneficiary under a trust may constitute a further trust of his equitable interest, thereby creating a subtrust. Subtrusts are common in tax-avoiding settlements. The beneficiary under the subtrust can himself repeat the process, creating a further subtrust, and there is no limit to the number of times this process may be repeated.

(c)   The example above is of a private (i.e., non-charitable) trust. If the trust is charitable (see chapter 8), there may be no true beneficiaries at all. Yet charitable trusts are perfectly valid, enforcement being by the Attorney-General.

(d)   The example above also assumes that the beneficiary has a full equitable interest in the property and that there is no restriction, for example, on the purposes to which he can put it. As we will see in the next chapter, however, it seems also to be possible to have private purpose trusts, benefiting a defined group of people. These people are not true beneficiaries because they are constrained to use the property for a particular purpose. An example might be a conveyance of land to A and B, in trust to be used as a football pitch for the employees of X Ltd. The employees are not true beneficiaries because they cannot use the land in any way they wish. Nevertheless, the trust is probably valid because, in spite of this, they have sufficient interest in the property to be able to enforce the equitable obligations owed by the trustees.

(e) There may also be an anomalous category of unenforceable trusts, which, however, share the other characteristics of ordinary trusts. These seem to be limited to trusts for the benefit of animals and the maintenance of tombs, and should be regarded as exceptional. They are considered in chapter 3.

2.3 TRUSTS DISTINGUISHED FROM SIMILAR COMMON LAW CONCEPTS

The division of ownership, and the nature of the enforcement, serve to distinguish the trust from other concepts with which trusts share common factors.

2.3.1 Trust and bailment

For example, possession of personal property is often separated from ownership of the property—as in common law bailment, for example, hiring or hire-purchase—but both legal and equitable ownership remain in the bailor or hirer; so the relationship of the bailee to the property is quite different from that of a trustee, who is the legal owner.

To some extent this is manifested in differences in the duties of bailees and trustees—those of bailees are beyond the scope of this book, while those of trustees are considered in chapters 9 and 10. Additionally, the position of third parties is different. If a bailee sells the goods, where this is unauthorised by the terms of the bailment, then unless the buyer can benefit from the provisions of the Factors Act 1889, ss. 2, 8 and 9, or the Sale of Goods Act 1979, ss. 21 to 26, he gets no title, even if he acts in good faith and has no notice of the existence of the bailment. This is because a bailee has no title, legal or equitable, to sell, so a purchaser from him gets neither legal nor equitable title. The statutory provisions, incidentally, allow transfer of title by non-owners (as here) in limited circumstances, and are dealt with in detail in sale of goods textbooks.

If, on the other hand, a trustee sells goods in breach of trust, the buyer obtains legal title from the trustee, and is bound by any equitable title and interests only if he is unable to show that he is a bona fide purchaser for value without notice (see section 1.4.6). If he is a bona fide purchaser etc., he obtains legal title unencumbered by equitable interests.

Another difference between trust and bailment is that trusts can apply to land and goods, whereas bailment can only apply to goods.

A particular variety of bailment is sometimes used in commercial sales of goods, in order to protect the seller against the possibility that the buyer goes bankrupt after the seller has parted with the goods, but before full payment has been made. A clause is written into the contract of sale reserving to the seller the legal title in the goods until payment is made, although the buyer obtains possession of the goods. The point of the clause is that if the buyer goes bankrupt the trustee in bankruptcy cannot claim the goods for division among the general creditors, because they are the property not of the buyer, but the seller. These clauses are often called Romalpa clauses after the name of the leading case: *Aluminium Industrie Vaasen BV* v *Romalpa Aluminium Ltd* [1976] 1 WLR 676.

In effect, the buyer is constituted bailee for the seller. Bailor-bailee relationships are fiduciary in nature (as to which, see section 9.5) and a consequence of this is that if the buyer resells the goods and then goes bankrupt, the seller can use the equitable tracing remedy to secure property in the proceeds (see section 11.4).

A full review of Romalpa clauses can be found in any sale of goods textbook and is beyond the scope of this book, but the orthodox view was restated by the Court of Appeal in *Clough Mill Ltd* v *Martin* [1984] 1 All ER 721. In effect, the court gives effect to the intention of the parties as expressed in the sale contract (i.e. Romalpa clauses work) so long as the goods are not destroyed by the buyer in a manufacturing process (*Borden (UK) Ltd* v *Scottish Timber Products Ltd* [1981] Ch 25). A device sellers sometimes use to guard against the latter eventuality is an additional clause attempting to obtain and retain property over all the newly manufactured goods incorporating the seller's product. These clauses apparently do not work—indeed, one could envisage problems if they did, where a product is manufactured out of materials supplied by a number of different sellers, all of whom attempt to use such a clause!

Romalpa clauses have been criticised (e.g., by the Cork Report on Insolvency Law and Practice, Cmnd 8558, 1982) because they do not require to be registered under the Companies Act 1985, s. 395, in order to be effective. Creditors of the buyer, therefore, may be unaware of their existence yet, of course, they are affected by them. Although the provisions of the Insolvency Act 1985 might affect tracing aspects of Romalpa clauses, they will render them no less effective in securing this priority.

Theoretically, there would seem to be no reason in principle why the same result cannot be reached through a trust, rather than a bailment. This would allow legal property to pass to the buyer while equitable property was retained, constituting the buyer trustee for the seller. The position in the event of the buyer's bankruptcy would be the same as before. But the courts seem unwilling to split legal and equitable ownership in the case of goods. In *Re Bond Worth Ltd* [1980] Ch 228, for example, Slade J was most reluctant to hold that a seller could retain equitable title in goods which had been delivered to a buyer; legal title had passed to the buyer and he thought that legal and equitable title could be separated only by a fairly clear declaration of trust. The result was that the seller did not jump the queue of creditors on the insolvency of the buyer.

2.3.2 Trust and contract

A private trust, then, is created either by a declaration of trust by the settlor, in which case he becomes trustee himself, or by his arranging for someone else to act as trustee. The beneficiary (or, if a purpose trust, the person who can enforce it) need not be a party to the arrangement at all. Yet it is he, and not the settlor, who can enforce the trust, because the settlor retains no interest in the property (*qua* settlor—he may, of course, be trustee). This is so whether or not the beneficiary has given any consideration, because he is in effect the recipient of a gift. So it is only the third party to the arrangement who can enforce it.

While a third party (X) can benefit from a contract, on the other hand, he generally cannot enforce it himself by legal action, by virtue of the privity of contract doctrine. However, the creation of a trust in favour of X is similar to making him a gift: X need do nothing in return; the gift gives him enforceable rights and a gift once made cannot be revoked.

As a general conclusion, then, whereas contracts cannot be enforced by third parties, trusts are enforceable by beneficiaries who need not be parties to the arrangement. Furthermore, trusts are unenforceable by anyone else, even the settlor, who is always party to the arrangement.

Of course, if the trustee is acting by virtue of a contract with the settlor, for example, if he is acting as his solicitor or banker, then the settlor can enforce this contract. It may also be that a settlement of property by A on B, subject to a condition that B holds it for the benefit of C, always leads to the implication of a contract between A and B. A's remedies are in contract, however, and these are quite different from those available to a beneficiary for breach of trust.

2.3.2.1 A contract example
Suppose, for example, A contracts with B that, in consideration of a payment by A to B of a sum of money, B will pay C an annuity for the rest of C's life. No trust is constituted. Assume also that C does not provide consideration for this benefit, and is not party to the arrangement. C is therefore unable to enforce the contract in his own right. This is shown diagrammatically in Figure 2.1.

Figure 2.1

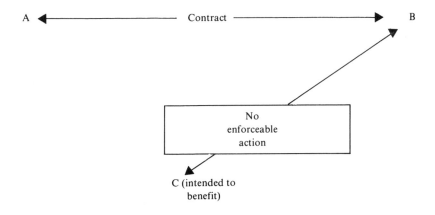

A can enforce the contract, however, and there are three points to note about enforcement of the contract by A:

(a)   Often such arrangements are made in favour of wives, sons or nephews, in which case A may well predecease them. In that event, after A's death A's personal representatives will be able to enforce the contract on A's behalf. As a third party, C cannot force them to do so, however, or sue B directly (*Beswick* v *Beswick* [1968] AC 58).

(b)   There may be difficulties over the appropriate remedy. In *Beswick* v *Beswick*, specific performance was obtained, and if this remedy is available, A can ensure that C obtains the benefit that has been bargained for. But the result in *Beswick* v *Beswick* depended, among other things, on the fact that B had actually received all the consideration (the transfer of the goodwill in A's business). Also, the remedy depends in general upon the mutuality requirement being satisfied, that is to say that the same contract would also have been specifically enforceable by B. This was the case in *Beswick* v *Beswick* because A had promised to transfer the goodwill of a business, but it will by no means always be so. In particular, the mutuality requirement is unlikely to be satisfied where the consideration moving from A is money alone.

If A cannot obtain specific performance and B does not perform the bargain at all, then A can get the property back on the ground of a total failure of consideration. This may be of no benefit to C, of course, unless A now makes another similar arrangement. In any case, if B has partially performed the bargain, A cannot obtain this remedy, and is forced to rely on contractual damages. Here the difficulty arises that personally he has suffered no loss, so the damages will be nominal, and the action may therefore be of limited value. The problem arises from the nature of damages in contract; arguably substantial damages should be available to A in these circumstances.

(c)   A and B may subsequently agree to vary the agreement, to C's detriment, and they can do so because C has no enforceable rights. Indeed, the most plausible reason for not making B a trustee in the first place would be that A and B wish to retain such flexibility. It is also a convincing reason, as a matter of policy, for the retention of this aspect of the privity doctrine.

2.3.2.2   A trust example

If A make B a trustee for C, however, the position is quite different. Not only can C sue B in his own right, but A and B can no longer vary the arrangment to C's detriment: to do so would be akin to making C a gift and taking it back again. In effect, the creation of a trust avoids the privity of contract rules. There is no objection to this, of course, so long as A and B clearly intend this to happen.

2.3.2.3   Trusts of promises

It is even possible to create trusts of promises. In other words, a cause of action in contract can itself be held in trust for a third party, at least if the contract involves payment of money or transfer of property. Again, this device avoids the privity doctrine. This is frequently done with the benefits of life insurance policies. It is not entirely clear how the courts view this device, but they do not appear very enthusiastic, and it seems that a clear intention to create an irrevocable trust benefiting the third party must be shown: it was not, for example, in *Re Schebsman* [1944] Ch 83. In effect, the same rules as to certainty and constitution (see chapters 3 and 4) apply to trusts of promises as to any other trust.

This device in any event will not help in the contract example discussed above if A's remedy in contract is itself useless. To constitute a trust of this remedy in C's favour would clearly achieve nothing.

2.3.2.4 Privity: burdening third parties

Since trusts bind not only the original trustee, but also anyone else who comes into control of the property, subject to the bona fide purchaser rule discussed in chapter 1, they can also be used to bind third parties to contracts, avoiding the privity rules.

For example, suppose X owns an aircraft and agrees to charter it to Y for two years, Y paying a single lump sum in advance. If X now sells the aircraft to Z, Y can sue X in contract but cannot sue Z. If, on the other hand, the courts hold that X has made himself a trustee of the aircraft in Y's favour, Z may find himself bound by the agreement. This may not be unjust in cases where a trust has been clearly created, but equally obviously, if the courts were over-zealous to infer trusts, it would become more difficult to sell aircraft, or other property.

2.3.3 Trust and loan

When you loan money to a friend or business partner, or deposit money in a bank account, your friend, business partner or bank becomes a debtor, not a trustee, and you become a creditor, not a beneficiary. It should be clear from the above that a debtor will be in a very different position from a trustee. A debtor's liability to repay a loan is contractual, and therefore strict, subject to the terms of the loan. In other words, it does not require proof of negligence or bad faith. It is not avoided, for example, by the theft by a third person either of the money loaned, or of any property purchased with the money, however innocent the debtor may be. On the other hand the property the creditor has loaned passes to the debtor, so if the debtor goes bankrupt, the creditor takes his place as one among many unsecured creditors, and will not see the return of some or all of his money.

A trustee's duties are less strict (see chapters 9 and 10) but in the event of a trustee's bankruptcy, a beneficiary is in the position of a secured creditor, because he has retained equitable property, which will be protected from the claims of the general creditors. In effect, the property never becomes part of the debtor's estate.

Both legal and equitable obligations can coexist, however, so that a loan can also constitute a trust. Thus, a creditor can also be a beneficiary, and this protects him in the event of the debtor's bankruptcy. I suggest that the courts have gone too far in this direction, because trusts are being more readily construed in these situations than in most others. It might be thought that only the clearest intention to create a trust should be manifested, but it seems only to be necessary that the loan is for a specific purpose for a trust to be construed. Thus a loan to pay a dividend was held to constitute a trust in *Barclay's Bank Ltd* v *Quistclose Investments Ltd* [1970] AC 567 (HL) as was an advance to pay off an antecedent debt to third parties in *Carreras Rothmans Ltd* v *Freeman Matthews Treasure Ltd* [1985] 1 All ER 155. In both cases the debtor had gone into liquidation, but the money advanced was secure from distribution to the general creditors by the trustee in bankruptcy.

One can see the force of Lord Wilberforce's remarks in the earlier case that the creditor had not the slightest desire to make his money freely available for the borrower's creditors, and that the decision in *Quistclose* gave effect to his intention. On the other hand, surely a general desire to achieve a particular result should not be regarded by itself as sufficient evidence of intention. In neither case, for example, was the word 'trust' used, and indeed a trust was apparently created by vaguer words than normally required (see section 3.1 on the attitude of the courts towards precatory words). In the more recent case it was by no means clear that Carreras Rothmans actually wished to give enforceable rights to the third parties in favour of whom the trust was held to be created. Rather, Peter Gibson J held this to be the inevitable consequence of creating an irrevocable trust. In effect, a trust was created *contrary to* the intention of the creditor. Also, of course, if loans of this type became commonplace the general law of bankruptcy would be seriously jeopardised, especially if insufficient assets remained to cover all such loans.

So far as dwelling-houses are concerned, contributions to the purchase or improvement of such houses have been held to give rise to resulting or constructive trusts, where the purpose of the contribution has been to enable the creditor to live in the house. The cases are probably suspect, but if correct it seems that if there is no intention that the money be repaid, the trust will attach to the house itself, whereas if the money is advanced as a loan, the trust attaches to the money. In either case the creditor becomes secured against the bankruptcy of the debtor. Examples of such trusts are *Hussey* v *Palmer* [1972] 1 WLR 1286 and *Re Sharpe* [1980] 1 WLR 219. This line of authorities will be further considered in section 5.5 and chapter 6. In *Re Sharpe* an aged aunt, who had taken no precautions to secure her loan in the event of her nephew's bankruptcy, became in effect a secured creditor. I suggest that the general creditors could justifiably have felt hard done by, and it is to be hoped that the courts will tread carefully before extending this line of development.

2.4   EXPRESS, IMPLIED, RESULTING AND CONSTRUCTIVE TRUSTS

So far we have considered only express trusts, where the settlor has expressed an intention to set up a trust. They are not the only variety, however, and the distinctions are important because implied, resulting and constructive trusts are not subject to the same formality requirements as express trusts (see section 3.5).

An implied trust arises where the settlor's intention is inferred from his words or conduct, rather than being expressed. A resulting trust arises where the settlor also becomes a beneficiary. This may have been his implied intention from the start, as where he contributes to a joint purchase of a house where the legal estate is conveyed into the name only of the other party. Alternatively, it can arise where a trust fails, either because it is void for uncertainty (see chapter 3), or because some or all of the beneficial interest is not disposed of for some other reason or because the underlying purpose of the trust has gone. A gift of land to a football club would result were the club wound up, for example. Resulting trusts are considerd in detail in chapter 5.

A constructive trust is imposed by the courts irrespective of the owner's intention. A particular variety will be considered in detail in chapter 6.

2.5   TRUSTS AND POWERS

2.5.1   Fixed and discretionary trusts

So far the assumption has been made that the extent of the beneficial interests under a trust has been known at the outset and, indeed, many trusts are of this nature. An example might be property divided equally among the sons of the settlor. Each son has an interest which is fixed and ascertainable from the outset. Statutory trusts for sale, arising from undivided shares in land, are normally fixed trusts, because each co-owner will have a defined share from the start.

This situation is by no means universal, however. With many trusts, the trustees are given a discretion as to how the property is to be distributed, usually within a defined class of possible beneficiaries. This type of trust is usually termed a discretionary trust, though the term 'trust power' has recently crept into occasional usage. Obviously, nobody within the class of possible beneficiaries (such people are referred to as 'objects', as we shall see in section 3.1.4) can claim a defined interest, or indeed any interest at all, unless and until the trustees' discretion is exercised in his favour. Yet though the trustees have a discretion as to *how* the property is distributed, that discretion does not extend to a refusal to distribute it at all. The trustees *must* administer the trust. They *must* appoint (i.e., decide who from within the class will benefit and also the size of beneficial interest). Who they appoint, and in what proportions, is up to them.

Family trusts are often of this nature for tax reasons. There are a number of advantages in giving discretion to the trustees. One is to enable them to alter the beneficial interests to take advantage of changing tax circumstances. Another is that tax liability attaches in some circumstances only where rights are created, and none of the beneficiaries has any right to the property at all unless and until the discretion is exercised in his favour.

As we shall see in chapter 3, the distinction between fixed and discretionary trusts is important as the orthodox view is that different requirements of certainty of object apply.

2.5.2   Nature of powers

A power (sometimes called a mere power) is similar to a discretionary trust, subject to the following differences. First, the legal title is given, not to trustees, but to donees of the power. They have a discretion not only as to *how* to distribute the property, but also as to *whether* to distribute it. They are under no obligation to appoint at all. In other words, whereas a trust is *imperative*, because the trustees have to appoint, a power is *discretionary*, because the donees of a power need not appoint at all—the choice is theirs.

If the donees of a power do not appoint, a gift or trust over may have been provided for in default of appointment. A gift or trust over is a gift or trust which takes effect where the property has not otherwise been fully disposed of. It must be provided for in the original trust instrument, and if it has, it will take effect. If not, the property goes on resulting trust to the settlor.

A power to distribute property to a limited class of persons (called the objects of the power) is called a 'special power of appointment'. If there is no limit as to whom the objects may be, it is called a 'general power of appointment'. There is also a category of intermediate, or hybrid, powers, where a donee is given power to appoint to anyone except those within a particular class. In each case a donee may also be an object of the power. Obviously, a donee under a general power of appointment is in a position akin to that of an absolute owner. The distinction between general and special powers of appointment is of importance when considering perpetuities (section 3.7).

The purpose of mere powers is not immediately apparent. Probably they are a hangover from days when testators did not trust wives and eldest sons to administer family property in the manner that they regarded as sensible. So, although the settlor in general terms wished to benefit his wife or eldest son, he did not wish to give them enforceable rights. Therefore the property was settled on somebody else, who had the power to appoint to the wife or eldest son, but did not need to do so if such an appointment appeared unwise.

In recent years the practice has arisen of creating intermediate powers with discretionary trusts over, in default of appointment, where the donees under the power are the same people as the trustees under the discretionary trust. In most respects this has an identical effect to a discretionary trust. For example, if A is given power to appoint to B, C or D, with a trust over in default, in favour of E and F, A cannot avoid appointing altogether, and this is no different from a discretionary trust in favour of B, C, D, E and F. The only exception might be where A refuses to carry out his duties at all, and the court is required ultimately to distribute the property. In the case of a power with a trust over, B, C and D would have no claim. If the instrument was in the form of a single trust, they would. But it is unlikely that settlors have frequent regard to this extreme and pathological situation.

So why use a power and trust over in default? One possible reason is that, as we shall see in the next chapter, between 1955 and 1971 the certainty of object test for powers was thought to be less stringent than that for discretionary trusts. In other words, an instrument which was valid as a power might be invalid as a discretionary trust, if there was a wide range of objects. It therefore became common practice to draft powers with a wide range of objects, which was valid, while confining the trust over to a narrow range of objects. Such an instrument could be valid, whereas if drafted as a trust alone would fall foul of the certainty-of-object requirements. If this is indeed the explanation for such instruments, one might expect that they will become less common now that, since 1971, the certainty tests for trusts and powers have been regarded as being practically the same.

As with discretionary trusts, the objects of the power have no definable interest in the property unless that power is exercised in their favour. The objects can come to court to enforce the power, however, to the very limited extent that the court will restrain disposal of the property otherwise than in accordance with the terms of the power.

2.5.3 Extent of discretion and nature of enforcement

For mere powers, the donee's discretion seems to be unfettered except to the extent that he must not dispose of the property otherwise than in accordance with the terms of the power.

So far as discretionary trusts are concerned, though, members of the class of possible beneficiaries have no defined interest in the property unless and until the trustees' discretion is exercised in their favour, nevertheless, they have sufficient *locus standi* to come to court to enforce the trust. Clearly the degree to which enforcement is possible is limited by the discretionary nature of the arrangement, but the courts will restrain the trustees from acting contrary to the terms of the trust instrument. And if they refuse to distribute at all, a court can remove them and appoint new trustees, or in the final analysis distribute the property itself. Furthermore, unlike donees of mere powers, the trustees' discretion is not absolute. In considering its exercise, they must make a survey of the entire field of objects, and consider each individual case responsibly, on its merits: per Lord Wilberforce in *McPhail* v *Doulton* [1971] AC 424. The requirement that discretion must be properly exercised is not merely academic. In *Turner* v *Turner*

[1984] Ch 100, the trustees simply acted on the instructions of the settlor (i.e., did not exercise their own discretion at all, but effectively delegated it to him). Mervyn Davies J held that the appointments they made were invalid.

We saw above that a power with discretionary trust over, where the donees of the power and the trustees are the same people, is very like a discretionary trust. On principle, therefore, the exercise of the power should be controlled in the same way as that of a discretionary trust rather than a mere power. Sir Robert Megarry V-C provides some support for this view in *Re Hay's ST* [1982] 1 WLR 1202, holding that the extent of the duty to consider both whether or not a power should be exercised, and how it should be exercised, is stronger when the power is given to someone who is also a trustee than when a mere power is exercised. For example, it is not sufficient simply to appoint to the objects who happen to be at hand, whereas the donee of a mere power can do this. It seems that it is necessary periodically to consider whether or not to exercise the power, and at least to appreciate the width of the field of objects, even if it is not possible to compile a list of all the objects or ascertain accurately their number. Also, individual appointments need to be considered on their merits. It is not clear whether Sir Robert Megarry V-C regards this duty as the same as in the case of discretionary trusts, or a lesser duty, though still more stringent than in the case of a mere power.

The extent of the duty is important, at least on the orthodox view, when considering certainty of objects, and we shall return to it in chapter 3.

2.5.4 Distinguishing between trusts and powers

The distinction between discretionary trusts and powers is often extremely fine. It is a matter of construing the settlor's intention, and therefore no precise criteria can be laid down. The courts have no particular presumption one way or the other, and in the days when certainty requirements used to be much stricter for discretionary trusts than powers, the courts refused to spell valid powers out of invalid trusts (see the equitable maxims referred to in section 1.4.1).

If the settlor provides for a gift over or trust over in default of appointment, or has otherwise provided for this contingency, a power must be intended. This is because a trustee *must* appoint. The converse statement does not follow, however, and the courts will by no means presume a trust because there is no gift over in default. If in this case a power is construed, a failure to appoint leads to a resulting trust in favour of the settlor.

There are a number of reasons why it is necessary to distinguish between trusts and powers:

(a)   The duties of donees and trustees and the method of enforcement are different (see above).

(b)   The certainty of object rules used to be different and may still be in detailed respects (see chapter 3).

(c) Suppose an appointment has become impossible, perhaps because the donee or trustee has died. In default of appointment under a power, either the instrument will provide for a gift over, or there will be a resulting trust back to the settlor. The objects have no claim. In the case of a discretionary trust, however, the property will ultimately be distributed among the objects. If the discretion is given to one person in particular, say a particular member of a family, and he dies without exercising that discretion, the court itself must do so, and in *Burrough* v *Philcox* (1840) 5 My & Cr 72 Lord Cottenham held that the property should be divided equally among the objects. This solution will not always be sensible except in family-type trusts, however, and where it is not the courts will not adopt it (*McPhail* v *Doulton* [1971] AC 424).

2.6 PROTECTIVE TRUSTS

This special type of trust was developed as a method of protecting family property against the consequences of the family falling into debt. Generally speaking, any property owned by a debtor can be taken to satisfy his creditors and in the extreme event of bankruptcy all of the debtor's property becomes vested in his trustee in bankruptcy, including, of course, any interest under a family settlement.

In the 19th century, when family settlements were commoner than today, such an interest would usually be a life interest, and where improvidence was feared, this interest might be made determinable upon the bankruptcy or attempted alienation of the interest on the part of its owner. At first, the practice was to provide for a gift over to some other member of the family if the life interest was thus brought to an end, but by the latter part of the 19th century a more satisfactory solution was discovered, and today a protective trust consists of a determinable life interest, the determination of which brings into play a discretionary trust in favour of the former life tenant, his spouse and children (if any) and ultimately his next of kin who would inherit in the event of his death.

The obvious advantages are that upon the bankruptcy or alienation of the interest, that interest simply ceases to exist and cannot be claimed by creditors or the trustee in bankruptcy. The property itself remains in the hands of the trustees who can distribute the income as they see fit in the circumstances. If the reason for the determination is the actual indebtedness of the former life tenant, it would clearly be pointless to make payments to him, as the creditors could then seize the money, but the lifestyle of the family can be maintained by paying the income instead to the wife, or directly to those who supply his needs, since they can apply it for the 'use and benefit' of the former life tenant without placing money directly into his hands. It is not even necessary to set out in express terms the nature of the trusts, since s. 33 of the Trustee Act 1925 provides a model form which can be invoked simply by directing that the property shall be held on 'protective trusts' for the benefit of the person who is to be the life tenant (called the 'principal beneficiary' in the section).

There are two main limitations. First, it is not possible to settle property upon oneself upon such trusts, and protective trusts would usually be created by the parent of the principal beneficiary on his behalf. Secondly, the life interest must be made *determinable* upon the relevant event—that is, so defined that it ends naturally upon the happening of the event. If on the other hand it is made subject to a *condition subsequent*, that condition may be void as a device to defeat one's creditors. The difference is purely one of language and is devoid of moral principle.

2.7   TRUSTS FOR SALE AND CONVERSION

Trusts for sale have become very important indeed over recent years, sufficiently so to justify separate consideration. In a trust for sale, the trustees are directed to sell the trust property and hold the purchase money on trust as directed.

Their original purpose, dating from around the beginning of the 19th century, was in settling commercial land. Unlike rural aristocratic estates, such land was not normally settled entirely on the eldest son and thereafter down the male line, but the intention rather was to share the wealth among all the sons equally. The best way to achieve this was to direct that the business be sold, each son to take a share of the proceeds.

2.7.1   Equitable doctrine of conversion

This doctrine is based on the maxim 'Equity looks on that as done which ought to be done' (see section 1.4.1). As we have seen (section 1.4.4) most contracts for the sale of legal estates in land are specifically enforceable, in which case, from the moment the contract is made, equity treats as done that which ought to be done and regards the property as if it were already sold. Thus a contract for a lease creates an equitable lease immediately, as long as the equitable remedies are available—they were not, for example, in *Coatsworth* v *Johnson* (1886) 54 LT 520 (see section 1.4.5.1).

Another result of the operation of the doctrine of conversion is that for some purposes the vendor's interest becomes an interest in money and that of the purchaser an interest in land. So, for example, the property is at the purchaser's risk as to damage and deterioration after contract. It also follows logically that a vendor of a legal estate in land holds it on constructive trust for the purchaser from the time the contract is made to the time of the actual conveyance of the estate in land. The trust is imposed on the vendor (who retains legal title until completion) by the courts because the purchaser is regarded as owner in equity.

Nevertheless, the two parties to the contract have conflicting interests before completion of the sale, so the trust that arises is of an unusual nature. The usual duties imposed on trustees (considered in chapters 9 and 10) do not apply to their fullest extent. For example, the vendor can retain any income on the property until completion.

There is still room, therefore, for at least some element of the disposition of the equitable interest to occur on completion. Though the purchaser is treated as equitable owner from the moment of contract for most purposes, he cannot be regarded as equitable owner in the fullest sense while the duties owed by the vendor are less stringent than those of other trustees. Thus the House of Lords held in *Oughtred* v *IRC* [1960] AC 206 (see section 3.5.4.2) that a disposition of an equitable interest in shares took place on completion—in other words a disposition of the entire equitable interest had not already occurred at the time of the contract (though it was specifically enforceable).

It is probable that the same principles apply to the sale of equitable estates and interests in land.

Applying the doctrine of conversion specifically to trusts for sale, equity regarded the interests of the sons (in the above example) as having been converted into personalty (i.e., money, not land) forthwith, even before the land was actually sold. One result of the operation of this doctrine is that a purchaser is not concerned with beneficial interests under a trust for sale, because they are regarded as being interests in money only. Another result is that it becomes personalty for other purposes also (e.g., taxation, or if 'all my personalty' is left to X in a will).

2.7.2 Trusts for sale and settled land

More recently, the function of the trust for sale has often been as a conveyancing device, in which case the direction to sell has become merely a fiction. 'Immediate binding trusts for sale' are exempted from the provisions of the Settled Land Act 1925 (see section 1.6.4). Since the purpose of that statute is to prevent land being tied up, and since trusts for sale are exempted from its operation, the paradoxical result is that if one wants to tie up land today, in such a way as to make it unsaleable, the trust for sale is the appropriate device for the purpose.

The reason this can be done is that into many trusts for sale is expressed a power to postpone sale, and indeed such powers are now implied by statute. Perhaps the original purpose of powers to postpone was to enable the trustees to sell at optimum market price. But it is even possible to direct the trustees that the sale shall be conditional upon the consents of named persons. The trick is to arrange for some such named person to have a vested interest in not consenting, for example, by giving him an interest in the property which is contingent upon it remaining unsold. Another possibility is to ensure that the extent of the interest is greater as long as the property remains unsold, and is reduced if it is sold. By this means it is possible to ensure that, in practice, the property cannot be sold, at least for a lifetime. A good example is *Re Herklot's WT* [1964] 1 WLR 583.

Thus the trust for sale has become an effective device to avoid the Settled Land Act, in cases where the last thing the settlor wants is for the land actually to be sold. This is not, however, the social evil that it may have been 100 years ago, because hardly anyone wants to tie up large estates today, and the Inland Revenue would be the main beneficiaries should anyone choose to do so.

2.7.3   Shared land

By far the most important function of the trust for sale today, however, is where land is shared. Matrimonial homes are frequently jointly held by husband and wife, for example, so this may well be one of the commonest forms of trust. The Law of Property Act 1925 provides that all shared estates in land are to be held on trust for sale with power to postpone sale. The people who share the land will usually be both trustees and beneficiaries, except that the legislation provides that there cannot be more than four trustees. So long as the purchaser pays the purchase money to at least two trustees he overreaches the beneficial interests in the property (see section 1.6.3).

As with settlements, the trust for sale is merely a conveyancing device, as it is not usually intended that the land be sold. This is especially the case where a matrimonial home is jointly held. Yet because the trust to sell is imperative, whereas the power to postpone is discretionary, the trust duty prevails unless the power is exercised unanimously by all the trustees. So in theory one trustee can force a sale, whatever the wishes of the others (*Re Mayo* [1943] Ch 302). The logical conclusion would be that one party to a marriage could force the sale of the matrimonial home (if jointly owned), whatever the wishes of the other party.

In fact, the courts have prevented this by not allowing a sale which is a fraud on the underlying purpose of the trust, so long as that purpose remains. For example, one party to a marriage cannot obtain an order for the sale of a matrimonial home while the marriage continues (*Jones* v *Challenger* [1961] 1 QB 176). Matrimonial homes are now covered anyway by later legislation but *Jones* v *Challenger* still applies to property held jointly by unmarried cohabitees. If the relationship terminates, arguably the underlying purpose no longer remains, in which case *Mayo* should apply, but the position can be complicated by any children of the liaison. The question then will be whether the underlying purpose included the provision of a home for the children also. This latter is a question of fact—the courts will not automatically protect the children: if the parents were married they would, however, because of the later legislation.

Suppose, on the other hand, the relationship still continues but one party (X) goes bankrupt. X himself would be unable to insist on a sale in these circumstances, but it seems the trustee in bankruptcy can, except in truly exceptional circumstances (*Re Turner* [1974] 1 WLR 1556; *Re Holliday* [1980] 3 All ER 385). He does not stand in X's shoes, in other words, but the interests of the creditors prevail. This result is unaffected by the marriage or otherwise of the parties.

One difference between statutory trusts for sale and other types is that the courts have recognised their fictitious nature, and that they are merely a device to make transfer of property easier. Consent requirements are more readily implied. Also, the doctrine of conversion may not operate to its full extent: the interests of the parties remain interests in land for some purposes (or at least 'subsisting in reference thereto' under the Land Registration Act 1925, s. 70(1)) until the land is actually sold—this can have important ramifications if the land is wrongly sold or mortgaged where questions of priorities are at stake (*Williams & Glyn's Bank Ltd* v *Boland* [1981] AC 487).

2.8 SUCCESSION

Trusts have a limited role to play in succession, but the main function of this section is to explain terms which will be used later in various parts of the book.

When a person dies, the legal and beneficial entitlement to all his property passes to his 'personal representatives'. If he made a will in which he appointed specific persons to be his personal representatives, they are known as his 'executors', and their first task is to obtain probate of the will (i.e., have the will registered at the principal or district probate registry). Thereafter, their duty is to meet the debts and funeral expenses of the deceased out of his property and then to distribute the rest in accordance with the instructions given in the will.

When a person dies intestate (i.e., without making a will), a statutory scheme provided by the Administration of Estates Act 1925 comes into play. This attempts to give effect to what most people are assumed to intend to happen to their property after their deaths by providing first for any widow or widower, then for children and so on, so that the closest relatives obtain the benefits which the deceased would probably have wished for them. The scheme extends outwards, so that if the deceased has no close relatives, his more distant relatives will benefit. If he has no relatives at all, the property passes to the Crown.

Since there is no will, his personal representatives will not be executors, but 'administrators', i.e., the persons who have obtained a grant entitling them to administer the estate. These will usually be the persons who are entitled to the property. If the deceased left a widow, she is entitled to a grant of administration, permitting her to distribute the property; if there is no widow, the right passes to the children, and so on.

Whether the personal representatives are executors of a will or administrators upon an intestacy, their duties are the same, and many of the rules which apply to trustees (see chapters 9 and 10) apply also to them. They hold their office for life but the active duties are usually completed within one or two years. They must collect in all the deceased's assets, pay all debts and expenses, and then distribute the property either in accordance with the terms of the will or the statutory scheme, as the case may be.

Wills commonly provide for specific gifts to relatives or friends. A gift of land is called a 'devise' and its recipient a 'devisee'; a gift of personal property, including money, is a 'legacy' and its recipient a 'legatee'. Property which is not specifically disposed of by will is called the 'residue', and the person(s) entitled to it the 'residuary legatee(s)'. If a specific gift fails for any reason (possible reasons appear in the following chapter), it is added to the residue. In practice, this often comprises the bulk of the property as it is usual to provide small specific gifts to selected friends and relatives and simply leave the rest to the person whom one most desires to benefit.

Trusts may arise on a death, either because the will specifies that some property is to be held on trust or because the intended recipient is under 18 so that the legal title must be held for him until he reaches that age. Where trusts are deliberately created, it is usual to name the persons who are to act as trustees and when the executors have completed their administration they must transfer that property to the trustees. Often, the same persons will be named as both executors and trustees and will continue to hold the legal title in their new capacity.

It is important to appreciate that the legatees, devisees and beneficiaries under any trust created by the will have no beneficial interest in that property until such time as the executors appropriate (i.e., earmark) property to meet the gifts or trusts created by the will. What they have is merely a right to demand the proper administration of the estate by the executors. Similarly, persons entitled upon an intestacy have no beneficial interest in the property until the administrators have paid off all the liabilities affecting the deceased's property and prepared their accounts, showing what is available for those persons. For the sake of convenience, the persons entitled under an intestacy are referred to as the 'next of kin' rather than legatees, etc.

It is possible for a partial intestacy to occur, e.g., where the deceased failed to specify in his will who the residuary legatee is to be, or where the residuary gift fails. In such a case, the property will pass to the next of kin, as provided by the statutory scheme.

3

Requirements for an Express Private Trust

Though this chapter explicitly concerns express private trusts, many of the same conditions need also to be met for other types of trust and power. Only express private trusts, however, are subject to all the requirements. Implied, resulting and constructive trusts (see chapters 5 and 6) are specifically exempted from the statutory formality requirements of the Law of Property Act 1925, s. 53 (see section 3.5) though, as we shall see, it is arguable that express trusts may also be exempt in some circumstances. Charitable trusts (see chapter 8) are exempt from the certainty of objects and purpose trust rules, and incidentally from the perpetuity rules (which are discussed in section 3.7). So it can sometimes be important to know whether a trust is or is not express—see, for example, the discussions of secret and half-secret trusts (chapter 7) and variation of trusts (chapter 12). 'Private' in this context means non-charitable.

For convenience, certainty of objects requirements for powers also are included in this chapter, by way of comparison with those for discretionary trusts.

3.1 CERTAINTY

3.1.1 The three certainties

The classification for certainty usually cited is that of Lord Langdale in *Knight* v *Knight* (1840) 3 Beav 148, 173: while the classification has been criticised, there is no doubt that it is the one adopted by the courts. The essential prerequisites of a valid private express trust are certainty as to the intention of the settlor to create a trust of property (sometimes misleadingly termed certainty of words), certainty as to the property to which the trust is to attach (also referred to as certainty of subject matter), and certainty as to the persons or 'objects' who are to benefit (certainty of objects).

3.1.1.1 Effect of absence of certainty
If any of the certainties is absent then no valid express trust will be created but the precise consequences will depend upon which of the three certainties is absent:

(a) If it is impossible to identify the property to comprise the subject-matter of the trust, the whole transaction will be nugatory and no property will leave the ownership of the would-be settlor.

(b)   If, on the other hand, the property is specified, but there is uncertainty as to the intention to create a trust (i.e., to separate the legal and equitable titles), then a person who has received the property will hold it free of any trust. In other words the legal title will pass but the equitable title will not pass separately from it.

(c)   Finally, if the intention to create a trust is clear and the property specified but it is uncertain who is to benefit from the trust, a valid trust will be created but it will not be the one intended by the settlor. In other words, the property will 'result' (i.e., return to the settlor) and anyone who has received it will hold it as trustee either for the settlor himself or, in the case of an attempt to establish a trust by will, for the residuary legatees of the estate.

3.1.1.2   Purpose of the rules

There are two main reasons for certainty requirements. The first and obvious reason is to ensure that property is dealt with in accordance with the wishes of the property owner (settlor if a valid trust is created). Thus, a doubt as to those wishes leads the courts to play safe rather than risk an unauthorised disposition of a person's property. Additionally, it must be clear to the trustees themselves exactly what are their duties. The difficulty is most acute in the case of testamentary trusts where those who have the duty of administering the estate have to rely for guidance upon whatever terms the testator may have chosen to express his desires, since obviously it is not possible to ask him.

The second reason is less obvious. Whereas today trustees usually act in a professional capacity, the typical trust of 200 years ago was very different in nature, and the rules originally developed around the older type of trust. These were often family arrangements and one of the main concerns of the courts was that the trustees might be fraudulent and keep the trust property themselves. Equity has been criticised for making essentially the same assumptions about, e.g., banks and company directors today; the problem stems from adapting to a modern situation a set of principles which were originally developed for quite a different purpose. Certainly a limited degree of successful adaptation has occurred but the same basic assumption remains, namely, that trustees are likely to be fraudulent.

Thus the courts tend to over-emphasise the pathological situation, where the trustees refuse to carry out the trust. The courts have insisted that there must exist someone with sufficient interest in the trust property to be able to come to court to compel them, and in the final analysis the courts must be able to administer the trust themselves. This emphasis has led to much more rigid certainty requirements than might otherwise have been the case.

3.1.2 Certainty of intention

3.1.2.1 Words or intention?
Although Lord Langdale spoke of certainty in relation to the words alleged to establish the settlor's intention, this is misleading in two respects. First, it is possible to establish a trust without any writing whatever, except where the statutory formality requirements obtain (see section 3.5). A trust need not even be orally declared, as it is possible to establish an intention of a settlor to create a trust (i.e., to separate legal and equitable titles) from words or conduct; this may be inferred from the nature of the gift as a whole. No doubt *in fact* most express trusts are created by means of written documents since they arise either by will or in a formal settlement, carefully documented to meet the settlor's tax-planning needs. A modern trust precedent will be highly intricate and will attempt to provide for almost all conceivable contingencies. But in principle technical words are not necessary since equity looks to the intention rather than the form of the transaction. It is not even necessary that the word 'trust' should have been employed if the intention to create a trust is clear.   *Paul v Waddell.*

The second reason why Lord Langdale's statement is misleading is that even where words are present the courts do not have regard to them alone, though they are important in construing the intention of the would-be settlor. Indeed, to rely on words alone as binding precedent would be dangerous as the attitude of the courts has changed considerably over the last 150 years or so, especially regarding precatory words (e.g., words expressing a wish, hope or request, rather than being imperative).

3.1.2.2 History of precatory words
So far as testamentary gifts are concerned, up to about the middle of the 19th century the courts were disposed to find that almost any expression of desire by a testator that his property should be used in a given manner was intended to create a binding trust of that property in the hands of an executor or legatee. The reasons historically can be traced to the fact that the administration of estates lay formerly with the ecclesiastical courts, which permitted the executor to keep for himself any undisposed-of residue of property left after the specific bequests had been satisfied. When this jurisdiction was taken over by the Court of Chancery, it preferred to treat the executor as trustee of such residue for the testator's family. Almost any expression of desire or hope would be seized upon to effect this policy. Even this solution was not entirely satisfactory. Widows and eldest sons of gentry were often provided for in any event by a marriage settlement, or entail of the estate, and the courts were suspicious of their ability to manage the family property in prudent fashion (that is to say, keeping it in the family). Therefore a similar principle was applied to legatees as had formerly been applied to executors. The outcome was that precatory words, like 'wish', 'hope' or even 'in

confidence' that the legatee would use the gift to benefit others, were taken to create binding trusts.

The rationale for the lenient view taken of precatory words largely disappeared with the Executors Act of 1830, which specifically required executors to hold property in an appropriate manner. Recently, therefore, the courts have felt able to tighten up their attitude, the modern view being stated in the judgment of Cotton LJ in *Re Adams and the Kensington Vestry* (1884) 27 ChD 394, 410, where it was established that beneficiaries were no longer to be made trustees unless this was the testator's clear intention, and a gift to the widow 'in full confidence that she would do what was right as to the disposal thereof between my children, either in her lifetime or by will after her decease' was treated as giving the widow an absolute interest unfettered by any trust in favour of the children. Cotton LJ thought that many of the older authorities had gone too far; he also thought that one should consider the total effect of the instrument (not only the particular words) to ascertain the testator's intention. Other cases around the same time made it clear that the attitude of the courts towards precatory words had changed.

3.1.2.3 *Law relating to precatory words*
Since intention is all-important, however, a trust may still be created by precatory words if such intention appears from the document (or settlor's conduct) as a whole. A modern example of the creation of a trust by precatory words is *Re Kayford Ltd* [1975] 1 WLR 279, where customers paid money to a company in advance for the supply of goods. This money was put by the company into a special account called a 'Customer Trust Deposit Account', the intention of the company being that this money should be kept separate from the company's general funds and withdrawn from the account only when the customers had received their goods. On the winding up of the company Megarry J held that a trust had been created and that the customers were not mere creditors of the company but beneficial owners of the moneys which they had paid until such time as their goods were delivered: a happy conclusion for the customers, whose rights would otherwise have been merely those of ordinary creditors claiming in the liquidation.

Because the whole document or transaction is to be considered, it does not follow that the same precatory words will always have the same effect. Thus in *Re Hamilton* [1895] 2 Ch 370, 373 Lindley LJ said (of a testamentary gift):

You must take the will which you have to construe and see what it means, and if you come to the conclusion that no trust was intended, you say so, although previous judges have said the contrary on some wills more or less similar to the one which you have to construe.

In *Cominsky* v *Bowring-Hanbury* [1905] AC 84, the House of Lords found a trust on the basis of words very similar to those employed in *Re Adams and the Kensington Vestry*: 'absolutely in full confidence that she [the widow] will make such use of [the property] as I should have made myself and that at her death she will devise it to such one or more of my nieces as she may think fit'.

If on the other hand, a testator reproduces the *exact* language of an earlier will which has previously been held to create a trust, it may be possible to infer that he intended to use the earlier will as a precedent. If so there is authority that the court in construing the later will should follow the earlier decision, at least unless that decision was clearly wrong (*Re Steele's WT* [1948] Ch 603). Though this case attaches great significance to the actual precatory words used, it is not really an exception to the flexible approach described above, because all the circumstances do indeed point to an intention to create a trust. It follows that draftsmen should make clear beyond doubt that precatory words are intended to indicate desire alone, unless of course a trust is indeed intended.

A further, somewhat technical, consideration is that the creation of a gift in a will, followed by the inclusion of a precatory expression in a codicil, raises a stronger inference of intention to create a trust than would be the case were both gift and precatory words to appear in the same instrument (*Re Burley* [1910] 1 Ch 215). Finally, it should not be forgotten that the testator, while not intending to create a trust, may have subjected the property to a power of appointment (see chapter 2) instead of making an outright gift to the legatee. In any case, the decision as to the testator's intention is a matter of construction of the document and no hard and fast rule can be laid down for determining when this intention is present.

3.1.3 Certainty of subject-matter

Two distinct difficulties can arise, and indeed it has been argued that the single test of certainty of subject-matter is deficient in that it confuses these (e.g., Williams (1940) 4 MLR 20; Watkin (1979) 8 AALR 123). The property to be subject to the trust may be uncertain. Alternatively, the precise extent of the beneficial interests may be uncertain.

3.1.3.1 Uncertainty as to the property
In *Palmer* v *Simmonds* (1854) 2 Drew 221 a testatrix left on trust 'the bulk' of her residuary estate, and Kindersley V-C, after consulting a dictionary, concluded that the word 'bulk' was inadequate to specify any portion of the property as trust property. Since it was not possible to carve out from the residue that portion which was to be held on trust, the trust failed and the residuary legatee took the whole absolutely. The same result was reached in *Curtis* v *Rippon* (1820) 5 Madd 434.

In both these cases, there was an ascertained beneficiary whose right to the whole of the property was made subject to the rights of others to a portion of it.

That portion was indefinite, so the gift to those ostensibly entitled to the portion failed. On the other hand, there is, of course, no reason why the whole of a person's property should not form the subject-matter of a disposition where there is an ascertainable beneficiary. Thus the beneficiary of the whole was entitled to take under a valid disposition, free from the gift of the portion, which failed because of uncertainty of subject-matter.

Where, however, the testator has failed to give any indication at all as to what property is to comprise the trust property, the whole transaction will fail, since there is nothing for any trust to fasten upon. This is not a case, as above, of a valid disposition of the whole, subject to an invalid gift of a part. There is no valid disposition of the whole or any part of the property.

It is clear, then, that a direction regarding all of a testator's property is workable (otherwise the beneficiaries would not have taken in the above cases) since it can be taken as meaning 'whatever it may be at the time of my death'. A direction regarding 'some' or 'most' of a testator's property, however, is unworkable and, unless (as occurred in the above cases) the property as a totality has been bequeathed to a specific individual, the whole exercise will be nugatory.

Another example, where the nature of the property itself was unclear, is *Re Kolb's WT* [1962] Ch 531, where the testator referred, in an investment clause in his will, to 'blue-chip' securities, a term generally used to designate shares in large public companies which are considered an entirely safe investment. The term has no technical or objective meaning, however, and Cross J held that its meaning in the context must depend on the standard applied by the testator, which could not be determined with sufficient certainty to enable the clause to be upheld. In this type of case, the uncertainty as to the nature of the property vitiates the whole transaction.

3.1.3.2   Uncertainty as to the beneficial interests
In *Curtis v Rippon* (1820) 5 Madd 434 not only was there uncertainty as to the property to be subject to the trust, but also as to the identity of the beneficiaries themselves. The widow received all her husband's property under his will, subject to an exhortation (using precatory words that were valid at the time) that she should use the property for the spiritual and temporal good of herself and the children, 'remembering always, according to circumstances, the Church of God and the poor'. The clause rendered uncertain even who was to benefit. Another possibility is that all the beneficiaries are known, but the amount of each beneficial interest is not. In these circumstances the courts can usually find ways of validating the trust.

An example is *Re Golay's WT* [1965] 1 WLR 969. The testator had directed his trustees to allow a beneficiary ('Totty') to 'enjoy one of my flats during her lifetime and to receive a reasonable income from my other properties'. The uncertainty of such a disposition, of course, is not confined to the beneficiary in question, since her eventual share to some degree determines the share of the rest in what is left. In such circumstances, however, since there is certainty as to the overall quantum of property available for distribution, the practice of the courts is to attempt to make a distribution in accordance with the settlor's wishes if they can be ascertained. In *Re Golay's WT*, Ungoed-Thomas J felt able to uphold the gift, as the trustees could select a flat and the income to be received by Totty could be objectively quantified by the court. In a case where property is left to a number of beneficiaries without any guidance as to how it is to be shared, the maxim 'Equality is equity' may be applied and the property divided between the beneficiaries in equal shares.

3.1.4 Certainty of objects

Certainty of objects rules serve two main functions. First, if a trustee, or a donee of a power, fails to carry out his duties, or exercises his discretion in an improper manner, it is important to be able to ascertain who has *locus standi* to come to court to remedy the situation. Secondly, a trustee, or a donee of a power, has to be able to ascertain who are the objects in order to be able to exercise his discretion in a proper manner.

3.1.4.1 *Rationale of the rules: enforcement*

Once a settlement has been made, whether it creates a trust or a power, the settlor ceases to have an interest in the property. Indeed, in the common case of a settlement by will he will naturally be unable to have any further personal say. The question then arises as to what happens if the trustee, or the donee of the power, does not carry out the trust or power. Sometimes a trustee will have agreed to act for consideration (e.g., a bank acting under a remuneration clause). In that case the settlor, or his personal representatives can sue at common law in contract. It is not an altogether satisfactory action, however, as we saw in chapter 2: unless he can obtain specific performance, he will be limited to claiming damages for his own loss, which will probably be nominal only. Therefore the courts have always been very concerned that someone who benefits in equity is able to enforce the trust.

The certainty requirements to achieve this end depend on the nature of enforcement by the courts. They have taken a more realistic and less rigid view in recent years as to the manner in which trusts are to be ultimately enforced. This has led to a relaxation of certainty rules, which in most respects is to be welcomed.

Generally speaking, all that is now required for this purpose is for it to be possible to tell, with certainty, whether any individual coming to court to enforce a trust or power has sufficient interest to do so: in other words whether or not he is within the class of objects. This test is called the individual-ascertainability test. It is not necessary to be able to draw up a list of all the objects, a much more stringent requirement called the class-ascertainability test. Further, in applying the individual ascertainability test, it is necessary only that definitions in the settlement be conceptually certain. The court itself can deal with evidential difficulties when an application for enforcement arises. Thus, a trust in favour of the first 20 people who crossed Clifton suspension bridge in 1983 should be enforceable; the class is conceptually certain even though proof may be difficult. A trust in favour of Mr Scargill's friends is conceptually uncertain, however, and ought to fail.

3.1.4.2   Rationale of the rules: administering the trust

Some writers argue (e.g., Matthews [1984] Conv 22) that this is not a proper function of certainty of objects rules at all but the orthodox view is otherwise (see, e.g., Jill Martin in her reply in [1984] Conv 304). The certainty test required to enable trustees or donees of powers to discover all that is necessary for them to be able to carry out their duties depends on the nature of their discretion. Generally speaking, however, if a trustee or donee has to get any impression of the size or composition of the entire class in order to carry out his duties, a more stringent test is required than individual ascertainability and both the above examples should fail (assuming no central record is kept of people walking over Clifton bridge).

3.1.4.3   The operation of the rules

Though there has been much litigation about certainty of objects in recent years, the operation of the rules is still unclear in detailed respects. The manner in which a settlement is ultimately enforced and the nature of the discretion given to trustees or donees of powers depend on whether a fixed trust, a discretionary trust or power has been created (see chapter 2 for the distinctions). So it is necessary to consider separately the certainty requirements for each of these categories.

3.1.4.4   Fixed trusts

Since it is of the essence of a fixed trust that the property is to be divided among all the beneficiaries in fixed proportions (e.g., in equal shares), it can only be workable if the entire class of beneficiaries is known; the conventional view, therefore, for which, however, there is little authority, is that the test of certainty is the class ascertainability test. In other words it must be possible to draw up a complete list of objects, and *McPhail* v *Doulton* [1971] AC 424 (discussed in detail below), which applies the individual-ascertainability test to discretionary trusts, does not apply to fixed trusts. Assuming the class ascertainability test indeed applies, it is stricter than the test adopted for discretionary trusts and powers.

Some writers (e.g., Matthews [1984] Conv 22) have argued that the distinction between fixed and discretionary trusts is artificial and that the less strict test applies to fixed trusts also. Two arguments can be advanced in response to the workability point. First, if the trustees cannot ascertain the identity of all the beneficiaries, it is not necessary to strike down the trust as they can protect themselves by insurance. I suggest, however, that this solution is not only inelegant, but also that it does not accord with the personal nature of trusteeship for trustees to be unable to discover the method by which their duties are to be performed.

The second objection to the orthodox view is that it is not the function of the certainty test to assist the administration of trusts; if a trust is unworkable, the courts can strike it down as capricious. If, however, the entire class of objects cannot be ascertained it will *always* be unworkable, so this solution is merely a disguised application of the certainty test itself.

Further, though it follows from the conclusion in the previous paragraph that the application of a public policy test *in this particular regard* would present no difficulties (because the trust would always be unworkable unless the class could be ascertained), there are difficulties *generally* in extending public policy tests too far. They are inherently vague and it could be impossible to know whether or not a trust is valid in the absence of litigation.

I suggest, therefore, that the orthodox view is also the best.

3.1.4.5 Powers

Since there is no obligation on donees to carry out a power, and since if they do not nobody else gains any interest in the property, it may be wondered why it is necessary to ascertain whether anyone has *locus standi* to sue them. Donees of powers are under limited duties, however (see chapter 2), to consider whether or not the power should be exercised and also not to dispose of the property apart from under the terms of the power. The duty to consider is probably not so stringent as to require the donees, in order to carry it out, to draw up a list of the entire class of potential beneficiaries. The limited negative duty concerning the disposal of the property can be carried out and enforced so long as 'it can be said with certainty that any given individual is or is not a member of the class', and this test of certainty (i.e., the individual ascertainability test) has been adopted by the House of Lords in *Re Gulbenkian's Settlements* [1970] AC 508.

3.1.4.6 Discretionary trusts

3.1.4.6.1 The old test Discretionary trusts differ from powers in that, as we saw in chapter 2, the trustees are under an obligation to distribute the property, although no given individual can claim any share until discretion is exercised in his favour. In earlier cases (see, e.g., the view of Jenkins LJ in *IRC* v *Broadway Cottages Trust* [1955] Ch 678), the courts concerned themselves with the problems of ultimate enforcement. Suppose the trustees refuse to distribute the property. It was thought that the court could not exercise their discretion for them; it could either remove the trustees and appoint others in their place, or if it could find nobody prepared to execute the trust, would have to divide the property equally between the beneficiaries. It was this last possibility that caused the difficulty, for unless the whole class could be ascertained, as with fixed trusts, equal division was impossible. The result of this was that the test for certainty was much more stringent for discretionary trusts than for powers. This had two main consequences: first, many perfectly reasonable trusts failed; secondly, the courts were at pains to construe doubtful dispositions as powers rather than discretionary trusts (while nevertheless denying that a valid power can be spelt out of an invalid trust, on the grounds that the settlor did not intend a power—see the maxims in section 1.4.1)—hence the litigation discussed in chapter 2.

It is in any event clear that ultimate equal distribution is a ridiculous solution; often it will not implement the intentions of the settlor and indeed is quite likely to frustrate them. It seems that the equality principle originated in 19th-century family settlements (e.g., *Burrough* v *Philcox* (1840) 5 My & Cr 72), where it may have been the most reliable method of carrying out the settlor's intention. It is much less likely to be appropriate, however, in modern settlements, for example, dividing proceeds among employees of a company. Furthermore, this justification of the class ascertainability test is based on pathological assumptions, to say the least!

3.1.4.6.2   The new test   In *McPhail* v *Doulton* [1971] AC 424, however, Lord Wilberforce decisively rejected the principle of equality of distribution in a case where equal distribution would have made a nonsense of the settlor's intention. The *ratio* of the case is that the test for certainty for discretionary trusts is essentially the same as that for powers, the individual ascertainability test, as applied in *Re Gulbenkian's Settlements* [1970] AC 508, not the class ascertainability test. *IRC* v *Broadway Cottages Trust* [1955] Ch 678 was overruled.

The settlement in *McPhail* v *Doulton* was further litigated to determine whether it was valid under the new test in *Re Baden's Deed Trusts (No. 2)* [1973] Ch 9. In this subsequent litigation the Court of Appeal decided that in applying the test the courts are concerned only that the class is not conceptually uncertain. A trust will not fail merely because there are evidential difficulties in ascertaining whether or not someone is within the class as 'the court is never defeated by evidential uncertainty'.

3.1.4.6.3   Problems with the new test   So far as enforcement goes, there is obviously much to be said for the new approach, because once the equality principle is rejected, the *Gulbenkian* test should follow in principle, as all that should be necessary is for a court to be able to tell if a particular individual coming before it has sufficient *locus standi* to enforce the trust.

The test is less satisfactory in terms of administration, however. The new test may put trustees in the position of not knowing, or being able to discover, the identities of all the possible beneficiaries. If their duties are such that they must survey the entire field, they may now be unable to carry out these duties. The precise extent of their duty to survey is not certain, but as we saw in chapter 2, it is certainly more stringent than that applicable to donees of powers, and it is possible to conceive of discretionary trusts which would be very difficult to carry out were the trustees unable to survey the entire field of possible beneficiaries. An example might be a discretionary trust to distribute property 'according to the age and ability of the potential beneficiaries'. Some writers have suggested that insurance is the answer, but it seems unsatisfactory for the reasons given in section 3.1.4.4.

Perhaps for this reason Lord Wilberforce thought that dispositions might fail if the class is so widely drawn as to be administratively unworkable, even if they otherwise satisfy the new test. An example he gave was a gift to 'all the residents of Greater London', but the acceptable width of the class presumably depends on the exact nature of the trustees' duties, and whether they must actually survey the entire field. In any event, if the terms of a trust (or power) negative any sensible intention on the part of the settlor then it has been suggested *obiter* by Templeman J in *Re Manisty's Settlement* [1974] Ch 17 (actually a case involving a valid power) that it may fail on the grounds of capriciousness (see section 3.4). Perhaps these qualifications are sufficient to give the trustees the protection they require, though at the expense of the vagueness inherent in tests of this nature.

Difficulties need still to be resolved in the actual application of the test. One is the exact nature of the proof required under the test (differing opinions were given in *Re Baden's Deed Trusts (No. 2)* [1973] Ch 9). If it is necessary to be able to show that any person definitely is or is not within the class, then that effectively returns to the rejected class ascertainability test. Sachs LJ avoided that difficulty by placing the burden of proof, in effect, on someone claiming to be within the class. This seems acceptable if ultimate enforcement is the issue, and the test is of the *locus standi* of the claimant, but it does not help the administration of the trust. Megaw LJ adopted a different solution, however, requiring that, as regards a substantial number of objects, it can be shown with certainty that they fall within the class. This is rather a vague test—clearly it is not enough to be able to show that *one* person is certainly within the class, as this test was rejected in *Gulbenkian*. It is also difficult to see what policy Megaw LJ's test promotes. It cannot, of course, be predicted which, if either, of these tests of proof will be adopted in future.

Another difficulty is whether the inclusion of invalid classes invalidates otherwise valid gifts, or whether they can be severed. Megaw LJ's substantial number test may save such dispositions in some circumstances, if it is correct, and there seems to be no reason of policy to strike down the entire trust, assuming it is otherwise administratively workable.

3.2 PURPOSE TRUSTS

It is possible to argue that the law allows purpose trusts so long as their terms are sufficiently certain and they are either charitable or otherwise within the limited category of private purpose trusts of which the law approves. In other words, the test of validity is one of policy. Certainly a limited number of pure private purpose trusts have been upheld, and in cases where trusts have been struck down there have usually been good policy reasons for so doing. But though policy plays a limited role in this area of law (see section 3.4), it is not the main test of the validity of pure private purpose trusts.

The lack of ascertainable beneficiaries is, however, a reason why private (non-charitable) purpose trusts are usually struck down, because for that reason they are not enforceable by anyone. Charitable trusts (which are dealt with in chapter 8) are always purpose trusts and are valid, but there problems of enforcement do not arise as the Attorney-General has *locus standi* to sue. Charitable trusts are also exempt from the perpetuity rules.

Two separate problems arise with private purpose trusts. Sometimes humans are not intended to benefit at all, in which case no one has any interest in enforcing the trust. Another category is where, although humans are intended to benefit, and can be ascertained with sufficient certainty, they do not have full beneficial interests.

3.2.1   No human beneficiary

In general, trusts without human beneficiaries are void. A classic example is *Re Astor's ST* [1952] Ch 534, where trustees were instructed to hold a fund upon various trusts including 'the maintenance of good relations between nations [and]...the preservation of the independence of newspapers'. The purposes were not charitable, but the settlement was drafted so as to be valid under the perpetuity rules. The trust was held by Roxburgh J to be void because there were no human beneficiaries capable of enforcing it. Another example is *Re Shaw* [1957] 1 WLR 729, where Harman J held void on the same principle a trust to research the development of a 40-letter alphabet.

In both cases the courts may have been reluctant to uphold the trusts for other reasons also. For example, Roxburgh J thought that it was against public policy to allow large accumulations of private capital to be dispersed with no administrative state control. These reasons cannot be decisive, however, as they could be applied to all non-charitable trusts, whether or not purpose trusts. The courts exercise general control over useless or capricious purposes (see further section 3.4) and if policy arguments are to be advanced, that would seem to be the appropriate place for them.

On the other hand, trusts to erect tombs and monuments have been upheld, as have trusts for specific animals (e.g., *Re Dean* (1889) 41 ChD 522). It is difficult to reconcile these with the general principle; on the other hand too much reliance has been placed upon them for them now to be regarded as wrong, and they are usually regarded as exceptions.

3.2.2   Purpose trusts for human benefit

Here the problem is different. There are people (who must be ascertainable within the certainty tests discussed in section 3.1.4) with an interest in enforcing the trust, but none is entitled to a full beneficial interest. The law applicable to such a settlement was considered in *Leahy v Attorney-General for New South Wales* [1959] AC 457, where property was to be held on trust for 'such order of nuns of the Catholic Church or the Christian Brothers as my executors and trustees shall select'. The trust was not charitable, and Viscount Simonds thought that it failed as a private trust on the grounds that though the individual members had an interest in enforcing the trust, they were not granted a full beneficial interest. Since this is invariably the case with purpose trusts of this nature, the reasoning leads to the conclusion that such trusts are never valid.

Privy Council cases cannot of course be ignored, however inconvenient, but the decision probably does not go this far; if a purpose trust is certain in its terms and capable of being enforced, it is difficult to conceive of good reasons of policy to strike it down (subject to section 3.4), and *Leahy* is explicable on other grounds. The settlement was in fact validated by the New South Wales Conveyancing Act. In any event, it is not clear from the facts that the individual members were ascertainable, and the gift may also have failed for perpetuity.

In fact there have been many cases where purpose trusts have been upheld so long as ascertainable people have been able to benefit. In *Re the Trusts of the Abbott Fund* [1900] 2 Ch 326 a trust for the maintenance of two old ladies was upheld, and Goff J in *Re Denley's Trust Deed* [1969] 1 Ch 373 made clear that the test was not whether a full beneficial interest was granted, but whether individuals who were ascertainable had *locus standi* to sue. They will have, he thought, so long as the benefit is not too indirect or intangible. The trust in the case was 'for the purpose of a recreation or sports ground primarily for the benefit of the employees of the company' and that was held to be sufficient to give the employees *locus standi* to sue.

It is submitted that the *Denley* approach is justified in terms of logic and principle. It can be argued that it does not much matter if private purpose trusts are struck down, as charitable purpose trusts are valid anyway. As we will see in chapter 8, however, the test for these has to be stringent, because as well as determining validity, charitable status also allows tax advantages. The only reason for not allowing non-charitable purpose trusts, assuming that they are not capricious, perpetual or unworkable, is if they are unenforceable—by adopting a *locus standi* test Goff J ensures that such trusts will indeed fail; otherwise the courts can give effect to the intention of the settlor.

3.3   GIFTS TO UNINCORPORATED ASSOCIATIONS

Another related problem occurs where property is conveyed to an unincorporated association (e.g., a society, social club or religious group), which will, of course, exist to use the property for a particular purpose. Unincorporated associations cannot themselves own property, not having legal personality (unlike companies). If the purposes of the association are charitable, its officers may hold property as charitable trustees, so no difficulties arise over gifts to charitable associations.

In other cases, it might be thought that the *Denley* principle allows property to be held in trust for the members of the association, for the purposes of the association, so long as the identity of those members is sufficiently certain. This is indeed the case so long as the gift is intended for present members only, but a gift to members for the time being (i.e., present and future) will usually infringe the perpetuity rules (discussed in section 3.7: one of the difficulties in *Leahy* v *Attorney-General for New South Wales* [1959] AC 457, discussed in section 3.2.2).

It is true that future associations may be able, by clever drafting, to find a solution to this problem (see Warburton [1985] Conv 318, 321) but most existing associations have not drafted their rules so as to allow a trust solution which also avoids perpetuity difficulties.

A better way round the perpetuity problem is to construe the gift as being to the existing members, but subject to their contractual duties as members of the society or club. These will be determined by the rules of the association, and may well prevent them from severing their interests.

This possibility was alluded to by Cross J in *Neville Estates* v *Madden* [1962] Ch 832, *obiter* because he held that the property, held by the trustees of Catford Synagogue, was held on charitable trusts, an aspect of the decision which is further discussed in chapter 8. A similar approach was taken by Brightman J in *Re Recher's WT* [1972] Ch 526, a case concerning a gift in trust for the London and Provincial Anti-Vivisection Society. Technically his view is also *obiter*, because the society had been dissolved at the date of the gift, but in principle it is correct, and in any event the approach has been approved in *Re Lipinski's WT* [1977] Ch 235 and *Re Grant's WT* [1980] 1 WLR 360.

Yet further support may be derived from the judgments of the Court of Appeal in *Conservative & Unionist Central Office* v *Burrell* [1982] 1 WLR 522. This case involved a statutory definition of an unincorporated association for tax purposes. The Conservative Central Office was held not to be an unincorporated association, and so outside the tax provision, because there were no enforceable mutual understandings between the members. The court proceeded on the assumption that the usual basis of enforcement would be contractual, though in the case there were no mutual understandings at all between the members, contractual or otherwise. Thus the case is direct authority only for the proposition that for a body to be an unincorporated association for the purposes of that particular statutory provision, there must be enforceable mutual rights and obligations between the members. It is not a direct authority on the basis of enforcement, though it was certainly assumed that it would usually be contractual.

It therefore seems to be possible to give money or property to a non-charitable unincorporated association so long as the gift can be construed in that manner, as a gift to the existing members absolutely, subject to the contractual rules of the association.

3.4 PUBLIC POLICY, CAPRICIOUS TRUSTS

3.4.1 Public policy: void conditions

Various trusts, which would otherwise be valid, are void for reasons of public policy, in which case the property will be held on resulting trust for the settlor. Trusts for illegitimate children as yet unborn fell into this category before 1970 because it was supposed that they tended to encourage immorality, and the old law still applies to pre-1970 dispositions. Since that date they have been validated by s. 15 of the Family Law Reform Act 1969.

Conditions affecting dispositions may also be struck down on public policy grounds, in which case the result depends on whether the condition is construed as a condition precedent or a condition subsequent. If the former, the entire gift generally fails (though the statement must be qualified in relation to personal property), and the property results to the settlor. If the latter, the gift, but not the condition, is valid.

Examples of invalid conditions are trusts tending to prevent the carrying out of parental duties, trusts in restraint of marriage and trusts which are fraudulent. Testators sometimes leave property to children subject to a condition subsequent relating to their religious upbringing. In *Blathwayt* v *Lord Cawley* [1976] AC 397, for example, a large estate (valued in 1975 at £2 million) was left in 1936 on various entailed trusts, but such that any person who became entitled was to forfeit his interest if he became a Roman Catholic (or disused the name and arms of Blathwayt). It was argued that with respect to the present children, the religious condition tended to restrain the carrying out of parental duties, and was therefore void on public policy grounds, but the House of Lords held otherwise. The effect of the clause may have been to force the parents to choose between material and spiritual welfare for their offspring, but this was not necessarily contrary to public policy. In the event, however, the House of Lords held by a 3–2 majority (Lords Wilberforce and Fraser of Tullybelton dissenting) that the clause did not apply on its construction.

Conditions subsequent can still be struck down on the grounds of uncertainty, as in *Clayton* v *Ramsden* [1943] AC 320, which concerned a forfeiture on marriage to a person 'not of Jewish parentage and of the Jewish faith'. This was held to be conceptually uncertain. But it seems that so long as a clause is not uncertain the courts will be slow to strike it down on grounds of public policy, and a somewhat similar clause to the above was upheld by the Court of Appeal in *Re Tuck's ST* [1978] Ch 49, where 'an approved wife' of Jewish blood was precisely defined, cases of dispute being dealt with by the Chief Rabbi in London. Names and arms clauses (such as the other clause in *Blathwayt*) have also been upheld (for example, *Re Neeld* [1962] Ch 643, CA). It may be, though, that such leniency by the courts is misplaced because social conditions change and clauses of this nature arguably allow the dead too much freedom to interfere in the lives of the living.

3.4.2 Capricious or useless trusts

There is no doubt that the courts can also strike down capricious or useless trusts. An early example is *Brown* v *Burdett* (1882) 21 ChD 667, which was an attempt to create a trust to block up windows—surprisingly, this was not an attempt to avoid window tax. It may be, though, that as well as being a public policy test, the courts will use this ground to strike down trusts if no sensible intention can be imputed to the settlor. Perhaps with the relaxation of certainty of object and purpose trust tests (see sections 3.1.4 and 3.2) this jurisdiction will become more important than it has been in the past. It is a method by which the courts can reserve to themselves extensive discretionary powers.

It is to be hoped that the courts tread warily where the validity of a trust itself is at issue, however. Public policy tests are inherently vague, and in this area in particular there is an acute shortage of judicial definition. Certainty as to the law is important in property transactions, especially for testamentary dispositions where there is no opportunity for the settlor to correct any mistakes or failures. Public policy is always supposed to be an unruly horse and I would suggest that extensive use of such a jurisdiction would be most inappropriate in this area.

3.5 FORMALITIES

3.5.1 Introductory

There are no formality requirements for express trusts, except those laid down by statute; these are now contained in the Law of Property Act 1925, s. 53. The important distinctions to bear in mind are between land and other property, and between declarations and dispositions.

Implied, resulting and constructive trusts are expressly exempted from the statutory requirements, and so, it appears, are variations of trust carried out under the Variation of Trusts Act 1958 (see chapter 12). As appears below, however, the distinction between implied, resulting and constructive trusts on the one hand, and express trusts on the other, may be less important than appears at first sight; it is probable that express trusts can also, in some circumstances, fall outside the operation of s. 53, even though they are not expressly exempted.

The area of formalities is often especially feared by students. Yet while the facts of the main House of Lords cases are very complex, the main principles are not especially, though it is true that some of the conceptual difficulties remain unanswered by those decisions. So long as the student keeps in mind the main distinctions drawn by the section, and does not become too immersed in the factual complexities of the cases, this subject is not as formidable as is often thought.

3.5.1.1 Reasons for the rules

Land is subject to special rules because of its value, and also because real property (i.e., land) transactions are sufficiently complex for it to be undesirable for them to be taken lightly. So far as other property is concerned, the purpose of legislation on formalities is twofold. Bear in mind that equitable interests are intangible, and that it may not be possible to trace their movement unless that movement is evidenced by written documents. The primary purpose of a writing requirement is to prevent fraud—indeed the original statute was entitled the Statute of Frauds 1677. The secondary purpose is to enable the trustees to ascertain where the equitable interests lie, to enable them to carry out the trusts.

3.5.1.2 The tax angle

The litigation has borne little relation to these primary and secondary purposes, however. It will become apparent that whereas declarations of trusts do not (generally) require writing, dispositions of equitable interests do. The question of what amounts to a disposition has received attention from the courts in recent years, due in part to attempts by settlors to avoid payment of *ad valorem* stamp duty. Stamp duty is imposed, not upon a transaction itself, but upon the written instrument by which property is transferred. All documents under seal, whatever their value, require a nominal 50p stamp, but more important is the additional *ad valorem* duty, whose amount is calculated as a proportion of the value of the interest being transferred. If the value of such interest is nothing, as (for example) where a bare legal estate carrying no right to beneficial enjoyment is transferred, no *ad valorem* duty is payable, but taxpayers obviously prefer to avoid transferring the valuable beneficial interest in writing if they can.

3.5.1.3 Exceptions

3.5.1.3.1 Part performance   None of the statutory requirements affects the equitable doctrine of part performance. This doctrine is expressly exempted from the operation of the Law of Property Act 1925, s. 40 (see section 3.5.2), by virtue of s. 40(2) of the Act, and is exempted from s. 53 by virtue of s. 55(d). It is described in detail in land law books, usually in relation to estate contracts (i.e., contracts for sale of leasehold or freehold estates in land).

In this context the doctrine is used to stop people relying on formality provisions to get out of contracts from which they have had a benefit. It only avoids formality provisions, and does not, for example, validate a purported contract that is unenforceable for any other reason (e.g., that one of the parties is a minor). Because the doctrine is usually categorised into the compartment of land law, rather than trusts, I shall only outline it here. The leading case is the House of Lords decision in *Steadman* v *Steadman* [1976] AC 576, and the requirements are:

(a)   Taking all acts of part performance together, they point unequivocally to the existence of a contract. No special standard of proof is required, merely the ordinary civil standard of balance of probabilities.

(b)   The payment of money by itself is insufficient, though it can be relevant when considered along with other acts of part performance.

(c)   The acts of part performance must indicate that the contract relates to land. This is not clear from *Steadman* itself, as their lordships split 2–2 on this question, with the fifth expressing no firm view, but there is subsequent authority in *Re Gonin* [1979] Ch 16.

3.5.1.3.2 Fraud   The part-performance doctrine is itself probably a specific application of a wider doctrine that equity will not allow a statute to be used as a cloak for fraud (see section 1.4.1). Though the precise scope of this doctrine is unclear (it is discussed in greater detail in chapters 6 and 7), at the very least it applies where there is an attempt to use a statute intended to prevent fraud (as the formality provisions are) as a means of perpetrating a fraud. Thus the wider doctrine may enable express trusts to be established despite lack of writing in certain circumstances, even though they otherwise appear to fall within the s. 53 criteria.

For example, in *Hodgson* v *Marks* [1971] Ch 892, an old lady (Mrs Hodgson) was cajoled into making a voluntary conveyance (i.e., not for value) of her house to her lodger (Evans). Evans then sold the property to a third party (Marks). Two issues arose: first, did Mrs Hodgson have an equitable interest in the property, and secondly, did that interest bind Marks? Both issues were decided in favour of Mrs Hodgson in the Court of Appeal. The second issue is important for land lawyers, who will be interested in the application of s. 70(1)(g) of the Land Registration Act 1925 and the approval of this aspect of the decision by the House of Lords in *Williams & Glyn's Bank Ltd* v *Boland* [1981] AC 487. We are interested in the first issue.

In the Court of Appeal Russell LJ, who gave the only substantive judgment and with whom Buckley and Cairns LJJ agreed, thought that Mrs Hodgson's interest was by way of resulting trust, the principles of which are discussed in chapter 5. If that were all that there was to the decision then it would be of no importance for the purposes of this section of the book, as resulting trusts are expressly exempted from the operation of s. 53.

Mrs Hodgson did not argue a resulting trust, however, but an express trust and this was the basis of Ungoed-Thomas J's decision in the High Court. The trust aspect of the High Court decision was upheld in the Court of Appeal (though the land law aspect was not). Ungoed-Thomas J relied on such cases as *Rochefoucauld* v *Boustead* [1897] 1 Ch 196, where it was held that the Statute of Frauds 1677 could not be used to prevent the proof of a fraud. Russell LJ seemed unsure whether this principle could apply to Marks, the third-party purchaser, which is why he preferred to base his decision on resulting-trust reasoning, but he also said: 'Quite plainly Mr Evans could not have placed any reliance on s. 53, for that would have been to use the section as an instrument of fraud.'

It is clear, then, that even express trusts are outside the scope of s. 53 if the section is being used to prevent proof of fraud.

3.5.2 Land

All formalities required for personalty are also needed in the case of land but there are additional requirements. Section 40 of the Law of Property Act 1925 requires any contract for the sale or disposition of any interest in land (including equitable interests) to be evidenced in writing. The contract itself need not be in writing, and signature by an agent is allowed. Section 40 does not make contracts void, merely unenforceable.

Section 53(1)(b) of the Law of Property Act 1925 provides:

A declaration of trust respecting any land or any interest therein must be manifested and proved by some writing signed by some person who is able to declare such trust or by his will.

This provision applies to freehold and leasehold land, and also to a share in the proceeds of sale of land. The trust need not actually be declared in writing, since what is necessary is that the declaration should be evidenced in writing, and no special form of document is needed—indeed, the necessary writing may be supplied by an exchange of correspondence or the like. The writing must, however, bear the signature of the settlor and not, unlike s. 40, his agent. Failure to comply with s. 53(1)(b) will probably not render the trust void but (like s. 40 contracts) only unenforceable in the absence of evidence in writing.

Some declarations within s. 53(1)(b) may also come within s. 53(1)(c) (see section 3.5.4). There is little point in requiring writing twice, of course, but it may in fact be necessary to consider both paragraphs because failure to comply with s. 53(1)(c) renders a disposition void, not merely unenforceable.

3.5.3 Declarations of trust: personalty

A far as personalty is concerned, a settlor (assuming he is *legal* owner) may create a trust merely by manifesting the intention to create it, and no special formalities are required. So, for example, the simple declaration by the owner of, e.g., a stamp collection that he holds it in trust for his nephew will be effective to create a trust of the collection. Even personalty of great value may, in theory, be settled with no greater formality than this. This is true only for *inter vivos* gifts, however. If it is desired to create a trust by will, then the will itself must comply with the provisions of s. 9 of the Wills Act 1837, which will be dealt with in the chapter relating to secret and half-secret trusts (chapter 7).

In fact, as a matter of practice, even with *inter vivos* gifts, the intention to create a trust will usually be declared in a written document setting out in detail the terms of the trust: a major motive for the creation of settlements is tax planning, and documentary evidence for this purpose is often highly desirable.

3.5.4 Dispositions of equitable interests

Dispositions of equitable interests, whether in land or pesonalty, are void unless in writing. Section 53(1)(c) of the Law of Property Act 1925 provides:

> [A] disposition of an equitable interest or trust subsisting at the time of the disposition, must be in writing signed by the person disposing of the same, or by his agent thereunto lawfully authorised in writing or by will.

This provision is much more stringent than those discussed above. The disposition must itself be in writing, not merely evidenced by writing, and though the section does not expressly say so, failure to comply renders the disposition void, not merely unenforceable. Therefore a later written ratification will not do.

The difficulty is in defining a disposition. In the case law, which as stated above is primarily about forms of tax avoidance, the main problem has been in distinguishing between assignments and substitutions of equitable interests, which constitute dispositions, and creations and extinguishments which probably do not.

3.5.4.1 Dealings with equitable interests on their own

The usual interpretation of the House of Lords case of *Grey* v *IRC* [1960] AC 1 is that a transfer of an equitable interest on its own constitutes a disposition, and therefore must be in writing and attract consequent liability for *ad valorem* stamp duty. Here Mr Hunter was beneficial owner of shares, the legal estate being held, as is sometimes the case with shares, by nominees. In order to transfer his interest Mr Hunter orally directed the nominees to hold the shares on trust for beneficiaries under six settlements (the nominees were also the trustees under these settlements). Later the trustee-nominees executed deeds of declaration to this effect, which were, of course, in writing. If the oral direction had transferred the shares no stamp duty was payable; if the transfer had been effected by the written declaration, however, it was. In deciding in favour of the Inland Revenue, the House of Lords held that a direction by a beneficiary to the trustees to transfer his interest to someone else constituted a disposition and must therefore be in writing. While on a literal interpretation it may be difficult to regard this as being other than a disposition, it does not fall within the mischief of the legislation, as a request to trustees can hardly constitute a secret transaction.

Less clear is the position if a beneficiary declares that he himself will hold his interest on trust for another (rather than directing the trustees to do so), so creating, in effect, a subtrust. A commonly held view is that the issue depends on whether the equitable owner effectively gives away the totality of his interest, so that he, like the trustees who hold the legal title, becomes in turn a merely nominal owner. In this event, there is a strong argument for regarding this as a case of substitution of a new beneficiary, and thus a disposition within the meaning of s. 53(1)(c). If, on the other hand, the equitable owner purports to assume the active role of a trustee of his equitable interest, for example, by declaring discretionary trusts, the case resembles a straightforward subtrust and should arguably be regarded as a declaration of trust and not a disposition of an equitable interest at all.

It is clear that a disclaimer of an equitable interest is not a disposition (*Re Paradise Motor Co. Ltd* [1968] 1 WLR 1125). The same is probably true of the surrender of an equitable interest to the legal owner. Certainly if the purpose of formality rules is to prevent hidden transactions which prevent trustees from ascertaining who the beneficiaries are, there is no reason to require them where the legal and equitable interests merge. But since the legal owner can immediately declare new trusts (these not of course requiring writing), this result would allow for an easy way to achieve a *Grey* disposition without attracting stamp duty.

In principle, however, the courts should construe the formalities legislation on its own account, without regard to tax legislation which is parasitic upon it. If the Inland Revenue wishes to close this potential loophole there should be fresh legislation for the purpose. To interpret formalities legislation, which is intended for specific purposes unrelated to taxation, in such a way as to ensure a consistent tax position at the expense of those purposes is to allow the tail to wag the dog.

3.5.4.2 Contracts for sale

Contracts for the sale of personalty (unlike land: Law of Property Act 1925, s. 40—see section 3.5.1) do not require writing but equity recognises that the buyer has an interest as soon as the contract is made. The nature of this interest is discussed in chapter 2. One might therefore imagine that a possible route round s. 53 (and therefore stamp duty) is to have an oral contract for the sale of (say) shares followed later by a formal transfer. The argument is that the oral contract, not the written transfer, conveys the equitable title; the formal transfer merely conveys the bare legal title, which is worth hardly anything for the purposes of *ad valorem* stamp duty.

The argument was rejected by the House of Lords in *Oughtred v IRC* [1960] AC 206. Though equity may in appropriate circumstances grant specific performance of a contract for the sale of shares (at any rate in a private company, because the shares are unique, but not in a public company, where equivalent shares are freely available on the Stock Exchange), and the seller holds the shares for the buyer with some of the duties of constructive trustee up to the time when they are formally transferred, the buyer does not have a full beneficial interest until the formal transfer. The House of Lords held (by a 3–2 majority) that this situation is analogous to a sale of land, where there is no doubt that the deed of conveyance is the effective instrument of transfer (and so liable to stamp duty).

3.5.4.3 Transfer of legal and equitable interest

I suggested above that, in principle, the merger of legal and equitable interests, extinguishing rather than disposing of the equitable interest, should not require writing, on the grounds that it is not a hidden transaction of the type which the law would wish to prevent. On the same principle, it should also be possible for an equitable owner orally to direct the trustees to transfer both their legal and his equitable interest to a single third party. In this event also the equitable interest is extinguished and the transaction cannot be secret from the trustees. That this is in fact the law would appear to follow from the decision of *Vandervell v IRC* [1967] 2 AC 291.

The facts giving rise to the Vandervell litigation (two main cases) are quite complex. The cases are relevant not only to formalities and it will be necessary to return to them in chapter 5 (on resulting trusts). Nonetheless, the various transactions are not easily severable, and it is convenient at this stage to summarise all the main issues.

Vandervell No. 1 Mr Vandervell wished to endow a chair of pharmacology in a manner attracting least liability to taxation. He was also equitable owner of a substantial number of shares in Vandervell Products Ltd, a private limited liability company which he controlled.

The legal interest in Vandervell's shares was held by a bank as nominee. This arrangement appears to be fairly uncommon in private companies, though less so in public companies, but it is probably more common in family companies, especially where family settlements are envisaged.

In order to endow the chair, he arranged with the bank orally (presumably to avoid stamp duty) to transfer both legal and equitable interests in these shares to the Royal College of Surgeons. It was not Vandervell's intention that the College should receive the shares absolutely, with all the implications that would have had for control of Vandervell Products Ltd. The intention, rather, was that it should receive large dividends on these shares, upon which, as a charity, it was not liable to pay tax. It actually received some £266,000 by these means. Vandervell retained an option to repurchase the shares themselves for a nominal amount (£5,000), however. He did not retain it in his own name, for that would have left him liable to pay surtax on the dividends. Instead, he set up a trustee company, Vandervell Trustees Ltd, to whom the option was granted.

At this stage, therefore, the legal interest in the shares had been transferred to the Royal College of Surgeons. Vandervell Trustees Ltd had the legal interest in the option. If the equitable interest in either remained in Vandervell himself, however, he would be liable to surtax. This is clear from the diagram in Figure 3.1.

Figure 3.1

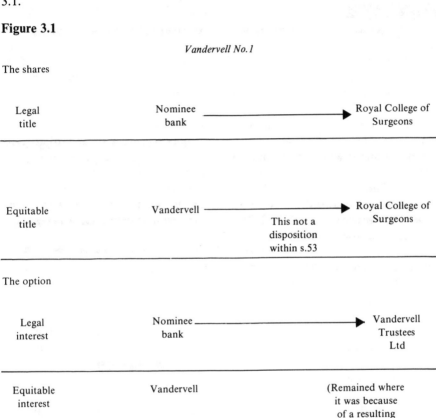

Vandervell No.1

The shares

| Legal title | Nominee bank ⟶ | Royal College of Surgeons |

| Equitable title | Vandervell ⟶ This not a disposition within s.53 | Royal College of Surgeons |

The option

| Legal interest | Nominee bank ⟶ | Vandervell Trustees Ltd |

| Equitable interest | Vandervell | (Remained where it was because of a resulting trust) |

The Revenue initially claimed surtax from Mr Vandervell. The ground that is of interest for the purposes of this section was that he remained the equitable owner of the shares, in the absence of a separate disposition in writing of his equitable interest. This argument failed before the House of Lords, which held that s. 53(1)(c) had no application to the case where a beneficial owner, solely entitled, directs his bare trustees with regard to the legal and equitable estate. This is the important point of the Vandervell litigation for these purposes—as far as the shares themselves were concerned, both legal and equitable interests had been validly transferred despite lack of writing.

Vandervell nevertheless lost, because the House of Lords held that he had not succeeded in divesting himself of the equitable interest in the option, as this was held on resulting trust for him. More detail on this aspect of the decision appears in chapter 5.

Vandervell No. 2   As a result of his dispute with the Inland Revenue, Vandervell in 1961 instructed the trustee company to exercise the option and repurchase the shares, and this gave rise eventually to further litigation (*Re Vandervell's Trusts (No. 2)* [1974] Ch 269, CA) about whether Vandervell had divested himself of the option and the whereabouts of the equitable interest in the shares thereby purchased. Clearly the legal interest in the shares was now vested in the trustee company.

In 1965 Vandervell clearly relinquished by deed any interest, legal or equitable, he may still have had in the shares, but liability to surtax from 1961 to 1965 depended on the whereabouts of the equitable interest in the shares during that period (although in the event the Inland Revenue was excluded as a party to the action). There was also another issue, because by the time of the action Vandervell had died and his executors claimed dividends on the shares from 1961 to 1965. In other words, they claimed that the equitable interest was vested in Vandervell himself from 1961 to 1965.

It should be noted that Vandervell Trustees Ltd were also trustees under a separate trust for Vandervell's children. The £5,000 purchase money came from the children's settlement, and the trustee company regarded themselves as holding the shares on trust for the children under this settlement.

The option   A formalities point arose over this. The option was destroyed when it was exercised by the trustee company in 1961, so Vandervell's equitable interest in it (resulting from the earlier litigation) was extinguished. This was not a disposition within s. 53.

The shares   The Court of Appeal held that the children had the equitable interest. Most of the argument concerned resulting trusts, and this aspect of the case is dealt with in chapter 5. The decision was that there was no resulting trust of the shares for Vandervell himself as there had been of the option. There was a related formalities point, however, which is that (per Lord Denning MR) writing is not required to terminate a resulting trust (not of land).

Alternatively, the appropriation of the shares to the children's settlement was a fresh trust of the shares, and this also was not a disposition within s. 53. There are difficulties with reconciling this alternative argument with *Grey* v *IRC* [1960] AC 1, however (see section 3.5.4.1), and I would suggest that it is wrong.

Figure 3.2 is an attempt to explain *Vandervell No. 2* diagrammatically.

Figure 3.2

Vandervell No.2 (1961–5)

The option was extinguished when exercised

The shares (on exercise of the option)

		Vandervell
Legal	Royal College of →	Trustees
title	Surgeons	Ltd

(who were also trustees
for the children under
a separate settlement)

Equitable   Royal College of   → Vandervell
title   Surgeons
(Vandervell's
estate's argument)

Equitable   Royal College of _____→ Children
title   Surgeons
(decision of CA)

3.5.4.4 *Conclusion*

Conclusions in this area are not easy to draw. It is likely, however, that neither the original creation of an equitable interest (by declaration of trust) nor its extinguishment (by merger with the legal interest) constitute a disposition, and it is difficult to see why writing should be required, given that the transaction cannot be hidden from the trustees. The same seems to apply to the creation (in the same way, but by the equitable owner) and extinguishment of sub-equitable interests. Transfers or assignments of existing equitable (and presumably sub-equitable) interests on their own do require writing, however, and are indeed within the mischief covered by the statutory provision.

3.6 CAPACITY

As a general rule, anyone who has the capacity in law to hold a legal or equitable interest in property has also the capacity to declare a trust of it. The old rules which placed married women in a special position have long been abolished and the repeal of the Mortmain Acts (by s. 38 of the Charities Act 1960) has removed former restrictions on trusts for corporate bodies. Two special classes of person require consideration, however: minors and persons suffering from mental abnormality.

3.6.1   Minors

A minor may hold the legal title to property other than land, and can therefore create a trust of such property *inter vivos*. Any such settlement is, however, voidable and the minor may repudiate it during his minority or within a reasonable time of attaining his majority.

Because a minor cannot make a valid will, he cannot therefore create a trust by will. Statutory exceptions are made in the case of soldiers on military service and sailors while at sea.

Since 1925 (Law of Property Act, s. 1(6)) a minor cannot hold a legal estate in land. He therefore cannot settle such an estate, but he may hold an equitable interest in land, and can settle this, subject to the possibility of repudiation of the settlement.

Before the coming into force of the Family Law Reform Act 1969, s. 9 of which reduced the age of majority from 21 to 18 years, the High Court had the power to approve settlements of real and personal property made upon or in contemplation of marriage by males not under 20 and females not under 17, and such approval made the settlement binding. These provisions were repealed by the Family Law Reform Act 1969, s. 11, without, however, affecting anything done before that Act came into force.

3.6.2   Persons suffering from mental abnormality

A mentally abnormal person may be unable to effect a valid disposition of his property where his condition can be shown to affect his understanding of the transaction. Some transactions call for a higher degree of understanding than others. In order to make a valid will, the testator must understand not only the nature of the document itself, but be able also to evaluate the claims of all the potential donees in relation to the sum of property to be disposed of. *Inter vivos* transactions may demand a lower degree of understanding, which depends upon the size of the contemplated transfer relative to the total assets of the donor. A low degree of understanding will be sufficient if the amount of the gift is relatively trivial, but if it comprises the donor's only assets of value, so as to pre-empt the devolution of his property after his death, then the same degree of understanding is required as in the case of a will.

The Mental Health Act 1983, replacing the 1959 Act of the same title, gives the Court of Protection wide powers to manage the affairs of a person whom the judge is satisfied is incapable of managing his property and affairs by reason of mental disorder. A judge may make orders or give directions for the settlement of any property of a patient of full age. These powers may provide for the maintenance or benefit of the patient or members of his family, or for persons or purposes for which the patient may be expected to provide but for his disorder, or otherwise for the management of his affairs. Such a settlement can be varied at any time up to the death of the patient if it appears that any material fact was not disclosed when the settlement was made or that there has been some substantial change of circumstances.

In exercising these powers, the court will be guided by consideration of what the patient would be likely to do if he were not under disability. In *Re TB* [1967] Ch 247 the court approved a revocable settlement of the whole of the patient's property in favour of the patient's illegitimate son and his family, the effect of which was to prevent the property passing to collateral relatives under the rules of intestacy at that date in the anticipated event of the patient's failure to recover testamentary capacity in his lifetime.

Since the Administration of Justice Act 1969 the court has had the power to make a will for a patient of full age whom the judge has reason to believe lacks testamentary capacity.

Applications for approval of schemes to deal with patients' property commonly have the aim of reducing tax liability, although the scheme must be for the benefit of the patient. It is not essential to provide for revocation if the patient should recover: it is sufficient that it is the sort of settlement which he would be likely to make in favour of his family if he were not subject to the abnormality.

3.7 PERPETUITIES

Apart from charities, all trusts have to comply with the rules against perpetuities. Traditionally this subject is dealt with in land law textbooks, because it is likely that the original policy behind perpetuity rules (in around the 17th century) was to prevent land being tied up for successive generations. However, at least until the Perpetuities and Accumulations Act 1964 it was a trap for unwary settlors of trust property also. Indeed, the rule against perpetuities used to be one of the commonest reasons for the failure of a trust.

Nevertheless, space considerations require that this book follows tradition to the extent that only an outline follows.

3.7.1 Interests which attract the rules

Perpetuities are about contingent interests, that is, interests which will arise only when a specified event occurs, such as reaching a certain age or getting married. It does not affect interests which are said to be already 'vested', even if the recipient's enjoyment of the gift is postponed until some prior interest comes to an end. To say that an interest is 'vested' in X means that X is an existing, identifiable person, that the size of the interest is known, and that there are no conditions to be fulfilled before X can take the gift.

For example, a gift to A for life remainder to B gives B a vested interest now, even though he cannot have the property until A dies. B's interest is part of his property, and he can sell or otherwise deal with it as he wishes.

A common situation where contingent interests are likely to arise is where some of the beneficiaries or potential beneficiaries are still unborn, as is often the case in family settlements. Gifts to unborn persons are necessarily contingent, because their identity is as yet unknown. So also could be the size of their interests as it will not yet be known how large a class of, e.g., A's grandchildren will be until the death of A and all A's children.

Perpetuity rules can also create a problem for trusts in favour of unincorporated associations, as we have seen, because if they are construed as trusts for the members for the time being, these members can fluctuate. Thus the gifts to future members are contingent, because their identities are not yet known and there is a condition to be fulfilled (membership).

The rule is not that all contingent gifts are invalid. They must vest, if at all, within the perpetuity period, however, which will be determined either by the common law, or by the 1964 Act.

3.7.2　Common law position

The pre-1964 (common law) position is important in two respects today. Old instruments are still governed by the common law and it is only when a post-1964 disposition fails at common law that the Act is applicable.

At common law an interest has to be certain to vest, if at all, not later than 21 years after the death of a person living at the creation of the interest (plus the 9 months an unborn foetus can exist in the womb). So, a gift to an existing person on reaching a certain age, or marrying, will always be valid, since the crucial event must take place if at all within his lifetime. If it does not take place, the gift will never vest, but this is of no consequence because the rule does not apply to gifts which do not vest at all, merely to those which are not bound to vest, *if at all*, within the relevant period. This is so however unlikely the condition. A gift to Y when he lands on the moon is valid, as is a gift to the first of my grandchildren to shake hands with John McEnroe (the relevant life in this case being that of the Mr McEnroe).

The appropriate lives for the purposes of the rule can be specified by the settlor (as commonly used to be done with Royal lives clauses, perhaps because Royalty usually lived longer than average) or deduced from the terms of the gift. In the latter case, the appropriate lives include any person or persons alive at the date of the instrument by reference to whom it is possible to identify the class of future donees. Thus if a living settlor creates trusts for his children, his own life is the life in being; if for A's children, A's life is the relevant life. If the gift is in a will, the testator is obviously not a life, so if a testator leaves property to be shared among his grandchildren, A's children will be the lives in being.

Where a gift or disposition cannot be related to any relevant lives, e.g., a gift to maintain a testator's tomb or pet animals, the perpetuity is an absolute period of 21 years.

However, the very possibility, however unlikely, that the gift *might* vest outside the period renders the disposition void *ab initio*, and this used frequently to operate as a trap. For example, whereas a trust in favour of the first child of A to reach 21 is valid, because it must occur no more than 21 years after A's death, a trust in favour of the first grandchild of A to attain the age of 21 is not, even if A is very old, and has grandchildren. Suppose, for example, A is 80, and has grandchildren (B, C and D) of 19, 17 and 15. The common law assumes that whatever A's age and sex, he or she can have further children (who are, of course, as yet unborn). These children can themselves have children (X and Y) in more than 21 years hence. If A and all his children and grandchildren then die, X and Y could theoretically reach 21 outside the perpetuity period, whereas B, C and D may all fail to reach 21. The purpose of this example is to show how the most unlikely possibilities can at common law invalidate a gift or trust, and why therefore settlors before 1964 needed to pay positive regard to the perpetuity rules.

Thus the common law has no regard for probabilities in the real world, and often used to hold gifts void because it was possible to imagine an outlandish set of circumstances which might cause them to vest outside the period. Further, the common law presumes every person to be capable of reproduction, regardless of age and physical condition. Gifts have been struck down on the assumption that women over 70, or three-year-old toddlers, can give birth. This make gifts to a class of persons especially vulnerable to the operation of the rule, since before a class gift can be said to have vested, it must have become possible to say that no more members of the class can come into being. Gifts to grandchildren, nephews and nieces etc., are especially likely to be caught by the fanciful possibility that geriatric relatives will produce offspring who in turn will add to the designated class after the expiration of the permitted period. Nor is it possible at common law to wait and see whether vesting actually takes place outside the period—if it *might* do so, the gift is void.

The rigidity of the rule with regard to class gifts is slightly mitigated, however, by the existence of a rule of executorship derived from *Andrews* v *Partington* (1791) 3 Bro CC 401, which states that where one member of the class has already met the specified condition, only such other members of the class as are already in existence may take. Any who are born later are excluded, even if in fact they too later meet the condition. This has the effect of closing the class at the date of the instrument, thus forestalling the possibility that others may join the class outside the permitted period and so render void the whole gift.

3.7.3 Perpetuities and Accumulations Act 1964

The Perpetuities and Accumulations Act 1964, which only applies to gifts which are void at common law, renders failure of a trust on grounds of perpetuity less likely, because its main effect was to enact a wait-and-see period. In other words, only if an interest *actually* vests outside the perpetuity period does the trust fail, not merely if it *might*. In order to operate a wait-and-see period, it is necessary to be able to determine who are the relevant lives, and these are defined in s. 3 of the Act. The settlor may, if he prefers, specify a fixed period of not more than 80 years.

The Act has made other changes also, one of which was to enact that some people are presumed to be incapable of producing children. The presumption is that male persons are fertile only after the age of 14, and females only between the ages of 12 and 55. Evidence of physical incapacity to have children is also now admissible.

A common reason for the failure of a gift was its postponement to an age greater than 21 years. Section 163(1) of the Law of Property Act 1925, which applies to pre-1964 instruments, provides that where a gift is void because of such a condition, the age of 21 is substituted for the age stated in the instrument. For post-1964 gifts, this section is replaced by s. 4 of the 1964 Act, which instead reduces the age only so far as is necessary to prevent the gift being void. The class-closing rules are also modified by s. 4(4) of the Act.

3.7.4 Powers of appointment

Appointments under special powers of appointment are subject to the rules, the perpetuity period running from the date of the creation of the power, not of its exercise. General powers of appointment are treated in the same way as out-and-out gifts, however. Thus, the perpetuity period runs only from the date of the exercise of the power.

3.7.5 Accumulation

Trusts commonly contain a power for trustees to accumulate the income of a trust, that is, to add it to capital rather than pay the beneficiaries. An accumulation and maintenance settlement, which allows trustees to accumulate the income of property held by an infant in so far as that income is not needed for his maintenance, is a popular form of trust today because it offers tax advantages.

The period for which income can be accumulated is limited by statute. Various periods are allowed under s. 164 of the Law of Property Act 1925 and, for post-1964 instruments, further periods are added by the 1964 Act. The settlor may select whichever period he wishes. The income must be distributed when the period allowed for accumulation comes to an end.

3.7.6 Charities

Charities enjoy some immunity from perpetuities. Unlike private trusts, charitable trusts may exist for ever. Also, once property has been given to charity, it is immaterial that it may pass from one charitable body to another at some future date, so that a gift over from one charity to another is exempt from the rule. However, if the gift to a charitable body is to take effect only after prior gifts to non-charitable bodies, the rule applies in the usual way, so the gift to the charity can fail if it falls outside the perpetuity period.

3.8 VOIDABLE TRUSTS

If a settlor goes bankrupt, transactions by way of gift, or at an undervalue, can be set aside within a certain time by the trustee in bankruptcy, and certain other people prejudiced by the bankruptcy. Trusts fall among such transactions. The relevant provisions are to be found in the Insolvency Act 1985.

4

Constitution of Trusts and Covenants to Settle

One of the major themes of the law of trusts (which has already been touched on in chapter 2) lies in a comparison between contracts and trusts. A beneficiary under a fully constituted trust (let us call him A) is in a very different position from someone (B) who is entitled to benefit as a party to a contract, but who is not a beneficiary under a trust. Somebody (C) who merely expects to receive a benefit as a third party to a contract between two other people is in a different position again. This chapter is essentially concerned with an analysis of those differences.

Section 4.1 details the requirements necessary for someone (let us call him X) to be in the position of A. If these requirements are not met, in other words if there is not a fully constituted trust, X may still be in the position of B or C. A likely possibility is that there is a contract to create a trust in X's favour, and if so X's rights and remedies (if any) are covered in section 4.2. X may have either legal or equitable rights and remedies, or both, and they will differ. Both therefore have to be distinguished and considered.

Yet another possibility is that there is a fully constituted trust, not of tangible property, but of contractual rights themselves. This possibility is considered, along with its implications, in section 4.3.

Section 4.4 is about mutual wills. These are a particular variety of contract to settle property, but deserve special treatment because a constructive trust may also be imposed on the surviving contracting party. Indeed, many writers prefer to deal with mutual wills along with constructive trusts, and some see them as being analogous to secret trusts. These views are perfectly supportable. It is also clear, however, that they are a variety of contract to settle property, and hence can be considered logically in this chapter. Indeed, my view (as will appear) is that though there now appears to be considerable authority for the imposition of trusts in this situation, the development is unfortunate, and a purely contractual solution would be preferable.

4.1 THE CONSTITUTION OF TRUSTS

In general, the legal title to trust property must be transferred to trustees for a valid trust to be constituted. The trustees must have control of the property. If formalities are required for this transfer, for example in the case of land or shares, then they must be complied with. In the case of land in an area of compulsory registration of title, the relevant register of title must be carried out. The effect of constituting a trust is:

(a)   Irreversible by the settlor; a gift once given cannot be un-given.

(b)   To give beneficiaries enforceable rights in relation to the property (assuming a private non-purpose trust), whether or not they have provided any consideration: *Paul* v *Paul* (1882) 20 ChD 742.

As we saw in chapter 2, a settlor can declare himself a trustee of property, in which case obviously there is no need to transfer the legal title to anyone else. This intention, which after all involves the settlor in onerous duties, is not readily construed, however.

It is not necessary that the property be transferred in the manner that the settlor intended. If it is conveyed to trustees in any manner, even accidentally, this is sufficient to constitute the trust: *Re Ralli's WT* [1964] Ch 288, and see also *Strong* v *Bird* (1874) LR 18 Eq 315.

Generally, then, if the trust property is not transferred to trustees, 'Equity will not perfect an imperfect gift' (see section 1.4.1), and no valid trust is constituted (*Milroy* v *Lord* (1862) 4 De G F & J 264). There are exceptional situations, however, where the settlor has done all that is within his power to constitute the trust by transferring the property to a trustee, but has been thwarted by formalities which are outside his control. Equity regards the trust as constituted by the last act of the settlor. An example is *Re Rose* [1952] Ch 449, CA, where the settlor intended to transfer shares, but where the directors of the company had an effective veto over any transfer. The Court of Appeal held that the date of constitution of the trust was when the settlor had done all he could, not when the directors consented to, and registered the transfer. The precise date was important for the purposes of assessing estate duty. This case is not without difficulty: for example, what would have happened had the directors refused to register the transfer? Probably in that event no trust would have been constituted.

4.2   CONTRACTS TO SETTLE

4.2.1   Common law and equitable remedies

Even if there is not a fully constituted trust, that may not be the end of the matter. Sometimes would-be settlors make contracts, either with would-be trustees or would-be beneficiaries or both, to settle property. Assume for the moment that the contract has not yet been carried out. Though some of the books, and indeed the cases themselves, refer to settlors, trustees and beneficiaries in this context, this is confusing where no trust is yet in existence. If the parties had actually become trustees and beneficiaries the position would be fundamentally different.

I will therefore, for clarity, preface the term with 'would-be' to indicate that no trust has yet been constituted. Clumsy English seems a reasonable price to pay for clarity of analysis, in an area where lack of clarity causes many difficulties for students.

Contracts to settle are especially common if the property has yet to be acquired by the would-be settlor, for example, an expected inheritance yet to be received, or expected royalties on a book, because it is the best that he can do. He has no existing property with which he can constitute the trust, and the courts have held, e.g. in *Re Ellenborough* [1903] 1 Ch 697, that future property, or expectancies, cannot themselves form the subject-matter of a trust. Additionally, however, such contracts are sometimes made to settle existing property, which is already owned by the settlor, expecially where the deal is that it will be settled by will on the death of the would-be settlor.

In principle, such contracts to settle ought to be enforceable by whoever is party to them. It may be that would-be trustees cannot enforce them, however, and even if they can, they may not always have a worthwhile remedy.

Most contracts (or covenants) to settle property are made either by deed or where the parties are within the marriage consideration (on which, see below). There is no reason why they should not be made for conventional consideration in money or money's worth, but in practice this is uncommon. The importance of this point lies in the availability of remedies.

It should be noted that whereas contracts under seal (or covenants by deed) are recognised as valid by the common law, even where no consideration moves from the promisee, they are not recognised as valid in equity. The result is that whereas the common law remedy of damages can be obtained for breach of such covenants by the would-be settlor, the equitable remedy of specific performance, which would require him actually to constitute the trust, is not. Further, as we shall see, a damages remedy is not always useful, especially at the suit of the would-be trustee.

Equity, on the other hand, recognises marriage consideration as valid, whereas the common law does not. Thus, even if they do not provide consideration in the conventional common law sense (e.g. money or money's worth), the husband, wife or issue of a marriage can sue in equity on a contract agreed to be made before, and in consideration of, such a marriage. In such cases specific performance can be obtained to force the would-be settlor to constitute the trust, or damages in lieu thereof under the Chancery Amendment Act 1858 (see section 1.4.5). As with all equitable remedies, however, they are discretionary, and cannot be obtained as of right.

Of course, if the contract is for ordinary common law consideration, conventional contractual principles apply, with a possible exception in the case of would-be trustees.

4.2.2 Would-be beneficiary party to the contract

If the would-be beneficiary is himself party to a covenant to settle, no problems arise, and he can enforce the contract in the same way as he could enforce any other contract. If he is party to a covenant by deed, he can obtain substantial damages at law if the would-be settlor fails fully to constitute the trust (*Cannon* v *Hartley* [1949] Ch 213). If he is within the marriage consideration, he can enforce the contract in equity (*Pullan* v *Koe* [1913] 1 Ch 9).

If he is neither party to a deed, however, nor within the marriage consideration, and has not provided any other consideration, he will be without remedy: 'Equity will not assist a volunteer' (see section 1.4.1). This was the result in *Re Plumptre's Marriage Settlement* [1910] 1 Ch 609, the facts of which were similar to those in *Pullan* v *Koe* except that the would-be beneficiaries were not within the marriage consideration and so could not enforce in equity. Nor had they a remedy at common law because on the facts it was barred by limitation (i.e., time-barred).

These cases appear in diagrammatic form in Figure 4.1.

Figure 4.1

A is the would-be settlor
B is the would-be trustee
C is the would-be beneficiary

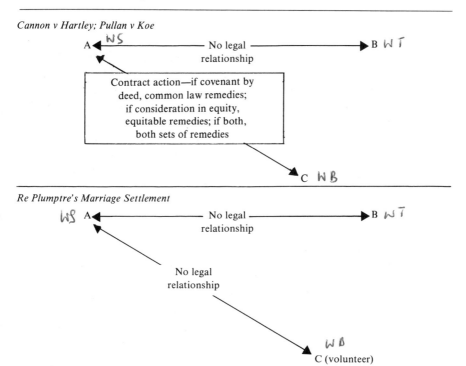

Cannon v Hartley; Pullan v Koe

A ◀—— No legal relationship ——▶ B

Contract action—if covenant by deed, common law remedies; if consideration in equity, equitable remedies; if both, both sets of remedies

C

Re Plumptre's Marriage Settlement

A ◀—— No legal relationship ——▶ B

No legal relationship

C (volunteer)

4.2.3   Would-be trustee party to the contract

The problem discussed in this section appears in diagrammatic form in Figure
4.2.

Figure 4.2

Re Pryce; Re Kay

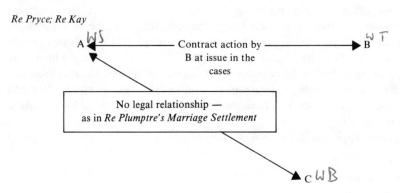

It might be thought that the same position should apply and that the would-be
trustee should be able to sue. Of course, the initiative would lie with him; the
would-be beneficiary could not force him to sue (assuming he has no action in his
own right, on the principles outlined above). There are two differences, however.
The first is that in cases where specific performance is not available, damages are
not necessarily a useful alternative. Damages compensate for loss suffered and,
since it is the would-be beneficiary who is intended to receive the benefit, the
would-be trustee personally suffers no loss if the trust is not constituted. Indeed,
if the duties under the putative trust are of an onerous nature, as they will often
be, the would-be trustee may actually gain from the settlor's breach. Thus,
damages are likely to be only nominal.

Secondly, however, even if the would-be trustee theoretically has a useful
action (as he would, for example, if specific performance were available), there
are dicta, which are, however, by no means conclusive, that he is not allowed to
bring it. In *Re Kay's Settlement* [1939] Ch 329, the would-be trustees were party
to a covenant under seal with the would-be settlor to settle after-acquired
property. No consideration moved from them, however. The would-be
beneficiaries were not party to the covenant, nor were they within the marriage
consideration, so were therefore volunteers. The would-be trustees requested

directions as to whether or not they ought to take steps to enforce the covenant or to recover damages. The court directed them not to do so. At the end of his judgment, Simonds J, following Eve J in *Re Pryce* [1917] 1 Ch 234, said [1939] Ch 329 at p. 342):

> [I]t appears to me that . . . I must direct the trustees not to take any steps either to compel performance of the covenant or to recover damages through [the settlor's] failure to implement it.

Though Simonds J talks of 'trustees', the plaintiffs never in fact became trustees. I would suggest that the terminology has given rise to confusion, in that arguments have been advanced, as we shall see, which assume that they are actually trustees. For this reason I prefer to use the 'would-be' preface.

This dictum, which was followed by Buckley J in *Re Cook's ST* [1965] Ch 902, seems quite extraordinary on its face. It appears to deprive a plaintiff of an otherwise perfectly valid contract action, for which very good reasons would have to be found. I will call this the 'wide view' of the case: on this view the would-be trustee is disallowed from bringing an action. It is not the only possible view, however; perhaps Simonds J does not go so far as is often supposed. In particular, the following points should be considered:

(a) Simonds J did not decide what the outcome would have been if the trustees had actually sued. They did not do so but merely requested directions. Obviously, the court would not direct them to sue, and force upon them the onerous burdens of trusteeship, in favour of volunteers. Professor Elliott has argued that the would-be trustees should have been directed that they need not sue, not that they ought not to sue, and perhaps this is what Simonds J meant: (1960) 76 LQR 100. On the other hand, they had requested directions, and arguably these ought to be mandatory in form. In any event, an explanation along these lines does not lead to the automatic conclusion that would-be trustees will be deprived of their contract action whenever would-be beneficiaries are volunteers. Given also that the dictum is not particularly considered, this seems to be the best explanation. I shall refer to this as the 'narrow view', which I prefer.

(b) One wonders whether the contract action would have been of any use anyway. Damages would have been the only available remedy and the would-be trustees had suffered no personal loss.

(c) The wide view has been supported on the grounds that the narrow view gives the trustees a discretion as to whether or not to enforce the trust, and that this is inconsistent with the very nature of a trust. Since the court will not force the trustees to act in favour of a volunteer, the only possibility is to deprive them of action. This is precisely the type of difficulty that arises, however, if the 'would-be' prefix is omitted. The plaintiffs are not yet trustees, so objections based on giving trustees discretion cannot apply. If they choose to sue and obtain specific performance (not a remedy available in *Kay* itself), then they become trustees. But at that point they no longer have a discretion; once they have taken this step, they have to carry out the trust. In other words, the narrow view does not give trustees a discretion as to whether or not they enforce the trust. The choice is given to people who are not trustees, as to whether or not they undertake the onerous duties of trusteeship. That choice is always given to would-be trustees, and is perfectly proper.

4.3 TRUSTS OF PROMISES

There is no reason in principle why a covenant to settle property should not of itself form the subject-matter of a trust. We know that in *Re Kay's Settlement* [1939] Ch 329, for example, no trust of the after-acquired *property* was constituted. But had it been decided that a valid trust had been constituted of the *covenant* (or promise), the result would have been very different: the beneficiaries, though volunteers, would have enforceable rights against the trustees of the covenant. Far from the trustees being directed not to sue on it, the beneficiaries could have required them to do so. A diagrammatic representation of this situation appears in Figure 4.3.

Figure 4.3

Substantive property as in Figure 4.2
B's action in contract against A

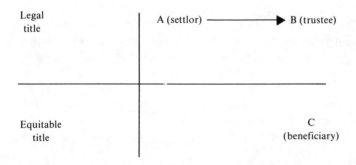

B holds the benefit of the contract on constituted trust for C, who can therefore force B to enforce it

This, as we know, was not the result in *Re Kay's Settlement*. We must assume, then, that the covenant was not held on a fully constituted trust. Even if it had been, the remedies question would still have remained. The two main issues that arise, then, are these: when will the courts construe a trust of a promise, and when are the trustees' remedies effective?

4.3.1 When do trusts of promises arise?

In *Fletcher* v *Fletcher* (1844) 4 Hare 67, the settlor covenanted by deed to pay £60,000 to trustees, on trust for Jacob (who was a volunteer, and outside the marriage consideration). Though the *money* was never settled, Wigram V-C held that the *covenant* was held on a fully constituted trust for Jacob. Thus Jacob could enforce it in his own right, despite being a volunteer. It seems from this case that the beneficiary can force the trustee to sue on the covenant, and that substantial damages can be recovered (at any rate where the covenant concerns the settlement of money), which will be held in trust for the beneficiary.

Though the principle of this case is no doubt sound, there are difficulties in construing a trust of the promise on the facts. A point often made is that the trustees knew nothing of the covenant until the death of the settlor and then were unwilling to enforce it. This is probably irrelevant, however, because one can argue (see Feltham (1982) 98 LQR 17) that the relevant intention is that of the settlor not of the trustee. If a trustee is unwilling to act, 'Equity will not allow a trust to fail for want of a trustee' (see section 1.4.1) and the courts will appoint another trustee.

Nevertheless in later cases the courts have demanded much more conclusive evidence before construing trusts of promises: e.g., *Re Schebsman* [1944] Ch 83, and see Smith [1982] Conv 352. I suggest that were the same facts to arise today, no trust would be construed, and *Fletcher* v *Fletcher* would be considered wrongly decided in this regard.

Fletcher v *Fletcher* involved a covenant to settle money. No doubt covenants to settle other property can also form the subject-matter of a trust, but there is some doubt as to whether a covenant to settle after-acquired property (i.e., mere expectations of the settlor) can be. Buckley J thought that it could not in *Re Cook's ST* [1965] Ch 902, and the same view has also been taken by Lee (1969) 85 LQR 213 and Barton (1975) 91 LQR 236, but this reasoning has been criticised, e.g., by Meagher and Lehane (1976) 92 LQR 427. Perhaps this is the explanation for no trust of a promise being constituted in *Re Kay*, which concerned after-acquired property, though I would suggest that on the question of evidence it is *Kay*, not *Fletcher*, which can best be reconciled with the later cases.

4.3.2 Remedies

In cases where the contract is for consideration, including the marriage consideration, specific performance may be available, in which case no *cavil-draft.*

difficulties arise. The problem area concerns covenants under seal (where there is no consideration), for which the equitable remedies are not available. Bear in mind that the covenant which forms the subject-matter of the trust is between settlor and trustee, and that the beneficiary is not a party (if he were he could sue in his own right on the principles discussed in section 4.2.2).

A distinction appears to arise between covenants to settle money, or existing ascertained property, and covenants to settle after-acquired property (i.e., mere expectations of the settlor). *Fletcher* v *Fletcher* (1884) 4 Hare 67 concerned a covenant to settle money and it is clear that a substantial sum could be recovered. This is possibly because the trust of the promise constituted the settlor as debtor of the trustees (see Friend [1982] Conv 280). Thus, because they could sue on the debt, it would not have been necessary for the trustees to rely on ordinary contractual damages, which as we saw above (section 4.2.3), are likely to be nominal only. It may be that the same principle applies with covenants to settle existing property, other than money, presently owned by the settlor. Some authority for this statement may be derived from the judgment of Younger J in *Re Cavendish Browne's ST* [1916] WN 341, but the report of the case is too short to place the position beyond doubt.

In the case of after-acquired property, however, it is probable that the trustees can only obtain damages, which will for reasons already discussed be nominal only, but see the contrary argument by Meagher and Lehane (1976) 92 LQR 427.

4.4   MUTUAL WILLS

Mutual wills are a particular variety of contract to settle property, to which special considerations apply. They are agreements, usually but not necessarily between husband and wife. Wills are made (or the parties agree to make them) by each party in (usually) the same terms, and there is a mutual agreement that neither party will revoke, but the essence of the transaction is an agreement that each party will settle his or her property in a particular (usually the same) way.

Mutual wills were fairly common between the last part of the 19th century and the First World War, when wives could own property in their own right but marriage was still regarded by many of the property-owning class partly (or even primarily) as a property transaction between families. Mutual wills were to protect the interests of the families. Probably they are rare today, but of course this cannot necessarily be inferred from a paucity of litigation.

4.4.1   Problems of mutual wills

It is difficult to conceive of any social value which is served by mutual wills today, and it is possible to envisage situations where they could operate in a most capricious manner. For example, suppose Mr X and Miss Y marry young, and enter into a transaction whereby each agrees to settle the whole of his or her estate on the other party on his or her death. Shortly afterwards, and before any children are born, Y dies. X and Y are still young and relatively poor, so X does not receive very much under Y's will. X, later in life, earns a great deal of money, marries Z and there are children of the second marriage. If the original agreement is fully enforced, Z and the children can receive nothing under X's will, whereas Y's family can claim his estate and receive a windfall. Since Y died before having children, this windfall could fall on, e.g., her brothers and sisters, or their children, who may have very little connection with X.

Though that conclusion may seem harsh on X, it is the inevitable consequence of enforcement of the mutual agreement, though the difficulty would be overcome either if the agreement could be construed in such a way that it was unenforceable for a public policy reason or if nobody was in a position to enforce it. Both these possibilities will be considered in the following section on mutual wills as contracts.

Additionally, however, the courts have imposed a constructive trust on X, and this can operate even more capriciously. Even during X's lifetime, Y's family may be able to restrain him to some extent from spending the money he later earns, on the grounds that to do so might diminish the estate, in which they have an interest. Exactly the same principle applies, of course, if the sex of the parties is reversed. The conclusion seems absurd, yet it is apparently the conclusion the law has reached.

4.4.2   Mutual wills as contracts

In the above example, while X and Y are alive each can revoke his or her will, and that revocation will be valid, but may commit a breach of contract by so doing. Whether there is a breach will depend on the construction of the agreement; this is simply an application of the ordinary law of contract.

In principle X continues to be contractually bound by the terms of the agreement after Y's death, the contract being enforceable by Y's estate (as in *Beswick* v *Beswick* [1968] AC 58, considered in chapter 2). When X dies, the action is by Y's estate against X's estate. In practice, this solution may not be as clear-cut as appears at first sight, however.

(a)   It depends on specific performance being available as a remedy. No theoretical difficulties arise if the contract can be construed as one to settle property on X's death. If, however, it is construed as a contract not to revoke an existing will, specific performance is unlikely to be available. Wills are in any event revoked automatically on remarriage and if the agreement were to be construed as one in restraint of marriage it would be void as an illegal contract on public policy grounds. No doubt it all depends on construction of the agreement and in principle mutual wills can be made which are contractually enforceable.

(b)   The intended beneficiaries themselves cannot enforce as they are not party to the agreement. In effect, they are in the *Re Plumptre's Marriage Settlement* situation ([1910] 1 Ch 609 see section 4.2.2). Probably it was for this reason that the trust action described below was developed but it is difficult to see why, in principle, they should be put into any better position than any other volunteers.

(c)   Enforcement then is at the discretion of Y's personal representative, who may be X. This may seem unsatisfactory, but if X then does anything inconsistent with the terms of the agreement, he will be liable in his capacity as personal representative directly to the intended beneficiaries.

Subject to the above, however, mutual wills are enforceable as contracts. It may seem harsh for X's future earnings to be tied to providing for Y's family, but if he has expressly so agreed, the common law will bind him to his agreement, even though it turns out to be a bad bargain. If no such term is expressed, however, only reasonable terms are likely to be implied into the agreement, and unless he has entered into a very unwise arrangement indeed, it is unlikely that X will be seriously impeded as regards spending his money during his (X's) lifetime.

4.4.3   Trust solutions

The law applicable in this area was fully reviewed by Nourse J in *Re Cleaver* [1981] 2 All ER 1018, noted by Hodkinson [1982] Conv 228. Unfortunately, the imposition of a constructive trust on Y's death leads, because of the inflexibility of the constructive trust, to consequences for X which are far harsher than those described above, which themselves result from the contractual solution.

The position appears to be that whereas X becomes absolutely entitled to any money received under Y's will (unless the will gives him a life interest only), he becomes bound by a trust regarding his other property and future earnings. In addition to being unable later to revoke his will (which he made before Y's death), he also becomes constructive trustee on the terms of the will, which of course, he undertook would be his last. The duties of trustees can be far more stringent than contractual duties (see chapters 9 and 10) and these duties may significantly affect his ability to dispose of his future income as he wishes. For example, he can only take reasonable expenses for himself and make small gifts in favour of his new wife and children. This result probably follows whatever the terms of the original agreement.

If X has genuinely agreed to such onerous duties, it is reasonable for the law to bind him to them, however bad the bargain he has made. The law of contract achieves this. It is unnecessary to impute a constructive trust, which can bind X in this manner whatever the agreement he has made. Probably the explanation for the development is that it occurred before the contractual position became clear (certainly it predated *Beswick* v *Beswick* [1968] AC 58). Perhaps also the courts wanted to give enforceable rights directly to the intended beneficiaries, which as we saw above the contractual solution does not do. But it is not easy to see why they should have enforceable rights.

As we shall see in chapter 6, the use of constructive trusts has been greatly extended recently. I suggest that this is not always to the good and this area is one example. The implication of the constructive trust here is based on a very general notion of fraud. Equity has had, as we shall see, a limited fraud jurisdiction for centuries. Recently this jurisdiction has been extended but mutual wills are an extreme example.

The basis is that X received property under Y's will because of the agreement. His conscience demands, therefore, that he be subject to the agreement, even to the extent that a trust is imposed on all his other present and future property. The fraud depends, it seems, only on there being a causal relationship between X's receipt of the property under Y's will and the making of the mutual wills agreement. This is quite a different concept from fraud in the common law or criminal law sense, which requires an element of intention and has connotations of extreme dishonesty.

As we shall see in chapter 7, secret and half-secret trusts are based on a similar notion of fraud. Special considerations apply there, however, in particular that the equitable jurisdiction prevents the use of a statute intended specifically to prevent fraud, actually to perpetrate a fraud. Furthermore, no alternative means of enforcement exists. Mutual wills extend the doctrine in two major respects. First, they are not otherwise unenforceable merely because of a statutory formality provision. Indeed, they are not otherwise unenforceable at all. Secondly, secret trusts are imposed only on the property actually received by the secret trustee, whereas in the present context of mutual wills, all the property of the trustee, present and future, appears to be subject to the trust.

Fortunately, *Cleaver* is not conclusive, as the remarks of Nourse J are dicta only. Nor are the earlier cases conclusive, though it can be stated with a fair degree of certainty that, as the law currently stands, a constructive trust is imposed. It is to be hoped that if the question ever arises in a higher court, its imposition in this situation will be seen as being inappropriate, however, because the contractual solution is adequate.

5

Resulting Trusts

The practical situations in which resulting trusts occur are quite diverse and it may well be wondered what they have in common. Section 5.1, for example, is about defective trust instruments. The settlor simply fails to dispose of some or all of the equitable interest in the trust property.

In section 5.2, there is nothing wrong with the trust instrument itself and the settlor does all he can to dispose of the trust property. This section discusses other reasons why the equitable interest is not properly disposed of.

There is nothing defective, however, about the transactions discussed in sections 5.3 and 5.4. The settlor successfully divests himself of the equitable interest in the property, which is usually a fund of money given to an unincorporated association. In section 5.3.1 the fund is collected for a particular purpose and all the objectives are later achieved. In section 5.4, the association is later wound up and so ceases to exist. In each case some of the fund is still left and the question arises what to do with the fund. If the association in question were charitable, then the cy pres doctrine, discussed in section 8.6, would apply. Where it is not, resulting trust principles are sometimes (but as we shall see not always) applicable.

Generally speaking, these situations divide into two types. Funds to which outsiders contribute (considered in section 5.3.1) are usually disaster appeals and, as we shall see in chapter 8, the organisers of such funds may have good reasons for not making them charitable. If they are not charitable the principles discussed in this chapter apply. The other common situation (discussed in section 5.4) is where people contribute to funds for their own benefit. Some of these may simply be clubs organising activities or whatever, but most of the cases concern mutual benefit or friendly societies providing relief against sickness or other misfortune. It may be presumed, incidentally, that the value of such societies has been diminished by the growth of State welfare provisions and modern insurance policies.

Finally, section 5.5 deals with a different situation altogether, that of the ownership of the matrimonial home or the home of unmarried cohabitees. It should also be appreciated that though the cases seem to have grouped themselves around the fact situations discussed above, resulting trust principles can apply in other situations as well, and are indeed of extremely diverse application.

Nevertheless, in all situations where resulting trusts occur, either the equitable interest never leaves the settlor or it returns to him. This can occur either because the settlor never disposes of his equitable interest properly in the first place or because some later occurrence takes place and there is nowhere else for the equitable interest to go, other than back to the settlor.

5.1 DEFECTIVE TRUST INSTRUMENT: INCOMPLETE DISPOSAL OF THE BENEFICIAL INTEREST

The settlor may have made it clear that property is intended to be held on trust, and may even have transferred the legal title to the trustee. There may be some reason, however, why the equitable interest is not properly disposed of. Obviously the trustee cannot keep the trust property for himself and so he holds it on resulting trust for the settlor. There is nowhere else for the equitable interest to go.

5.1.1 Formalities and certainty

Sometimes this can arise for technical reasons. For example, we saw in chapter 3 that formalities may be required for the disposal of an equitable interest. If these formalities are not complied with, there will be no effective disposal. In that case the equitable interest never leaves the settlor and there is a resulting trust. A similar result obtains if the certainty of objects requirement is not complied with.

5.1.2 Equitable interest undefined

Another possibility is where property is settled on trust but details of the trust are left unclear (i.e., the terms of the trust fail to provide for the totality of the beneficial interest). The Vandervell litigation provides a good example of this. All the relevant facts appear in section 3.5.

In section 3.5, we saw how Mr Vandervell made arrangements to endow a chair of pharmacology by transferring shares to the Royal College of Surgeons, to enable it to take the dividends declared on those shares. He did not wish to make an out-and-out transfer, however, and so gave an option to purchase (at a nominal cost) to a trustee company which was under his control. He left no clear instructions with the trustee company as to the terms on which the option was to be held by them.

The Revenue, as we saw in the earlier section, failed to show that he had not divested himself of the entire interest in the shares. The point that arises in the present context, however, is that they succeeded in showing that he had not done so with regard to the option, the legal interest of which was now in the trustee company (*Vandervell* v *IRC* [1967] 2 AC 291). The option was therefore held on resulting trust for him along with liability to pay surtax on the dividends.

Lord Wilberforce said that the trusts upon which the option was supposed to be held were undefined and in the air, possibly to be defined later. The trustee company itself was clearly not a beneficiary. An equitable interest cannot remain in the air and so the only possibility was a resulting trust in favour of the settlor. This is an example, then, of the trust being insufficiently defined.

To counteract the Revenue's claims to surtax on the dividends declared on the shares, Mr Vandervell in 1961 instructed the trustee company to exercise the option and repurchase the shares. The shares were then placed by the trustee company on the trusts of the children's settlements.

The Court of Appeal held in *Re Vandervell's Trusts (No. 2)* [1974] Ch 269 that Vandervell had now succeeded in divesting himself of the entire interest in these shares, there being no longer a resulting trust in his favour. The later trusts were precisely defined, in favour of the children's settlements, so that it was no longer necessary for this reason for the equitable interest to remain in the settlor.

As we saw in chapter 3, however, there are some formality difficulties about the actual transfer of the equitable interest in the shares to the children. It cannot have been the result of the creation of a new trust by Vandervell, as he (on the reasoning of the Court of Appeal) had no equitable interest to settle. It looks like a *Grey* style disposition, which ought therefore to have been caught by s. 53 of the Law of Property Act 1925. The decision of the Court of Appeal is therefore not easy to reconcile with other House of Lords decisions and may well be wrong.

Sometimes the settlor disposes of some, but not all, of the equitable interest. Here also, the undisposed of residue 'results'. An example is *Re Cochrane* [1955] Ch 309, which concerned a marriage settlement of the income of a fund. An unforeseen contingency arose so that for a time there was no clear disposition of the equitable interest; the contingency had simply not been provided for. During this time there was a resulting trust of the income to the settlor.

5.2 DISPOSITION FAILS FOR SOME OTHER REASON

There can be reasons apart from a defective trust instrument for a failure to dispose of an equitable interest. One possibility is that the body upon which money or property is settled has never existed or has ceased to exist. If a general or paramount charitable intention is shown on the part of the donor, a cy pres scheme may be applied (see section 8.6). Otherwise the property will be held on resulting trust for the settlor.

Another situation is where money or property is given for a purpose and the circumstances necessary to achieve the purpose fail to materialise or later cease. For example, in *Essery* v *Coulard* (1884) 26 ChD 191, a trust for the parties to an intended marriage could not take effect when the parties decided to live together without marrying, so the property was construed six years later to be held on resulting trust for the settlor. A similar result was reached in *Re Ames's Settlement* [1946] Ch 217, where, although the parties went through a ceremony of marriage, a court later declared tne marriage void ab initio, a decree of nullity having at that time retrospective effect. In other words, there had never been a valid marriage.

We have already come across (in section 2.3.3) *Barclays Bank Ltd* v *Quistclose Investments Ltd* [1970] AC 567, where a loan was made to Rolls Razor Ltd, a firm which was in difficulties, for the specific purpose of paying dividends previously declared on its shares. When Rolls went into liquidation before the dividends were paid the money was held on resulting trust for the settlor, Quistclose Investments, in preference to the general creditors, of which Barclays Bank was one. Here, of course, the resulting trust took effect in addition to the settlor's contractual remedy, which was, however, useless. Another similar case is *Carreras Rothmans Ltd* v *Freeman Matthews Treasure Ltd* [1985] 1 All ER 155.

Alternatively, the conditions necessary to achieve a purpose may come to an end, in which case again there will be a resulting trust. For example, in *Hussey* v *Palmer* [1972] 1 WLR 1286 a payment of £607 for improvements to property to enable a widow to live with her daughter and son-in-law was held on resulting trust for her when differences arose, and she had to leave the house.

5.3 SURPLUS AFTER PURPOSES ACHIEVED

Even where the equitable title is originally disposed of, it may later result to the settlor. Suppose money is given for a purpose, and a surplus is left over after the purpose has been achieved. Two solutions are possible. One is that the transaction will be construed as an out-and-out gift, the purpose being regarded merely as a statement of the testator's motive for making the gift. In that case the recipient can keep the surplus. If no out-and-out gift was intended, however, the surplus will be held on resulting trust for the donor.

An example of the latter construction being adopted is *Re the Trusts of the Abbott Fund* [1900] 2 Ch 326. A fund was collected for the relief of two deaf and dumb ladies. A surplus of some £367 remained when they died and this was held on resulting trust for the subscribers.

In reaching his decision in *Re Abbott*, Stirling J held that the ladies themselves never became absolute owners of the fund. Nor did the trustees once the purposes were accomplished. No resulting trust occurs if either beneficiary or trustee is intended to take absolutely, however.

The fund in *Abbott* was subscribed to by various friends of the Abbotts. On the other hand, where the whole of a specific fund is left by a single individual for the maintenance of given individuals, the courts are more likely to construe the transaction as an absolute gift to those individuals, even where the fund is expressed to be left for a particular purpose. An example is the Court of Appeal decision in *Re Osoba* [1979] 1 WLR 247, where a testator left the whole of a fund for the education of his daughter up to university level. On completion of the daughter's university education she was held entitled to the surplus beneficially, the educational purpose being regarded merely as a statement of the testator's motive — in other words, there was no resulting trust in favour of the testator's estate. No absolute rule can be stated, of course, since the question of whether there is an absolute gift depends on the intention of the donor, i.e., it is a question of fact. But where the whole of a fund is left by one person, rather than, for example, so much of a fund as trustees shall determine, the courts are more likely to infer an intention to make a gift.

The other possibility is a gift to the trustee. *Abbott* applies only where the property was intended to be held on trust, and so does not apply where an out-and-out gift is intended, subject to trusts (as opposed to a gift 'on trust', which is subject to the *Abbott* principle). In such cases the trustee is clearly intended to keep the surplus. An example is *Re Foord* [1922] 2 Ch 519, where the testator left in his will: 'All my effects including rubber and all other shares I leave absolutely to my sister Margaret Juliet on trust to pay my wife £300 per annum'.

5.3.1 Anonymous subscriptions to funds

Where money has been given to a fund, say a disaster appeal fund, one might infer the donor's intention from, among other considerations, whether the donation was anonymous (e.g., small change in a street collecting box). If so, and no means of tracing the donor has been left, then the contribution might be construed as an out-and-out gift. Clearly the donor cannot have intended that any surplus left over be held on resulting trust for him, when he has left the organisers no means of finding him in the event of there being a surplus. If there is a surplus left over after the fund has fulfilled his purposes, therefore, and the fund is not charitable, that part of the surplus attributable to his donation will have no owner. It therefore goes to the Crown as *bona vacantia*.

Nevertheless *Re Abbott* was followed in *Re Gillingham Bus Disaster Fund* [1958] Ch 300, and such donations were directed to be held on resulting trust. The case concerned a fund collected to defray funeral and other expenses incurred as a result of a disaster involving the deaths of 24 Royal Marine cadets in Gillingham. Far more money (about £9,000) was collected than necessary for these purposes and Harman J, following *Re Abbott*, held that the surplus should be held on resulting trust for the donors.

The difficulty was that although some of the money had been provided by identifiable people, most had been obtained from street collections. So many of the donors were anonymous and the trustees were therefore required to hold the fund on resulting trust for unknown people. Obviously this is most inconvenient administratively. As we will see in section 8.6, had the gifts been charitable, the cy pres doctrine could have provided a way of avoiding this difficulty, but the gifts in *Gillingham* were not charitable. As explained above, if people give money in an anonymous collection, surely it can be assumed that they do not intend to see it back again. In other words, an out-and-out gift seems a more sensible inference than a gift on trust. Had that inference been drawn by Harman J, the surplus would of course have gone to the Crown as *bona vacantia*.

This result (i.e., the out-and-out gift construction) was indeed reached by Goff J in *Re West Sussex Constabulary's Widows, Children & Benevolent (1930) Fund Trusts* [1971] Ch 1. The case concerned a fund for widows and dependants, and not only did members contribute but there were also outside contributions. The fund came to an end upon amalgamation with other police forces in 1968, and the question arose as to the distribution of the surplus. In this section we are concerned only with the outside contributions. The division of the surplus among the members themselves is considered in section 5.4.

So far as identifiable donations and legacies were concerned, Goff J thought these indistinguishable from *Re Abbott*, so the proportion of the surplus attributable to that source was held on resulting trust. But there were also collections from raffles and sweepstakes, which Goff J thought were out-and-out payments subject only to a (contractual) hope of receiving a prize. Thirdly, however, there were the proceeds of street collecting boxes, and here Goff J declined to follow Harman J's earlier judgment, on the grounds also that the intention to be inferred was also that of an out-and-out gift. Thus, nobody could lay claim to the proportion of the surplus attributable to the last two categories, so it went to the Crown as *bona vacantia*.

Clearly the *West Sussex* case is easier to justify in conceptual terms than the earlier case and, of the two, *West Sussex* is, I suggest, more likely to be followed in the future. Understandably, however, Harman J was concerned to ensure that the Crown were not the main beneficiaries of a fund collected in highly publicised and tragic circumstances.

5.4 WINDING UP FUNDS

We have already seen in section 5.3, the questions which arise when a fund to which *outsiders* have contributed folds, either because it is wound up, as in the *West Sussex* case, or because its purposes have been achieved, as in *Gillingham Bus Disaster Fund*. This section is about funds to which members have contributed for their own benefit, and considers the basis upon which property is distributed among the *contributing* members upon the winding up of a fund. We shall see that, generally speaking, the resulting trust has no application in this situation.

5.4.1 When is a fund wound up?

It is necessary first to consider when a fund may be wound up. According to Brightman J in *Re William Denby & Sons Ltd Sick & Benevolent Fund* [1971] 1 WLR 973, winding up of a fund is not at the discretion of the treasurer or trustees of the fund, but may occur only when:

(a)   the rules allow for dissolution, or
(b)   all interested parties agree, or
(c)   a court orders dissolution, or
(d)   the substratum upon which the fund is founded is gone. In some cases,
this can include the gift of a large windfall (*Re St Andrew's Allotment Association*
[1969] 1 WLR 229.

5.4.2   Why is a trust solution usually inappropriate?

The types of fund with which this section is concerned are members' clubs or
friendly societies, which are unincorporated associations. As we saw in section
3.3, the property of unincorporated associations is not normally held in trust for
the members. Instead, the relationship between the members is contractual.
Members' contributions or subscriptions are regarded as out-and-out gifts, each
member retaining contractual rights (based upon the rules) to use the property of
the club or society. On resignation from the club or society, though the gift of the
subscriptions remains (otherwise a retiring member could claim back a share of
these), the retiring member gives up any contractual claim on the property of the
association.

It follows, therefore, that when such an association is wound up, only existing
members have a right to claim any part of the fund. The basis of their claim is
contractual and the method by which the division is calculated is considered in
section 5.4.3.

It is nevertheless possible in theory for funds to be held on the basis of a trust,
even though it is rare in practice. The main difficulty is the rule against
perpetuities, considered above in section 3.7, but this will not necessarily apply
where the fund is intended only for the benefit of existing members, or is of short-
term duration. Otherwise, the normal requirements for constitution of an express
trust will apply. If such a fund is dissolved, the property will be held on resulting
trust. All contributors, including those who have ceased to contribute, will be
entitled to a share, and division will be in proportion to the *total amount* they
have contributed. Thus, assuming everyone pays subscriptions at the same rate, a
person who has contributed for 10 years is entitled to twice the share of the
proceeds as someone who has contributed for only five.

Such was the basis of division in *Re Hobourn Aero Components Ltd's Air Raid
Distress Fund* [1946] Ch 86, affirmed [1946] Ch 194. It seems that this fund was
limited to known and existing employees of a company who were on war service,
to compensate for air raid damage in the Second World War, and in this type of
case a trust solution can indeed be appropriate. The fund was unusual in that it
seems to have assumed no fluctuations in membership, and was probably
intended to be short term in duration, so that perpetuities difficulties did not
arise. *Hobourn Aero* cannot be regarded as laying down any principle applicable

to the majority of fund cases, however, as it is rare for a club or society to be limited in that way.

It is true that in *Re Printers & Transferrers Amalgamated Trades Protection Society* [1899] 2 Ch 184, the basis of division was also ostensibly decided on trust principles, but in fact only existing members were allowed to claim, whereas a trust solution should allow for distribution among both past and present members (unless, of course, you can imply an out-and-out gift on resignation). In actual fact, it appears that the basis of division there was probably consistent with contractual, rather than trust principles, whatever the views of Byrne J in the case to the contrary. The *Printers'* case has been severely criticised in subsequent litigation, e.g., by Walton J in *Re Bucks Constabulary Widows' & Orphans' Fund Friendly Society (No. 2)* [1979] 1 WLR 936, and it must now be assumed that division on a contractual basis is the norm, the fund in *Hobourn Aero* being exceptional.

5.4.3   Calculation of shares

We have already considered this in the rare situation where a trust solution is applicable. Normally, the basis of division is contractual and, of course, if the rules provide for the contingency of dissolution of the fund, division will be according to the rules, as they will form the basis of the contract.

Often the rules do not so provide, however, and in this event the courts are left to imply terms. In accordance with normal contractual doctrine, this will be on the basis of inferred intention, and since this is largely a question of fact, no rigid rules of law can be stated. Nevertheless, certain presumptions appear to apply:

(a)   Only existing members can claim, because it is assumed that past members gave up all claims on the fund on resignation. Sometimes the rules expressly so provide, as in the *West Sussex* case, considered in section 5.3.

(b)   Generally speaking, in the case of members' clubs, division is equally among existing members. In mutual benefit or friendly society cases, the prima facie rule also appears to be equal division (*Re Bucks Constabulary Widows & Orphans' Fund Friendly Society (No. 2)* [1979] 1 WLR 936), though there have also been cases where division has been proportional to total contributions — this seems appropriate where the benefit contracted for while the fund subsists is also proportional to total contributions. In *Re Sick & Funeral Society of St John's Sunday School, Golcar* [1973] Ch 51, there were two distinct classes of membership, one class of which (adults) paid twice the subscriptions of, and received twice the benefits of, the other (children). Division was such that adults received twice as much as children. It must be emphasised, however, that inferred intention is a question largely of fact, and that it would be a mistake to deduce rigid principles of law from these cases.

(c)   If the assumption can be made that a contributor has made an out-and-out gift of his contributions, retaining no rights at all, then the property will go to the Crown as *bona vacantia*, because nobody has a claim on it. This was the result reached in *Cunnack* v *Edwards* [1896] 2 Ch 679, where only the widows of contributors were entitled to benefit from the fund. The same result was reached in the *West Sussex* case, because again only dependants of the contributors could benefit, but on this point the case was criticised in the *Bucks Constabulary* case. The precise circumstances in which an out-and-out gift of this type will be inferred are therefore still to be authoritatively decided, but in principle such an inference should not be lightly drawn and, since it is possible to enforce contracts for the benefit of third parties (see *Beswick* v *Beswick* [1968] AC 58), the mere fact that benefit is for third parties should not be regarded as conclusive.

5.5 MATRIMONIAL PROPERTY AND COHABITEES

5.5.1 Voluntary transfers of legal title and presumptions of advancement.

Where there is a voluntary transfer of legal title (i.e., a gift rather than a transfer for value) then, unless there is a presumption of advancement (see below), the presumption is that the equitable title remains in the settlor, i.e., there is a resulting trust.

An example of the operation of this principle in a general context is *Re Vinogradoff* [1935] WN 68, where the testatrix had before her death transferred gilt-edged stock into the joint names of herself and her granddaughter. The granddaughter held the property on resulting trust for the estate, there being no presumption of advancement.

Another example is *Hodgson* v *Marks* [1971] Ch 892, where an old lady (Hodgson) conveyed the legal title of her house to her lodger (Evans), in order to protect him against her nephew, who disapproved of him. By oral agreement Hodgson was to retain beneficial title and the Court of Appeal gave effect to the oral agreement. The trust thereby created is usually regarded as a resulting trust, rather than an express trust, because, as we saw in chapter 3, an express (but not resulting) trust relating to land is required to be in writing by virtue of s. 53 of the Law of Property Act 1925. Russell LJ in the Court of Appeal thought that Mrs Hodgson's interest was by way of resulting trust and it is a resulting trust of the *Vinogradoff* variety.

Another explanation, however, which I suggest is preferable, is that there is also an express trust in Mrs Hodgson's favour and that s. 53 does not apply because equity does not allow the statutory formality provision to operate as a cloak for Evans' fraud. This argument is dealt with in much greater detail in section 3.5.1.3.2.

Let us now apply the general principle to the purchase of a matrimonial home or a home for unmarried cohabitees. We have seen that if a gratuitous transfer of property occurs where there is no presumption of advancement, or where such presumption is rebutted (see below), the law presumes that whoever acquires the legal estate holds the property on resulting trust for the donor. There is, as we shall see below, no presumption of advancement where a wife transfers property to her husband, or one unmarried cohabitee (of whichever sex) transfers property to the other. Like the presumption of advancement, the presumption of resulting trust is based on intention and can itself be rebutted.

Suppose, for example, the matrimonial home is purchased in the name of the husband alone, but his wife has contributed to the purchase price. The presumption is that the wife acquires an equitable interest in the home by virtue of the resulting trust doctrine and the husband will therefore hold the legal estate on trust for both himself and his wife in proportion to their contributions. They will thus hold the land as joint tenants or tenants in common in equity, and a statutory trust for sale will arise under the provisions of the Law of Property Act 1925, ss. 34 to 36 (see sections 1.6.3 and 2.7.2). A similar result may obtain if the wife makes financial contributions in other respects, for example, by payment of part or all of the mortgage repayments.

The same result obtains, of course, if the parties are living together but not married. The difference arises where the man pays the purchase money, the property being conveyed into the woman's name alone. If they are married, as we shall see, the presumption of advancement applies. If not, the presumption of resulting trust applies.

If, however, there is a presumption of advancement, the position is quite different, because the equitable title follows the legal title (i.e., the gift takes effect as an absolute transfer). Presumptions of advancement occur where the relationship between the parties is such as to impose a moral obligation upon one to provide for the other. Examples are the obligation of a husband to support his wife and the obligation of a father to support his children. The effect of the presumption is that where there is a voluntary conveyance of the legal title (i.e., without consideration, in effect a gift), the equitable title passes also. In other words, the presumption is that an out-and-out gift is intended, to fulfil the moral obligation to give, whereas in other voluntary conveyances there is a presumption of resulting trust. So, for example, if a husband provides the money for a home which is conveyed into the name of his wife, an out-and-out gift of the home is presumed. Or if it is conveyed into the joint names of husband and wife, the presumption will be that the equitable title also will be jointly held, even if the husband has provided all the purchase money.

The presumption only applies between husband and wife and between father and son (or any other person to whom he stands in *loco parentis*, e.g., an adopted child). It does not apply between mother and son, though in that case it is easier to prove an intention to make a gift than in the case of a stranger (*Bennet v Bennet* (1879) 10 ChD 474). Nor does it apply from wife to husband, nor at all between unmarried couples.

Like most presumptions, and any presumption based as this is upon intention, it can be rebutted. An example may be if a wife is allowed to draw cheques on a joint banking account for the convenience of the husband, perhaps because the husband is ill, as in *Marshal* v *Crutwell* (1875) LR 20 Eq 328. Clearly in such a case there is no intention to make a gift to the wife, unlike, for example, *Re Figgis* [1969] 1 Ch 123, where an otherwise similar arrangement on a joint account was not merely for convenience. It also appears that bank guarantees, for example, where a husband guarantees his wife's overdraft, do not attract the operation of the presumption but that ordinary rules of contract apply (*Anson* v *Anson* [1953] 1 QB 636).

It should be noted that property rights must be ascertained at the time of purchase or transfer, so the subsequent conduct of the parties (e.g., the breakdown of a marriage) cannot affect the operation of the presumption.

5.5.2 Agreements: express, inferred or imputed intention?

If the above presumptions operate, it will be by sole reference to the financial contributions of the parties. But, of course, whatever the contributions of each party, the parties can agree as to the equitable ownership of property. Such agreement will effectively rebut either of the above presumptions. It must be shown either that on initial acquisition of the property there was an agreement that the beneficial interest was to be shared in a particular way or that a subsequent agreement was made which had the effect of varying the interests.

Such agreements can be either express or, in some cases, inferred from the conduct of the parties, but if the agreement is of the first type, conduct after initial acquisition is unlikely to be relevant. With either type, two types of agreement are possible. If the nature of the agreement is that the parties are to be treated as having provided contributions in a different proportion to the actual proportion, this can be inferred from the conduct of the parties; the trust is not of land, so formality requirements do not arise. An agreement directly to vary beneficial interests in land, however, must comply with the writing requirements of s. 53 of the Law of Property Act 1925 (see section 3.5.2). Such an agreement probably cannot therefore be inferred from conduct alone. The law was reviewed and so stated by Bagnall J in *Cowcher* v *Cowcher* [1972] 1 WLR 425.

Suppose now that the wife does not directly contribute financially to the home and no agreement on the above lines can be inferred. She contributes indirectly, however, for example, pays household expenses, provides furniture, provides services as a housewife or brings up the children. Can the law impute an intention to the parties, regardless of whether or not they actually addressed their minds to the matter? It can be argued that such contributions should be valued, and that it is unjust to base the wife's interest on the limited grounds discussed above alone.

The House of Lords in *Pettit* v *Pettit* [1970] AC 777 and *Gissing* v *Gissing* [1971] AC 886 took the view that the rights of property of spouses in the matrimonial home depended on the above criteria of express or inferred intention alone. In other words, the courts have no discretion to vary these rights, or impute any intention, in the light of the subsequent conduct of the parties or what they may see as the injustice of the case. Mrs Gissing, for example, had been married to Mr Gissing for 16 years and had paid a substantial sum towards furniture and the laying of a lawn, but the house had been conveyed into the name of Mr Gissing alone and Mrs Gissing had made no direct contributions towards its purchase. On their divorce, the House of Lords held that she had no interest. The main importance of the case is that the courts will not impute intentions to the parties where no actual intention is expressed, or can be inferred, simply to do 'justice'. It was also said that there is no such concept as family assets. At the end of the day, therefore, the interests in the property are determined on the basis of expressed or inferred intentions of the parties (as affected by the presumptions as to intention) at the time of acquisition of the property or, if the interests are subsequently varied, then at that time.

Since *Gissing* v *Gissing* Parliament has given the courts greater discretion on the breakdown of a marriage by virtue of the Matrimonial Causes Act 1973, s. 23. The operation of this Act is traditionally dealt with in family law and is beyond the scope of this book. But the legislation has not altered the position where the marriage subsists or where there is no marriage (i.e., the position of cohabitees). These situations are still dealt with by the law of trusts.

5.5.3 Constructive trusts

A number of Court of Appeal decisions appeared subsequently to alter the position, however, in holding that the constructive trust remedy allowed greater flexibility in all cases. The assumption was made that the nature of the interest depended on all the equities of the case and that the law might consider not merely financial contributions at the time of acquisition of the property but all types of contribution, whether at that time or subsequently. The basis of these decisions is a passage from Lord Diplock's speech in *Gissing* v *Gissing* [1971] AC 886 which has been quoted out of context. The essence of the passage is that:

> A resulting, implied or constructive trust — and it is unnecessary for present purposes to distinguish between these three classes of trust — is created . . . whenever the trustee has so conducted himself that it would be inequitable to allow him to deny to the cestui que trust a beneficial interest in the land acquired.

These Court of Appeal decisions are premised on the assumption that equity is still able to develop in the flexible manner in which it did in early days. 'Equity', says Lord Denning MR in *Eves* v *Eves* [1975] 1 WLR 1338, at 1340, 'is not past the age of child bearing. One of her latest progeny is a constructive trust of a new model.' We saw in chapter 1 that this flexibility may no longer be as extensive as it once was. If the reasoning for the Court of Appeal decisions is correct then a great deal of uncertainty has been brought into this area of property law. Not only is it more difficult to advise the parties themselves but third parties may be adversely affected. Conveyancing may be made more difficult, contrary to the policy behind the 1925 property legislation (on which, see section 1.6).

The development is on similar lines conceptually to that discussed in section 6.3 but the factual situation is different and all the cases actually involve two parties only (e.g., no third-party purchaser).

The first of such cases is *Heseltine* v *Heseltine* [1971] 1 WLR 342. A wife, during the subsistence of a marriage, advanced some £40,000 to her husband to enable him to save estate duty and some £20,000 to him to enable him to raise sufficient security in his own name to become an underwriter at Lloyd's. On the principles discussed above, the husband would have taken this money beneficially. The presumption of resulting trust would have been rebutted because the purpose of these transactions would have been defeated unless the husband obtained the equitable interest in the money. Nevertheless, on a dispute between the parties after separation (but not divorce), the Court of Appeal (Lord Denning MR citing the passage of Lord Diplock quoted above) held that the money was held on constructive trust for the wife.

In other cases an unmarried female cohabitee has been given an interest on the basis of a constructive trust where almost certainly a different result would have been reached on strict *Gissing* principles. One such case is *Cooke* v *Head* [1972] 1 WLR 518, where though the lady concerned had provided only one-twelfth of the cost of a bungalow (the building of which had not actually been completed), the Court of Appeal awarded her one-third of the proceeds of sale. On the other hand, she had also greatly contributed to the labour of building itself and this may justify the result. Another case is *Eves* v *Eves* [1975] 1 WLR 1338. Here 'Janet', who had made no financial contributions towards the purchase price (though again she had worked on the house), was held entitled to a one-quarter share in the house under a constructive trust.

The problem with these cases is that, whereas they may strive to do justice between the parties, the implications of imposing a constructive trust upon a house are wider than that, affecting third-party purchasers and creditors. Nevertheless, the issue differs from that considered in section 6.3 in that there were *in fact* no third parties to consider, so one wonders whether a proprietary remedy is necessary or appropriate at all.

At the end of the day all these cases are about one party making financial provision for the other. In both *Cooke* v *Head* and *Eves* v *Eves* the relationship had terminated and the issue was essentially over money, whether by way of proceeds of sale or (as in *Eves* v *Eves*) otherwise. The same goes for *Hussey* v *Palmer* [1972] 1 WLR 1286, another case based on the passage from Lord Diplock's speech quoted above, though in this case, where £607 was provided specifically to improve a house, conventional *Gissing* reasoning may well have achieved the same result.

It is possible, of course, that the cases are simply wrong, as being inconsistent with House of Lords authority. If not, however, one wonders whether a contractual solution may have been more apt. If one party is unjustly enriched at the expense of the other (which appears to be the position in these cases), it ought to be possible in principle to imply a contract between them on the basis of their conduct, which would ensure justice between them without affecting third parties. Contractual, rather than trust solutions, are better suited to dealing with two-party situations.

In all of the above cases it may be that an agreement between the parties could have been inferred as to repayment of moneys, or compensation for work done, in the event of termination of the relationship. There is no doubt that the common law is extremely flexible in its ability to infer contracts from conduct. Why not, indeed, if property rights and third parties are not involved? A good example is the contractual licence terminable on twelve months' notice implied in *Chandler* v *Kerley* [1978] 2 All ER 443, another case involving an informal cohabitation arrangement. Certainly no agreement was *expressed* to that effect.

On this basis, it may have been possible to infer an agreement between the Heseltines that the money given beneficially (on ordinary trust principles) to the husband would be repaid if the marriage broke down, or that the men in the other cases would compensate for the money paid or work carried out on the property. If not, then the only reasonable assumption would be that a gift was intended from the woman to the man in each case, in which event the Court of Appeal decisions are wrong.

It is sometimes said that it is artificial to force unjust enrichment cases into the straitjacket of contract. Three answers can be made, however, to this criticism:

(a)   Contract is no longer a straitjacket. In a rather different type of case, Lord Wilberforce in the Privy Council made it clear that English law takes a practical approach to the implication of contracts, 'often at the cost of forcing the facts to fit uneasily into the marked slots of offer, acceptance and consideration' (*New Zealand Shipping Co. Ltd* v *A.M. Satterthwaite & Co. Ltd (The Eurymedon)* [1975] AC 154 at 167. In fact, a most unusual contract was implied in that case, on the basis of the conduct of the parties, where there was no question of there being any direct agreement expressed between them (indeed, they had probably never met). Uncertainty is of course less important where property rights as such are not at stake and third parties are not involved.

(b)   Contract requires an agreement, but if no agreement can be inferred, the only realistic possibility is that a gift was intended, in which case it is difficult to see how anyone is unjustly enriched.

(c)   If the intended solution (as in these cases) is financial, and the idea is to affect nobody but the parties to the action, a contract-based solution is really the only possibility. Trusts create property rights and affect third parties, and therefore give a remedy greater in scope than necessary.

In any event, it now seems that the Court of Appeal is moving back towards the conventional *Gissing* view: see, e.g., the reasoning adopted in *Burns* v *Burns* [1984] Ch 317, the facts and result of which were similar to *Gissing*, except that though the parties had lived together as husband and wife for 19 years, they were unmarried. All the cases considered above were explained on conventional resulting trust reasoning and the court reaffirmed that it is not possible to impute intention where there is none in fact. On the other hand, a strange result was recently reached by the Court of Appeal, apparently on *Gissing* principles. In *Winkworth* v *Edward Baron Development Co. Ltd, The Times*, 23 December 1985, an interest was inferred from a contribution not to the matrimonial home itself, but to pay off the overdraft of a company which owned the home. At the time of writing the case had not been fully reported, and in any event leave has been given for an appeal to the House of Lords, so it is perhaps too early to reach conclusions on it. If it goes to the House of Lords, perhaps some of the issues discussed in this section can be finally clarified.

Another recent example is *Bristol & West Building Society* v *Henning* [1985] 1 WLR 778. Here also, as in *Burns* and *Gissing*, the lady concerned (Miss Ingram) was an unmarried cohabitee, who had not contributed to the purchase money of the home, though she had made other contributions not directly of a financial nature. Again, she failed in the Court of Appeal on *Gissing* principles.

The case is less clear than *Burns*, however, because Browne-Wilkinson LJ ultimately refused to decide whether Miss Ingram actually had a beneficial interest in the property, preferring to rest his decision on the question of priorities, that is to say whether her interest (if any) bound the plaintiff building society, which was a subsequent mortgagee. On the facts, even if she had an interest, it did not bind the plaintiff, so the question *whether* she had an interest did not arise. It is a pity that the case was not clearer on the trust issue because the plaintiff here *was* a third party, so this is one case where contract reasoning would not have worked — to bind the plaintiff, Miss Ingram had to show either a beneficial interest or an estoppel licence (see section 6.3). The Court of Appeal also cast doubt on, but again without deciding, the correctness of *Re Sharpe* [1980] 1 WLR 219 a decision of the same judge (albeit when he sat in the High Court) discussed in detail in section 6.3.

The conclusion is, however, that the flexible approach adopted by the Court of Appeal in some of the cases discussed in this section is wrong. The decisions themselves may well be right, but the constructive trust reasoning is a wholly inappropriate method of achieving the desired result.

6

Constructive Trusts and Inequitable Conduct

Whereas express and implied trusts effect the express or implied wishes of the settlor and resulting trusts are also a consequence, albeit more remote, of the settlor's intention, constructive trusts are imposed by the court as a matter of law. They depend on principles of equity and conscience and are independent of the settlor's intention.

The circumstances in which constructive trusts can arise are many and varied, and rather than attempt to cover all situations in this chapter, many have been dealt with elsewhere in the book. Some trusts which are arguably constructive, for example, secret trusts and mutual wills, are dealt with, not in this chapter, but in their appropriate place in the book. Trusts imposed on third parties in connection with the tracing remedy appear in the chapter on trustees' duties.

There is, however, a residue of cases which are based on similar principles and which fall within this chapter: trusts that are imposed by the courts specifically because of the conduct of the legal owner of property.

6.1 CRIMINAL ACTS

Equity will not allow a person to retain the benefit of criminal activities: property received criminally is held on constructive trust for those entitled to it. Thus in *Re Crippen* [1911] P 108, Crippen murdered his wife and attempted to escape abroad with his mistress, Miss Ethel Le Neve. He failed, and was caught and hanged, leaving his property to Miss Le Neve. The question arose regarding that part of Crippen's property to which he was apparently entitled on the death (intestate) of his murdered wife. Evans P held that Crippen could not take the property and that it could not therefore pass to Miss Le Neve. Instead it passed to his wife's next of kin. It must be assumed that if Crippen had actually received the property he would have held it on constructive trust for his victim. There was no evidence, incidentally, that the murder was in any way motivated by a desire to inherit Mrs Crippen's property.

It is not entirely clear which crimes attract the principle. There is no difficulty with crimes requiring an element of intention, such as murder or theft, because a connotation of unconscionable conduct can be presumed. A principle based on unconscionability ought to require a subjective element of intention, and in recent cases the courts are apparently moving towards the view that only criminal acts committed with such an intention are indeed included within the principle.

6.2   FRAUD

There is some recent authority for a general principle that property obtained by fraud is to be held on constructive trust for the victim of the fraud. This general principle seems to be relatively new, however, and to have developed from other more specific principles. I suggest that it is still possible to argue that the jurisdiction is in fact limited to the specific cases, especially that equity will not allow a statute to be used as a cloak for fraud, and that he who seeks equity must come to the court with clean hands (see section 1.4.1).

6.2.1   Equity will not allow a statute to be used as a cloak for fraud

This principle was developed by the courts of equity to prevent people from taking unfair advantage of statutory formality provisions, which are of course intended to prevent, rather than encourage fraud. There are two main lines of authority.

First, there are express trusts which are enforced despite the fact that they do not comply with statutory writing requirements. Examples may be found in section 3.5.1.3. They are not authorities for any general fraud principle involving the imposition of constructive trusts. The second strand of cases concerns secret and half-secret trusts, where the doctrine avoids the formality provisions of the Wills Act 1837 (see chapter 7). I suggest that these are also really examples of express trusts and therefore provide no authority for any general principle of imposition of constructive trusts.

In any event, both types of case apply only where there is an attempt to use a statute intended to prevent fraud as a means of perpetrating fraud. Far from being authority for any general principle, therefore, they may not even apply to every statutory provision. Indeed, it would be difficult to argue that the principle applies to the Land Charges Act 1925 (which was intended to simplify conveyancing, not prevent fraud), following the House of Lords decision in *Midland Bank Trust Co. Ltd* v *Green* [1981] AC 513. There a sham sale between husband and wife, intended specifically to defeat a third party's valuable option to purchase a farm, succeeded in its purpose, solely because the option had not been properly registered under the Act. Lord Wilberforce said (at p. 531) that in general it is not 'fraud' to rely on legal rights conferred by Act of Parliament. Thus equity's intervention is by no means as universal as some of the recent cases suggest.

6.2.2 He who seeks equity must come to the court with clean hands

This principle prevents people from enforcing fraudulent trusts. It, too, has nothing to do with the imposition of constructive trusts.

6.2.3 A general principle of fraud?

It follows that the development of any general principle seems unwarranted by earlier authority. Furthermore, there is as we shall see no need for it, and indeed it can cause injustice. It must be remembered that the imposition of a constructive trust is an extreme step. As between the parties, it creates all the incidents of a trustee-beneficiary relationship (this was the difficulty encountered with mutual wills in chapter 4). More importantly, it creates a property interest, which binds third parties also.

Mutual wills cases themselves may seem to provide the necessary authority for a general fraud principle (see section 4.4). It is probable that mutual wills are special cases, though, because before the Executors Act 1830 the survivor would often have also been executor, and therefore also residuary legatee under the other party's will. Thus enforcement may have been justified on a similar basis to early secret trust cases (see section 7.1.1). Later, it has been assumed that there is no alternative enforcement, though, as we saw in section 4.4, this assumption is probably mistaken. In the cases that follow, there are alternative and better means of reaching the appropriate conclusion.

If there is a general principle, it has been expanded to form the basis of some of the cases on new varieties of constructive trust (discussed in section 6.3).

The case most often relied upon is the Court of Appeal decision of *Bannister* v *Bannister* [1948] WN 261, [1948] 2 All ER 133, though the judgment of Scott LJ is actually fairly limited in its scope. The defendant was negotiating to sell two cottages to the plaintiff, her brother-in-law, and it was understood that after the sale she would be able to continue to live in one of the cottages rent-free for as long as she wished. Because of this oral arrangement the plaintiff obtained the cottages for only £250, as compared with their true market value of around £400. No written agreement to this effect was included in the conveyancing, however. After the sale, the plaintiff claimed possession of the cottage. Obviously the plaintiff had obtained the property cheaply by fraud. The Court of Appeal therefore decided that he held it as constructive trustee of the defendant for her life.

In fact, though there are passages in the judgment which appear to suggest a general principle, and though the trust was said to be constructive, the case is actually about an attempt to use the writing provisions of the Law of Property Act 1925 as a cloak for fraud. It is really only an application of the principle in section 6.2.1, therefore, and is similar to *Hodgson* v *Marks* [1971] Ch 892 (see section 3.5.1.3.2). Though the trust was described as being constructive, this was probably only because such trusts are expressly exempted from s. 53 of the Law of Property Act 1925 (requiring writing, which there was not in the case). It is reasonably clear from *Hodgson* v *Marks*, though, that express trusts also avoid the provision as explained in section 6.2.1.

Even so, though the result is clearly correct and justified on the basis of previous authority, it shows how the imposition of a constructive trust can be an extreme remedy. Its effect was that the defendant became a tenant for life under the provisions of the Settled Land Act 1925 and therefore had power to sell it. Clearly this is a much more extreme result than the parties intended.

There were only two parties in *Bannister* v *Bannister*, i.e., there were no complications involving purchasers. The case, I suggest, is not an authority for any new general principle. It is the extensions of the reasoning in section 6.3, however, which give rise to the real problems, especially where it is carried over from situations with two parties to situations with three parties.

6.2.4 Why no contract?

We saw in section 5.5 that in cases in which there are only two parties, such as *Bannister* v *Bannister* [1948] 2 All ER 133, contract reasoning is preferable to trust reasoning. There was clearly a contract in *Bannister* v *Bannister*, which could have been enforced to give the defendant exactly what she had bargained for. True, it was not in writing, but nor did it need to be. The Court of Appeal could have reached the desired result by treating the agreement as giving rise to a contractual licence to remain in one of the cottages. Contractual licences do not need to be in writing, and the defendant would have had exactly what she had bargained for. The constructive trust reasoning actually adopted by the court gave her far more, because of the Settled Land Act implications.

Perhaps the case was not argued on this basis because it was not clear at that time (unlike today) that it was possible to have a contractual licence, not in writing, giving a right of exclusive possession in land. It was probably (wrongly) assumed that an estate contract would be required, which would have been caught by the writing provisions of s. 40 of the Law of Property Act 1925 (see sections 3.5.1.3 and 3.5.2).

In mutual wills cases also there is, as we saw in section 4.4, an enforceable contract, and the difficulties arise because of the constructive trust which is imposed. In this area also, the contract possibilities do not seem to have been fully examined, and less appropriate trust remedies have been adopted instead.

6.3 DEVELOPMENTS OF FRAUD JURISDICTION – A NEW VARIETY OF CONSTRUCTIVE TRUST?

As we saw in Chapter 1, equity has traditionally provided an element of flexibility to a common law that has in the past sometimes been too rigid. I argued then that such a role is probably no longer appropriate today, but since *Bannister* v *Bannister* [1948] 2 All ER 133 there is further authority that constructive trusts are still developing in this way, especially in cases concerning land.

As with any rapidly developing area of law, it is very difficult to state with any precision what the law is at any given time. Indeed, one of the difficulties over the development is precisely that it creates uncertainty. It is not even possible to state a conventional view, because there is little agreement, among judges or academics, either as to what the law is or what it ought to be.

There is of course no reason why major new developments should not take place by means of case law, for example, the torts of negligence, interference with contract, conspiracy, intimidation and negligent misstatement are all creatures entirely of fairly recent case law. The difference is that all those tort actions either developed initially, or have been approved, by the House of Lords. In this area the authorities are relatively few in number and none goes higher than the Court of Appeal. Given that the development is so radical it is legitimate, in my view, to question whether the cases are in fact correct. One cannot rule out the possibility that the House of Lords might in the future overrule them.

By and large the decisions are based on a notion of what the court considers to be the just result. It would certainly be a pity if some of them were overruled. Again, however, given the lack of previous authority and (I shall suggest) the inappropriate character of the constructive trust as a remedy in these situations we should also consider whether the same decision could have been reached on other grounds.

6.3.1   Why is the constructive trust inappropriate?

The proponents of the new variety of constructive trust base their views especially on American experience, where general theories are developing about liability based on unjust enrichment. English law, however, recognises no such general theories of liability, and nor should it. Such liability is inevitably defined vaguely and in dealing with matters involving property, a unique and expensive commodity, certainty as to liability is immensely important. I would in any event suggest that it is not easy to make out a case of unjust enrichment unless either there is some kind of agreement or request for a benefit to be conferred, in which case either there will be a contract action or the situation will fall within the usual trust criteria (see section 5.5).

Again, in some other jurisdictions a constructive trust can be used simply as a remedy, without any wider consequences. In English law this is not the case, however, because a constructive trust creates a property right just like any other trust. It has, as we have seen, consequences for third parties, for creditors and so on. It is not merely a remedy, as may be the case in the United States. Many of the new constructive trust cases, while apparently doing justice as between the parties, seem to take little account of the wider consequences that inevitably follow from the creation of a property interest.

There is also an assumption that the common law is inflexible. In fact this is not so, and in many of the situations considered in this section, not only has the common law a perfectly satisfactory answer, but it is not fraught with the difficulties of the constructive trust approach.

6.3.2 Nature of the problem

The problem stems from around the time of the Second World War, when Rent Act protection for lessees became increasingly widespread, and landlords sought to evade it. One possibility was the contractual licence, giving rights of exclusive possession to the licensee. It was then, and is now, possible to use the licence rather than a lease as a method of avoiding some or all Rent Act protection, though the House of Lords decision in *Street* v *Mountford* [1985] 2 All ER 289 may make the operation of the dodge more difficult.

Once the principle had been established that rights of exclusive possession of residential property could be licences, rather than leases, the contractual licence began to crop up in other circumstances, in particular in informal arrangements, particularly of the family kind. The difficulties spring from the fact that unlike a lease, a licence is usually regarded as a personal not a property right, and the privity of contract doctrine demands that contracts are usually enforceable only by and against the contracting parties. While this is of no consequence so long as the property does not change hands, if the landlord sells, the question arises as to enforcement against the purchaser. Similarly, if the landlord dies, the question is as to enforcement against his successors in title. The contract will not bind purchasers and other third parties so, unless the licence itself can constitute a property right, the privity doctrine works in favour of the third party.

While this may cause no great injustice with non-exclusive possession licences, it is quite a different matter if the licensee loses his home, especially where he has given valuable consideration for the licence. Not surprisingly, therefore, the courts have sought solutions to the problem. An early approach was that of the Court of Appeal in *Errington* v *Errington* [1952] 1 KB 290, which sought to make contractual licences property rights. This development has probably been curtailed, however, by *dicta* in the House of Lords in *National Provincial Bank Ltd* v *Ainsworth* [1965] AC 1175, where support can be found for a traditional view (namely, that licences are personal rights only). The issue is still alive, however, because there was no contractual licence in *Ainsworth*, merely a deserted wife's equity of occupation. The issue did not directly arise, therefore, and *Errington* was not overruled.

Another development was the estoppel licence, to which the hostile remarks in *National Provincial Bank Ltd* v *Ainsworth* did not apply. The estoppel arises where the licensee relies to his detriment on a representation by the licensor, and is a form of promissory estoppel. It is easier to argue that these bind third parties because there is no applicable privity doctrine and no reason in principle why a third party claiming through the licensor should not be bound by representations made by him (if he knows about them), even if the licence itself is only a personal right. The authorities, while not being conclusive for that proposition, generally support it, but there are a number of ways in which estoppel rights and remedies are weaker than those in contract. For example, permanent rights are probably not created. Further, it is possible that estoppels create no cause of action, so that their only value is in defending other people's claims, e.g., an action for possession or trespass, and nearly all the cases are of this type.

6.3.3   Constructive trust as a solution

This is the scenario in which the new variety of constructive trust was developed. At first sight it seems to be the ideal solution because trusts clearly create proprietary rather than personal interests and so are capable of binding third parties. Furthermore, all the trust remedies apply. However, the difficulties alluded to in section 6.1.3.1 are exacerbated, precisely because the device is so extensive in its scope. A particular problem is that if purchasers and other third parties are to be bound, conveyancing becomes more difficult, this being contrary to the policy of Parliament in its enactment of the 1925 property legislation (see section 1.6).

There are only a few cases, and it is doubtful whether constructive trusts can or should be used in this area and if so, to what extent. The position is complicated further by the fact that there were alternative, and even conflicting, reasons given for the leading decision, that of the Court of Appeal in *Binions* v *Evans* [1972] Ch 359. There is little doubt that 79-year-old Mrs Evans should have won in that case, as she did. The issue is over the correct reasoning to achieve that result.

Binions v *Evans*   The trustees of the Tredegar Estate, near Newport, entered into an agreement with Mrs Evans (the defendant), whose husband had worked on the estate for many years and had a tied cottage, that Mrs Evans could continue to live in the cottage for the rest of her life. It is not entirely clear what consideration Mrs Evans provided for this licence but she was required to keep the property in a proper manner. Anyway, the Court of Appeal accepted that she had a contractual licence to remain.

The trustees sold the cottage to the plaintiffs, Mr and Mrs Binions, expressly subject to Mrs Evans's 'tenancy agreement'. The plaintiffs, having thereby obtained the cottage more cheaply, six month later claimed possession from Mrs Evans. They failed in the Court of Appeal. A diagrammatic representation of the case appears in Figure 6.1.

The reasoning of Megaw and Stephenson LJJ seems to be that the original agreement between the trustees and the defendant created a life tenancy. Thus at that stage the trustees held the property on trust for Mrs Evans for her life,

Figure 6.1

Binions v Evans

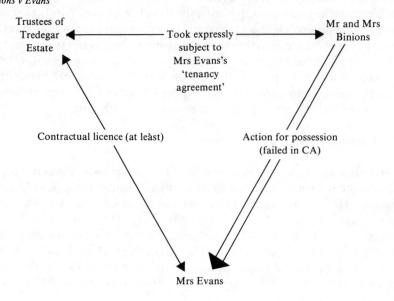

thereafter for the Tredegar Estate in fee simple. This is a succession of equitable interests, so Mrs Evans had an interest in land coming within the provisions of the Settled Land Act 1925 (see section 1.6). *Bannister* v *Bannister* [1948] 2 All ER 133 was treated as authority in this (at this stage two-party) situation, Mrs Evans's interest arising by way of constructive trust. The purchasers were therefore bound by an existing trust on the ordinary principles of the equitable notice doctrine (see section 1.4.6).

This view is not without its problems, representing as it does an extension of the reasoning in *Bannister* v *Bannister*. The agreement here was in writing, so there was no question of a formalities statute being used as a cloak for fraud. Maybe it is possible to infer constitution of a trust from the agreement on conventional principles but it would be necessary (because no legal title was conveyed at this stage) to infer that the trustees of the estate were constituting *themselves* also trustees for Mrs Evans. As we saw in section 2.2 this inference is not readily made because it imposes an onerous obligation on the trustees.

The reasoning of Lord Denning MR was very different. He thought, relying on *Errington* v *Errington* [1952] 1 KB 290 (see section 6.3.2), that the contractual licence could of itself have bound the purchaser with notice. Though Lord Denning took this view, Stephenson LJ was less sure on this point. In any event such reasoning on its own would have been unlikely to be upheld, had the plaintiffs appealed to the House of Lords, because of *National Provincial Bank Ltd* v *Ainsworth* [1965] AC 1175 (see section 6.3.2).

Lord Denning MR therefore also adopted a second approach, that because Mr and Mrs Binions had purchased expressly subject to the agreement, equity would impose upon their conscience, so that they held the property on constructive trust for Mrs Evans. This approach, like that of the other judges, is an extension of the fraud reasoning discussed in section 6.2 and seems to depend on him taking expressly (or according to Lord Denning MR impliedly) subject to the agreement. It differs from the views of the other two judges, and any previous authority, in that the trust arose not under the original agreement, but *on the sale of the property to the plaintiffs*. It is also far wider in its scope than any previous case. Indeed, the Master of the Rolls thought that a constructive trust could be imposed whenever the trustee had conducted himself in an inequitable manner — this would give enormous discretion to the courts. His citation of American authority (Cardozo J) suggests that he regarded such a trust as a remedy only (see section 6.3.1) without the wider property consequences usually attendant upon creation of trusts, which is perhaps why he was so keen to impose it. As we have seen, however, this is not the position adopted in English law.

The difficulty with constructive trust reasoning, of either variety, is that it is too extreme. For example, it is, as we have seen, at least arguable that the Settled Land Act 1925 applied in the case, and indeed Megaw and Stephenson LJJ thought that it did. The result of this is that Mrs Evans, as tenant for life, could have the legal estate vested in her and has extensive powers to sell the land, overreaching the Binions' interest. Such a result is clearly far more extreme than the parties intended. Lord Denning MR thought that the Act did not apply, however, effectively because he said it applies only to expressly created settlements (though the Act itself does not say this).

Yet obviously the result in *Binions v Evans* is to be welcomed. How, then, can the decision be justified? The assumption is always that the common law is unable to cope with situations such as these, yet Megaw LJ expressly mentions a common law solution which admirably fits the bill without all the difficulties of the trust. There was a contract between the trustees of the Tredegar Estate and Mrs Evans giving her an irrevocable licence. That remained binding on the trustees even after the sale to the plaintiffs, because otherwise the trustees could have evaded their obligations by the unilateral act of selling the property. The plaintiffs knew of this contract and deliberately caused it to be broken. They were therefore guilty of the tort of interference with contract. Megaw LJ wondered whether the ordinary principles of the tort action should apply in a land law situation, but in fact this would have been the best reason for the decision. All the usual common law and equitable remedies are available for this action, and in one land law case (concerning an induced breach by a purchaser of a solus agreement between a garage and an oil company), a mandatory reconveyance was ordered (*Esso Petroleum Co. Ltd v Kingswood Motors (Addlestone) Ltd* [1974] QB 142). Not all third parties would be bound; the tort seems to require express knowledge of the existence of a contract and constructive knowledge of its terms (*Emerald Construction Co. Ltd v Lowthian* [1966] 1 All ER 1013). Because of the express knowledge requirement, the difficulties of conveyancing are not significantly increased.

Lord Denning's view in *Binions* v *Evans* was, however, followed by the High Court in *Lyus* v *Prowsa Developments Ltd* [1982] 1 WLR 1044, though in one respect a limited view was taken of the earlier decision. *Lyus* v *Prowsa Developments Ltd* is a most extraordinary decision and is almost certainly wrong. Certainly if it is correct it makes conveyancing much more risky and, unlike *Binions* v *Evans*, it is difficult to see how the result could have been arrived at by any other reasoning.

The plaintiffs, Mr and Mrs Lyus, had an estate contract, as prospective purchasers of property from a firm of builders. The builders became insolvent, however, before completion, and the prior mortgagees, National Westminster Bank, exercised their power of sale under the mortgage. From this point, of course, the plaintiffs were entirely at the mercy of the bank, and no longer had any enforceable rights. The purchasers from the bank purchased subject to the plaintiffs' contract, however, in so far as it was originally enforceable. Dillon J held, on the basis of *Binions* v *Evans*, that they therefore held the benefit of the original estate contract on trust for the plaintiffs and that Mr and Mrs Lyus were entitled to specific performance of it.

Unlike the earlier case it is not clear that any policy demanded that the plaintiffs should win. The dispute was essentially about money, as the property had significantly increased in value. The effect of the decision was, therefore, a substantial windfall for the plaintiffs and probably a substantial loss for the defendants.

Dillon J limited the operation of *Binions* v *Evans* to cases where the purchaser took subject to a right. It is not enough that he merely knew of it. He also took the view that this is an extension of the fraud jurisdiction discussed above. In another respect, however, the case is an extension of *Binions* v *Evans*; the plaintiffs had no rights at all before the purchase from the bank, as they were before then entirely at the mercy of the bank. Here the right was apparently created by the sale. This seems an unwarranted extension, in that the obligations of the purchaser are greater than those of the vendor.

It is also because of this that no alternative reasoning would work. There was no interference with contract, because there was no enforceable contract before the sale. Another possibility that has been argued is that the case depends on a good faith requirement being written into the Land Registration Acts (such has been held to be the case by Graham J in *Peffer* v *Rigg* [1977] 1 WLR 285). Here the land was in an area of compulsory registration of title (i.e. the Land Registration Act 1925 applied — see section 1.6). The purchaser was not acting in good faith so should, on that argument, be bound by the plaintiffs' prior rights whether they were registered or not (they were not). The difficulty with this reasoning is that the plaintiffs had no prior rights.

The conclusion I would draw is that where there are existing rights before the sale a purchaser who takes expressly subject to those rights may be bound by them, and it is not necessary to extend the constructive trust to achieve this result. Where there are no existing rights it is difficult to see why the purchaser should be bound at all, and I suggest that *Lyus v Prowsa Developments Ltd* is wrong. Also, there are no obvious reasons of policy for the result in that case.

Re Sharpe   Another difficult case is *Re Sharpe* [1980] 1 WLR 219, where an 82-year-old lady, who was not in good health, loaned a large sum of money (£12,000) to her nephew to enable him to purchase a house in which they could both live. The nephew later went bankrupt and the question arose whether the old lady's money was secured or whether it formed part of the nephew's assets to be divided among his general creditors. Browne-Wilkinson J found for the old lady on the basis that she was a beneficiary under a constructive trust, which bound the trustee in bankruptcy. His views on when a constructive trust might arise were much wider than earlier views. It seems that a constructive trust can be imposed simply because a licensee expends money or otherwise acts to his detriment. In other words this encompasses pretty well any estoppel licence of residential property.

Though Browne-Wilkinson J had to hold that a property interest arose in order for the trustee in bankruptcy to be bound, again it may be wondered whether constructive trust reasoning is appropriate. In fact, the exact nature of the aunt's interest was not made clear in the judgment (for example Browne-Wilkinson J would not say whether a purchaser could be bound) but unlike some of the cases in section 5.5 it should be noted that contractual reasoning will not work in this situation. Trustees in bankruptcy are not bound by contractual rights.

But if it was the intention of the aunt and nephew that the old lady should have an interest in the property, then she has an interest on conventional resulting trust principles, as discussed in section 5.5. If not, it is difficult to see why her interests should prevail over those of the other creditors, unless the facts of her age and health are considered decisive. In other words, the case should have been decided on resulting trust principles; it is not clear whether the result would have been the same if it had been.

Alternatively, it has been argued by Jill Martin [1980] Conv 207 that an estoppel licence or proprietary estoppel was created, and that this is the true explanation of the decision. Certainly this view is arguable. Estoppel licences and proprietary estoppels are outside the scope of this book (they are traditionally land law) but I would suggest that there are problems with this approach, in particular whether estoppel licences can in fact be proprietary so as to bind a trustee in bankruptcy.

In conclusion, constructive trusts have been argued in these cases to do what is seen as justice between the parties without sufficient regard for wider issues. Mrs Evans could have been protected on other, less extensive reasoning, and it is not clear whether the decisions in *Lyus v Prowsa Developments Ltd* [1982] 1 WLR 1044 and *Re Sharpe* are correct in any case. The courts should be careful before continuing along the constructive trust road and it is beginning to look as if a judicial reaction is indeed setting in: e.g., *Bristol & West Building Society* v *Henning* [1985] 1 WLR 778, CA — see section 5.5.

6.4 UNDUE INFLUENCE

If one party uses undue influence to force the other party (whom I will call for these purposes the 'victim') into an agreement or transaction, equity will unravel the transaction. This is most likely to occur when the victim is in a very weak bargaining position by comparison with the other party.

If a contract is entered into under conditions of undue influence, it is voidable at the instance of the victim. The contract is not void at common law, however, so in accordance with equitable principles, the victim's rights will be defeated by delay or affirmation, so long as the affirmation is not itself affected by undue influence. If property has changed hands, equity can set aside the transaction by imposing a constructive trust on the transferee to hold the property for the victim. Third parties may also be affected on ordinary equitable principles but if the property has passed to a bona fide purchaser for value without notice the victim loses his remedy.

The doctrine bears some factual similarities to the common law doctrines of duress and restraint of trade but it must be distinguished from them. Contracts entered into under duress or in restraint of trade are void at common law. The doctrines are narrower than undue influence, however.

Duress in particular is a very narrow doctrine, being limited to threats of violence or of catastrophic economic consequences. Commercial pressure and mere inequality of bargaining power are not sufficient to vitiate a contract on the grounds of duress. It is true that both may be factors for the purposes of the common law restraint of trade doctrine, but there are some types of agreement (e.g., most leases) to which that doctrine is not applicable at all. And, of course, an agreement can be the result of unfair pressure without having anything to do with restraint of trade — a purchase of goods from the victim at well under their market value would be one example. The Court of Appeal has recently reviewed the restraint of trade doctrine in *Alec Lobb (Garages) Ltd* v *Total Oil (Great Britain) Ltd* [1985] 1 All ER 303, on which see also the author's note in [1985] Conv 141. All that we need to note for present purposes, however, is that the common law doctrines by no means apply to all unfair practices.

The equitable doctrine of undue influence operates in circumstances where the common law duress doctrine does not. Some forms of pressure, e.g., a threat to prosecute the weaker party or a close relative, come within the equitable but not the common law doctrine. Apart from that, though it is not possible to state exactly when the doctrine will apply, the law has recently been reviewed by the House of Lords in *National Westminster Bank plc* v *Morgan* [1985] 1 All ER 821, and some general statements can be made.

(a)   It is not enough that a bargain be merely unreasonable: the test, unless there is a special relationship as considered below, is one of unconscionability, which is more difficult to prove. The courts seem reluctant to extend the doctrine on the ground that that is the function of Parliament in specific instances. The language used by Lord Scarman suggests that the influencer must use an unfair advantage, putting the victim at a manifest disadvantage as a result of which he enters into a hard and inequitable agreement. In particular, inequality of bargaining power, though a relevant factor, is not by itself enough to attract equitable intervention, even where the victim did not have independent legal advice, despite the remarks of Lord Denning MR (but not the other judges) to the contrary in *Lloyd's Bank Ltd* v *Bundy* [1975] QB 326.

(b)   In some fiduciary or other special relationships (e.g., doctor and patient, solicitor and client), but never in commercial dealings (e.g. bank and customer), a presumption of undue influence arises. In other words, the transaction is allowed to stand only when the presumption is rebutted. The general test is whether it is the free exercise of independent will of the victim. The presumption is likely to be rebutted if independent advice is given, so long as it is given in full knowledge of the relevant facts, but possibly if the influence is especially strong, or a large amount of property is at stake, it is also necessary that the adviser approve the transaction. A recent example is the Court of Appeal decision in *O'Sullivan* v *Management Agency & Music Ltd* [1985] 3 All ER 351, where a management agency, which was in a fiduciary relationship with a composer of music (Gilbert O'Sullivan), persuaded him to enter into various contracts without independent professional advice. The contracts were set aside by the court on the basis of the principles discussed above. We come across the case again in the next section because the management agency was nevertheless allowed some remuneration for the benefit conferred on Mr O'Sullivan.

7

Secret and Semi-Secret Trusts

As with *inter vivos* transactions (see section 3.5), there are formality requirements where property is left by will. The usual justification for formality requirements is that they prevent fraud. As in other areas, however, those relating to wills can sometimes encourage fraud. 'Equity will not permit a statute to be used as a cloak for fraud', (see section 1.4.1 and also the discussion in sections 3.5.3 and 6.2), and the doctrines of secret and semi-secret trusts have evolved in this area to prevent this.

To be valid, wills have to be made in writing and properly signed and witnessed, as required by s. 9 of the Wills Act 1837, as amended by s. 17 of the Administration of Justice Act 1982. If the provisions are not complied with, the will is completely void, and any trusts which it purports to create will be invalid also. As will be seen, however, the doctrine of secret trusts permits the creation of a trust to take effect on the death of the testator without the need to specify the terms of the trust in the will, or indeed to reveal its existence.

The purpose of this section, as we have already seen, is to prevent fraud. To make a will is to enter into a major transaction. This must not be done in a light-hearted manner but must be the result of a deliberate act. Formality requirements are supposed to ensure this. It is also more important than with *inter vivos* gifts to remove the possibility of false claims as the testator himself obviously cannot refute them. There may, however, be at least two reasons why a testator may wish to avoid formality provisions (on this see, e.g., Sheridan (1951) 67 LQR 314).

First, he may wish the identity of the beneficiary to remain secret. This was especially common in the 19th century, if a gift of land to a charity was intended, when the Statutes of Mortmain (which prevented testamentary gifts of land to charities between 1736 and 1891) were in force. Another common situation was (and still is) where the beneficiary is to be a lover or mistress or illegitimate child. Perhaps the need for secrecy has diminished since 1969, because until then there was a presumption that a gift to children in a will excluded illegitimate children. Thus it was necessary to identify them to include them. That presumption was reversed by the Family Law Reform Act 1969, s. 15, so a gift to children on its own will now suffice. Even so, secrecy may still be desired if it is wished to keep their very existence secret.

Secondly, the testator may simply not have made up his mind at the time of making the will about the details of all the dispositions. It has been argued (e.g., Watkin [1981] Conv 335) that, whereas the law should indulge secrecy, it should discourage indecision and, to at least a partial extent, it has taken this line.

There are two methods by which the Wills Act can be effectively evaded. A can leave property by will to B, in a manner which complies with the provisions of the Act but having come to an (unwritten) understanding with B that he is merely trustee of it in favour of C. The understanding does not, of course, comply with the formality requirements of the Act. This is called a fully secret trust. Alternatively, A can leave property by a valid will 'to B on trust', but leave the beneficial interest under the trust (for example, in favour of C) undeclared. This is called a half-secret (or semi-secret) trust because, while the details of the trust are secret, it is made clear that B holds as trustee and not beneficially. For clarity, A, B and C will be used in the same fashion throughout the chapter.

While secret and half-secret trusts are quite rare today, they are traditionally covered in courses on trusts because they illustrate important equitable principles. What therefore follows is a discussion of the validity and basis of these dispositions.

7.1 FULLY SECRET TRUSTS

These are generally speaking valid — in the above example C can enforce the trust against B. The leading authority is the House of Lords decision of *McCormick* v *Grogan* (1869) LR 4 HL 82. Though in the case itself it was held that no secret trust was created in C's favour (an illegitimate child) but merely a moral obligation imposed on B, the court made it clear that had the facts been different a fully secret trust would, in principle, have been enforceable by C, in spite of the provisions of the Wills Act 1837. In fact, the principles go back at least as far as *Thynn* v *Thynn* (1684) 1 Vern 296.

It is by no means self-evident that equity should uphold a trust, apparently in spite of a clear statutory provision to the contrary. Clearly, the basis of such an equitable doctrine requires close examination. In *McCormick* v *Grogan*, Lord Hatherly LC and Lord Westbury emphasised that the doctrine should be limited to cases where B had committed a personal fraud. In other words, secret trusts should only be enforced where B had deliberately induced the testator to leave the property to him in the will, on the clear representation that he would hold it in trust for C. 'Equity will not permit a statute to be used as a cloak for fraud' (see section 1.4.1). In several places in his speech, Lord Westbury in particular emphasised the need for a '*malus animus*' to be 'proved by the clearest and most indisputable evidence'. In effect, this means that an intention to deceive must be shown on B's part, and that the standard of proof is as in common law fraud; in other words, a very high standard is required.

The principles enunciated in *McCormick* v *Grogan* beg an important question, however. If the only basis of the doctrine is to prevent B from fraudulently

keeping the property for himself, why is it necessary to enforce the trust in C's
favour? Why is it not enough for there to be a resulting trust in favour of the
testator's estate? We must consider this, and also developments in the law since
McCormick v *Grogan*.

7.1.1 Why no resulting trust?

One might imagine that if equity's only concern is to prevent B from committing
a personal fraud, it would be enough to require him to hold the property on
resulting trust for the estate. This solution would deprive B of his personal gain
and the policy of the Wills Act 1837 would appear to be effected. Yet even before
McCormick v *Grogan* (1869) LR 4 HL 82 it was clear that the courts did not
favour the resulting trust solution, and that equity would enforce the trust in
favour of C. An early example is *Thynn* v *Thynn* (1684) 1 Vern 296. The testator
(A) had made his wife sole executrix — it should be noted that at that time, before
the Executors Act 1830, the executor (or if female, executrix) was entitled to
retain the residuary estate (i.e., the estate not otherwise disposed of by will) for
himself (or herself). The son (B) persuaded the wife to make him sole executor
instead, upon a completely fraudulent pretext. The Lord Keeper held that the
property must be held in trust for the wife (C). A resulting trust in favour of the
estate would not have answered, because B would himself have benefited from
that as residuary legatee. A more recent example is *Re Rees* [1950] Ch 204, where
a solicitor was both trustee and residuary legatee.

  Thynn v *Thynn* was decided before the Wills Act 1837. Also, of course, had the
same facts arisen after the Executors Act 1830, B may not have personally
benefited in the same way from a resulting trust. Yet *McCormick* v *Grogan*
applied the same principles to a case under the Wills Act. This appears to go
further than necessary, and to defeat the intention behind the Act.

  It is possible to justify such enforcement on policy grounds. If C is (say) A's
mistress (in 1869 A would usually have been male) or illegitimate child, a
resulting trust in favour of his estate, which, of course, benefits (typically) his wife
and legitimate children, is the very last thing the testator intended. In *McCormick*
v *Grogan*, C was in fact an illegitimate child, so had the facts suggested the
imposition of a legally binding obligation on B, enforcement in C's favour could
have been justified on this basis.

  More importantly, however, we must examine the nature of the fraud, upon
which the doctrine is based. Just because Lord Westbury insisted on an element
of intention to deceive, it does not follow that the nature of that deceit rests only
in the personal gain of B. Rather, it must be defined much more widely than this.
It should be remembered that the gift to B depended in the first place on B's
promise to carry out the wishes of the testator. B's fraud, in equity, lies in the
defeat of these wishes, not necessarily in his own personal gain. In *McCormick* v
Grogan, had the facts suggested fraud, it could only have been resolved by the

enforcement of the trust in C's favour: a resulting trust would not have sufficed. This line of reasoning is not universally accepted, but has been further developed by, e.g., Hodge [1980] Conv 341.

7.1.2 Developments since *McCormick v Grogan*

There is limited authority that, since 1869, their lordships' stringent requirements concerning '*malus animus*' have been relaxed. Before considering the law itself, however, which is not yet clear, it is necessary to consider why Lord Westbury was so concerned to limit the doctrine as he did, and what has altered since 1869.

As we have seen, *McCormick v Grogan* (1869) LR 4 HL 82 concerned an attempt to make a secret gift in favour of an illegitimate child. Secret trusts were also frequently used, however, in providing for charity. Testamentary gifts of land in favour of charities were, at that time, void. Other gifts were not, however. The practice therefore grew up whereby A left property to B, who was a trusted friend, on the understanding that he would later give the property to the charity. There was no question, in such cases, of B being fraudulent. He had every intention of carrying out the testator's wishes.

Why, then, did any problem arise? The charity would receive the property — why any need for litigation? It must be appreciated, however, that it was not the intended beneficiary in these cases who brought the action. Rather, it was A's family who attempted to show that the secret trust was enforceable. This can be seen from the case of *Wallgrave v Tebbs* (1855) 2 K & J 313, where the secret trust failed, for reasons discussed in section 7.2.

The reason for this extraordinary state of affairs was this. If the secret trust was unenforceable, B took the property beneficially and he could be relied upon, as a friend of the testator, to carry out A's wishes. If, however, it was enforceable, then, by virtue of the Statutes of Mortmain, it was void. Thus, there would be a resulting trust to the estate (i.e., A's family)! This accounts for the surprising circumstance that it was the very last people who might at first sight be expected to benefit from the secret trust being enforceable who argued that it was. On the other hand, it was in the interests of the charity for it not to be enforceable because the charity could rely on B carrying out A's wishes.

The House of Lords in *McCormick v Grogan* did not wish to allow gifts to charities to be defeated in this way. On the other hand, if B was really on the make, they did not wish to see a mistress or illegitimate child deprived of his rightful interest because of the provisions of the Wills Acts 1837. In the first case B was far from being fraudulent — indeed, he only wished to carry out the trust. In the second case, he was. Hence the stringent limits placed on the doctrine in that case.

The position changed in 1891, and the last vestiges of the mortmain legislation disappeared in 1960. Only the second type of secret trust remains today, therefore. Arguably, their lordships' limits to the doctrine are no longer appropriate. They are, of course, dicta, albeit from the House of Lords, because in the event C lost on other grounds. There is some authority that the limitations will no longer be stringently applied.

Though it seems that the doctrine is still based on fraud, in so far as equity will not allow a statute intended to prevent fraud to be used to perpetrate fraud, it is possible that fraud in equity is nowadays a wider concept that it was in 1869. Today, there is some authority that it bears little relation to the common law or criminal law concept of the same name. It imposes on B's conscience but may not necessarily demand the same degree of *mens rea* as fraud in the common law or criminal sense. Because of this, it may also demand a lower standard of proof.

Ottoway v *Norman* [1972] Ch 698 was a case involving a rather unusual family arrangement, where a secret trust of land was enforced. Brightman J imposed on B (Miss Hodges) a constructive trust in C's favour. Yet Miss Hodges probably did not intend to deceive the testator, at least at the time when he made his will. In other words, she did not obtain the property under A's will by deceit, although she later changed her mind and decided not to carry out his intentions. In any event, the evidence was insufficient to surmount the stringent standard of proof required for common law fraud. Yet Brightman J was prepared to enforce this secret trust of land. Far from requiring fraud in the sense required in *McCormick* v *Grogan*, he held that enforcement of a secret trust in C's favour depended only on:

(a)   The intention of the testator to subject B to an obligation in favour of C.

(b)   Communication of that intention to B.

(c)   The acceptance of that obligation by B, either expressly or by acquiescence.

These criteria were derived from *Blackwell* v *Blackwell* [1929] AC 318, a case discussed in section 7.3. Further, Brightman J held that it is immaterial whether these elements precede or succeed the will. This is fair enough: if acceptance of an obligation by B persuades A not to revoke an existing will in B's favour, for B to break this obligation is quite as clearly a fraud on A as it would have been had A been persuaded, by B's acceptance of obligation, to make a will in his favour.

Since fraud in so wide a sense was enough, it was also held that it need only be proved on the ordinary civil standard of balance of probabilities.

It cannot be said that the position is yet clear, however, and that fraud in Brightman J's sense is indeed enough. Megarry V-C partially dissented from this view in *Re Snowden* [1979] Ch 528. He thought that a higher standard of proof was required where fraud (which seems to be viewed in the narrower sense) had to be proved, and further thought that it did for some, but not all secret trusts. In other words, in his view, there are two classes of secret trusts, some of which require a more stringent burden of proof than others. Unfortunately, he did not go on to elaborate on the distinction. In any event, Megarry V-C's views are *obiter* because in the case before him there was really no evidence at all on which a secret trust could be established.

I suggest that contrary to the views expressed by Megarry V-C, however, there is in fact only one basis for secret trusts. The policy reasons for limiting the operation of secret trusts as in *McCormick* v *Grogan* no longer apply. Whether or not the law has in fact moved away from those limitations, however, is not yet clear. To some extent the *Ottoway* v *Norman* reasoning parallels the development of constructive trusts described in section 6.3. As we saw in the previous chapter, that debate also is by no means over.

huuy

7.2   LIMITATIONS ON ENFORCEMENT OF SECRET TRUSTS

Whether or not the limitations of *McCormick* v *Grogan* (1869) LR 4 HL 82 still apply, it is clear that once B has received a gift absolutely, any subsequently imposed obligations cannot deprive him of that gift. Apart from the principle that gifts are irrevocable, there is no reason, in such a case, to impose on B's conscience. Thus in *Wallgrave* v *Tebbs* (1855) 2 K & J 313, the existence of the secret trust, in favour of a charity, was not communicated to B until after A's death. B was entitled to the property absolutely. Any other decision would have been a derogation from A's grant and there is a general legal principle that a grantor (A in this case) shall not derogate from his grant. In any event, as we saw above, there were good policy reasons for this decision, since B intended to carry out the trust anyway. Had the trust been held to be enforceable, as A's family argued, it would have been void under the Statutes of Mortmain, so the property would have gone on resulting trust to the estate.

A more difficult decision is *Re Boyes* (1884) 26 ChD 531. Here B was told of the existence of the trust before A's death, but was not informed of the terms (in favour of a mistress) until after the death of the testator. Kay J held that B held as trustee, but on resulting trust for A's estate. This is a difficult case to fit into the general scheme of things, because A obviously did not intend the property to go to his estate, and arguably the court actively sanctioned a fraud on A. There are two possible explanations:

(a)   It is wrong: after all, it is a High Court case only, which has not been followed.

(b)   Alternatively, other policy considerations outweigh that of enforcement of the trust in C's favour. In particular, to enforce the trust would sanction indecision by A, which is arguably bad policy. Also, the court has to set a limit on the time for which trustees are required to hold property without knowing who the objects are, and it is a reasonable solution to insist that they know from the outset (though this may be not until the estate has been administered — i.e., later than death, so arguably this rather than death should be the deadline).

I suggest that *Re Boyes* is correct.

It is enough, incidentally, for the terms of the trust to be placed in a sealed letter to be opened after the testator's death (*Re Keen* [1937] Ch 236, 242). Though B is not informed of them until after A's death (as in *Re Boyes*), the policy reasons discussed above, against enforcing the secret trust in C's favour, do not apply. A is not being indecisive and B is not being asked to hold property for any length of time as trustee without knowing the identity of the objects of the trust.

In *Re Stead* [1900] 1 Ch 237, Farwell J made various distinctions where property was given to two persons (B1 and B2) as joint tenants or tenants in common, but where only one (B1) had promised to hold the property on a secret trust. The question at issue is whether B2 is bound by the trust. The distinctions were said to be based on older cases and are difficult to support as a matter of policy. Perrins argues, however, (1972) 85 LQR 225, at 228, that Farwell J's distinctions are wrong and that the cases actually show that B2 is bound if his gift was induced by the promise of B1 on the grounds that he should not profit from another man's fraud but not otherwise. If Perrins is correct, then these cases fit into the general scheme of things, so long as the criteria for enforcement advanced in *Ottoway* v *Norman* [1972] Ch 698 (see section 7.1) are correct.

7.3   HALF-SECRET TRUSTS

These are also valid in principle, and like secret trusts, can be enforced by the intended beneficiary. The leading House of Lords authority is *Blackwell* v *Blackwell* [1929] AC 318. The justification for enforcement of half-secret trusts is exactly the same as that for fully secret trusts, as Lord Buckmaster made clear in that case. Equity imposes on B's conscience in order to prevent fraud by him. So secret and half-secret trusts should be regarded as similar creatures.

Some writers have argued that fraud cannot be the justification, because B cannot in any event take beneficially himself, whereas he could if fully secret trusts were not enforced. This is because half-secret trusts differ from the fully secret variety in that the will makes it clear that B takes as trustee only. So, if half-secret trusts are not enforced, B holds the property, not beneficially, but on resulting trust for the residuary legatee. Therefore, there is no possibility of personal gain by B (unless, of course, B is also residuary legatee).

It is no answer to say that a resulting trust would be a fraud on C, the intended beneficiary. As an argument in favour of enforcement, the reasoning is circular, because if a half-secret trust is not enforceable there is no beneficiary to make the argument work. C is only a beneficiary if the conclusion has already been reached that half-secret trusts are to be enforced.

There is an answer to the resulting trust argument, however, which is exactly the same as the one we have already considered for fully secret trusts. The resulting trust is a fraud on the testator (A) and the property has only been given to B because of an express or implied promise made by B to A. This is clear from the facts of *Blackwell* v *Blackwell* itself. A intended to benefit his mistress and illegitimate son. A resulting trust would have given the property to his wife and legitimate child — indeed, it was they who argued for a resulting trust. Clearly, A did not intend that they should benefit. He would not have settled the property on B had he thought that the result would be a gift in favour of his wife and legitimate child. B's acceptance of the property would have been a fraud on A unless the trust was enforced in favour of C. The justification for the enforcement of half-secret trusts, therefore, is exactly the same as that for fully secret trusts.

7.4   LIMITATIONS ON ENFORCEMENT OF HALF-SECRET TRUSTS

It appears, however, that half-secret trusts differ from their fully secret cousins in one respect. It is necessary, for their enforcement, for B to have accepted the obligation before the will is made. This distinction is difficult to justify in principle, because a will is a revocable instrument having no legal status until death. And if it is argued that the contrary result allows the testator to alter the identity of the beneficiaries every day, at any time up to his death, then why not have the same rule for fully secret trusts?

Nevertheless, there are dicta supporting the distinction in *Blackwell* v *Blackwell* [1929] AC 318, and the leading authority is *Re Keen* [1937] Ch 236. The remarks in *Re Keen* are also dicta because the trust there failed on other grounds (the terms of the will were inconsistent with the directions given to B). There can be little doubt that they represent the law, however, because they have been followed in *Re Bateman's WT* [1970] 1 WLR 1463.

A possible explanation is that there is a second principle at work, in addition to the fraud principle already discussed. This is that where reference is made in a will to a document, that document must already be in existence, otherwise the possibility exists of testators creating unattested codicils. It may be that of the two principles, the latter prevails where there is conflict. With fully secret trusts, the question does not arise because the will is silent. Thus the distinction between half and fully secret trusts is justified. It must be admitted, however, that this explanation lacks credibility.

Watkin [1981] Conv 335 argues for the *Bateman* position on policy grounds, namely, that whereas the law should and does not object to secrecy it should not encourage indecision. A testator should have made up his mind by the time the will is made. The logic of this reasoning (if correct) applies to fully secret trusts also and Watkin argues that they should be brought into line by statute. While not dissenting from these arguments of policy, I would suggest that there may be theoretical problems in legislating in this area, as will appear in section 7.6.

7.5   BASIS OF SECRET AND HALF-SECRET TRUSTS

It is now generally thought that the reason that these trusts need not comply with the provisions of the Wills Act 1837 is that they take effect outside the will. They take effect independently of it, except that the will is necessary to constitute the trust on A's death. In other words, if the will was invalid, B would not receive the property at all and any secret or half-secret trust would necessarily fail.

Once the trust is constituted, however, the will has no further relevance. Thus, not only the requirements of writing, but also other provisions affecting wills (i.e., rules of probate) are avoided. One such rule of probate is that a beneficiary cannot attest a will. It does not invalidate a half-secret trust, however, for a beneficiary under the trust to attest the will (*Re Young* [1951] Ch 344). The reasoning of Danckwerts J there also applies in principle to fully secret trusts.

A more difficult case is *Re Gardner (No. 2)* [1923] 2 Ch 230. Here the beneficiary (C) under a fully secret trust predeceased the testator (A). It is impossible to leave property by will to somebody who is already dead. Yet Romer J upheld the secret trust. His explanation was that C acquired an interest as soon as the secret trust had been accepted by B, but this cannot be correct because, until A's death, no trust was constituted. There are two possible views to take on this case:

(a)   The orthodox view is that it is wrongly decided. This is also my view. Many of the writers who advance theories explaining the law in this area frankly admit that their theories do not account for *Re Gardner (No. 2)*.

(b)   Oakley's view (*Constructive Trusts* (London: Sweet & Maxwell, 1978), p. 93), as I understand it, is that though it is impossible to leave property by *will* to a dead person, it does not follow that it is also impossible to constitute a *trust* in favour of someone already dead. Though there is no authority on the question, in principle it ought to be possible. On this view, *Re Gardner (No. 2)* is correctly decided and also applies to half-secret trusts, but not on Romer J's reasoning. C's interest does not arise until constitution of the trust on the death of A, but the fact that by then C is dead is not decisive. If Oakley's view is correct, this is simply another example of a case where the rules applicable to wills are not applicable to half or fully secret trusts, which take effect outside the will.

7.6   EXPRESS OR CONSTRUCTIVE TRUSTS? DOES IT MATTER?

We have seen that the basis of enforcement of both fully and half-secret trusts is B's fraud, defined in a wide equitable sense. Additionally, both varieties implement the express intentions of the testator, even though those intentions may not be expressed correctly, in writing, signed and attested etc. Each takes effect outside the will. It is said that it matters whether they are classified as express or constructive trusts because the formality requirements of the Law of Property Act 1925, s. 53(1) (see section 3.5), apply to express, but not (by virtue of s. 53(2)) constructive trusts.

Section 53(1)(b) requires express trusts of land to be declared in writing, yet a fully secret trust of land was enforced in *Ottoway* v *Norman* [1972] Ch 698 despite being oral. Further, that case ostensibly rested on constructive trust principles. This is therefore apparently authority that fully secret trusts at least are constructive. Yet, as we saw in section 7.1.2, the case stands rather on its own and probably should not yet be regarded as a conclusive authority. Further, it applies directly only to fully secret trusts, and some writers distinguish between the two varieties. Indeed, *Re Baillie* (1886) 2 TLR 660 suggests that writing is required for half-secret trusts of land, though not too much emphasis should be placed on cases prior to *Blackwell* v *Blackwell* [1929] AC 318. Indeed, I have already argued that the basis of half and fully secret trusts is the same.

My view is that writing is never required for any secret trust of either variety. I am not, however, convinced that they should be classified as constructive simply because they are based on fraud — as we saw in sections 3.5.3 and 6.2, express trusts have been enforced also on this basis. *Hodgson* v *Marks* [1971] Ch 892, discussed in those sections, is a good example, and I would also suggest that *Bannister* v *Bannister* [1948] 2 All ER 133 was an express trust. In any event, as we saw in section 6.2.3, there is little authority for any principle of imposition of constructive trusts on the basis of fraud.

I suggest, however, that the issue is wholly academic and of no practical importance. The classification is relevant only to the formality requirements of s. 53 of the Law of Property Act 1925. Yet the validity of half and fully secret trusts depends on a principle of equity, which is not defeated by s. 9 of the Wills Act 1837. Surely it will also not be defeated by s. 53 of the Law of Property Act, or any other statutory formality provision intended to prevent fraud. If equity will not permit a statute intended to prevent fraud to be used as an instrument for fraud, there is no reason why it should distinguish between statutes for these purposes. The principle applies as much to s. 53 as to s. 9. This will be so however secret trusts are classified, because it is not therefore necessary that they fall within the s. 53(2) exception to avoid the requirements of s. 53(1). See further on this point, Oakley, *Constructive Trusts*, p. 101, and Perrins [1985] Conv 248, 256–7.

The conclusion is, then, that, whether secret and semi-secret trusts are express or constructive, they are not affected by any enactment requiring formality.

I have argued in section 6.2 that the equitable fraud jurisdiction is probably limited to preventing use of statutes intended to prevent fraud, to perpetrate fraud. Nevertheless, there are many, as we saw in the earlier section, who argue that the principle is of wider application, and on the basis of existing authority either view is tenable. It is for this reason that I suggested, in section 7.4, that the legislative proposals of Watkin [1981] Conv 335 may be difficult to implement, as indeed may any legislative proposals in this area. Enforcement of secret trusts is based on an equitable fraud jurisdiction, and it may be (though I would argue otherwise) that equity allows no statutory provision to curtail that jurisdiction.

8

Charities

8.1 LEGAL BASIS OF CHARITIES

8.1.1 Charities and the trust

It is usual to deal with charities as an integral part of the law of trusts. It is not necessarily the most appropriate classification, however, because, though many charities exist in the form of a trust, this is not universal. Also, historically the law has recognised charities for even longer than the trust itself.

In its earliest institutional form, charity was the province of the medieval Church and its supervision the responsibility of the Ecclesiastical Courts. It was the secularisation of charitable donation during the Tudor Period, and the contemporaneous growth of the jurisdiction of the Court of Chancery by way of the use (see sections 1.2.5 and 1.2.6), which brought the administration of charity under the control of the Chancellor. He began to enforce uses relating to land. The attractive simplicity of the use, and later the trust, for philanthropic donors, coupled with the effectiveness of equitable remedies (see section 1.4.5), meant that the trust rapidly became the commonest method of dedicating property to worthy causes.

Charitable trusts are, of course, a variety of purpose trust, and as we saw in section 3.2, there are difficulties in the enforcement of purpose trusts, especially as with charities there will probably not be easily identifiable human beneficiaries. However, since the early 17th century the Attorney-General has undertaken the enforcement of charitable trusts as representative plaintiff and, as we shall see, since 1960 the Charity Commissioners have been given supervisory powers over charities. Because the Attorney-General has powers of enforcement, there is no need for charitable trusts to be subject to the same certainty of objects requirements as private purpose trusts, and they are not. Indeed, because of the public character of charitable trusts, we shall see that they are also exempt from other requirements to which private trusts are subject, and in addition enjoy certain privileges.

Although, as we shall see in section 8.1.2, not all charities exist in the form of a trust, the trust is still the most common medium of charity today, both numerically and in terms of value of funds. The trust seems to be most favoured on the one hand by private individuals and on the other by the largest and wealthiest of charitable enterprises, the foundations which often originate within international commercial corporations.

From the viewpoint of the private donor, the trust form is simple to create and sufficiently flexible to allow for a degree of individuality to be expressed in its provisions. For a large and well-funded organisation, the trust form offers the opportunity to maintain large capital funds producing high levels of income, which can be distributed on a discretionary basis. For these reasons the trust will probably remain the most usual form of charitable enterprise, and charity law will continue to take its direction from the doctrines developed in equity. Indeed, the courts have always shown a preference for treating all charities as partaking in the nature of a trust, even where their institutional arrangements are of a quite different sort.

8.1.2   The alternatives

The most common alternative forms for charity are the charitable corporation and the unincorporated association.

8.1.2.1   Charitable corporations

An increasing number of charitable ventures nowadays operate within a corporate structure, and this form is particularly well-suited to collective, active enterprises. A corporate charity will be a company limited by guarantee. A distinction between a charitable company and an ordinary commercial company limited by shares is that the constitution of a charity will forbid the distribution of profit among its members. Otherwise, the establishment of a company limited by guarantee is broadly similar in terms of formality to the setting up of an ordinary commercial company. As with a commercial company, the liability of the charity is limited to its assets, thus protecting its members from personal liability in the event of the charity becoming insolvent.

The advantage of corporate status is that the charity can operate as a legal person. So it has the capacity to make contracts, incur liabilities and hold property in its own right, without the need to involve trustees. Also, it does not need to effect alterations in the documents of title to its property at every change in personnel. It is therefore well suited to charities which undertake extensive long-term operations. These often have considerable assets, sufficient to make the expense of incorporation worthwhile.

8.1.2.2   Unincorporated associations

These are the other most common form, which may convert to corporate status if and when it becomes convenient. The less rigid framework offered by this form makes it attractive to groups of people wishing to undertake active charitable work in accordance with broadly democratic and flexible policies which may change and develop over time. Control of the organisation and its funds, if any, will typically be vested in a committee of managers who will probably be elected in conformity with the wishes of the current membership.

As we saw in section 3.3, the basis of this form of organisation is usually a contract between the members, formulated as the rules which are contained in the constitution of the association. This carries the advantage of extreme flexibility, allowing the terms of the contract to be modified to meet new situations. The main disadvantage is that the managers and members are exposed to unlimited personal liability incurred in the course of the organisation's activities. Nevertheless, the unincorporated association accounts for a moderate proportion of old-established charities, as well as some of the newer and most active charitable undertakings.

8.1.2.3   Other, unusual forms

3 .Mutual benefit organisations maintaining funds collected by subscription from members, and being intended to provide benefits during sickness, old age, etc., may be registered under the Friendly Societies Act 1974, and those which qualify as charitable according to the legal definition of that term, (see section 8.5) may have the status of 'benevolent societies'. Their significance appears to be declining in view of the growth in State welfare provision.

Another form available to charities, and apparently favoured by the growing number of housing associations, is the Industrial and Provident Society, a kind of hybrid with some of the features of both the friendly society and the guarantee company, and registrable under the Industrial and Provident Societies Acts 1965 to 1978.

Finally, there is the charitable corporation, which is not related to the guarantee companies discussed above. These are established either by charter from the Crown or else by government or ecclesiastical agencies having power to create corporate bodies. They include universities, hospitals and the British Museum. Such institutions are diverse in nature, and there is no standard form — each is endowed with a constitution specific to its own requirements. These charities are generally considered to enjoy high prestige by virtue of their unique character, and represent something of an elite category within the range of charitable organisations.

8.2   LEGAL REGULATION OF CHARITIES: ADVANTAGES OF CHARITABLE STATUS

Before considering the legal definition of charity (see section 8.5), we should consider the consequences that flow from charitable status. It will be seen that they are quite diverse, which has led to a confusion on the part of the courts as to the policy they should adopt. This helps to explain the apparently haphazard nature of the cases defining charity.

8.2.1 Tax advantages

Charities enjoy exemption from income tax on all income, rents, dividends and profits provided these are applied for charitable purposes, and may reclaim from the revenue any income tax already paid prior to receipt of the income. Nor is income tax chargeable on the profits of any trade carried out by a charity, so long as these are applied for charitable purposes only and the trade is either exercised in carrying out the primary purposes of the charity or the work is carried out mainly by its beneficiaries (e.g., workshops for the handicapped). Charitable corporations are exempt from corporation tax.

Gifts to charity are largely exempt from capital transfer tax (to be called inheritance tax), and capital gains tax is not payable where gains are applied to charitable purposes. No stamp duty is payable on conveyances, transfers or leases, nor were charities liable to pay development land tax. All charities are exempt from half of the rates on premises occupied in connection with the charity, including charity shops, and premises used for religious purposes are entirely exempt from rates. Generally, charities must pay VAT on goods and services but certain goods, such as some equipment for the handicapped, are zero-rated.

The annual cost to the Revenue of these tax concessions is of the order of half a billion pounds or, to put it into perspective, about £50 for every average-sized family in the UK.

8.2.2 Validity

Charities have three main advantages in this regard.

First, as we saw in section 8.1.1, charities are public trusts enforceable at the suit of the Attorney-General, so their lack of human beneficiaries is not fatal, as it is to private trusts. Indeed, only the Attorney-General can enforce charitable trusts; individuals who may benefit have no *locus standi*, by virtue of the Charities Act 1960, s. 28. The Attorney-General can be substituted as plaintiff for individuals, however (*Hauxwell* v *Barton-on-Humber Urban District Council* [1974] Ch 432, where he was substituted as plaintiff for two individuals).

Secondly, it is not necessary for the purposes of a charitable trust to be defined with certainty. A gift on trust 'for charitable purposes' will be valid, and the court and Charity Commissioners have jurisdiction to create a scheme for the application of the property donated. A gift to charity which is not expressed as a trust will be similarly disposed of by the Crown.

Thirdly, charitable trusts, unlike private trusts, may exist indefinitely. This being so, a gift over from one charity to another may take effect at any time in the future (*Christ's Hospital* v *Grainger* (1849) 1 Mac & G 460). Once property is dedicated to charity, there is no infringement of the perpetuity rules merely because it passes from one charitable body to another. A side result of this rule is that property may, in effect, be dedicated perpetually to a non-charitable purpose by attaching to the gift to a charitable body some requirement upon the failure of which the property will pass to a second charity. However, the rule against perpetuities applies as usual to prevent a too remote vesting of a gift to a charity in the first instance, and also to a gift over from a charity to a non-charity.

8.2.3 Policies adopted by the courts

Courts generally are unwilling to frustrate the wishes of a settlor and prefer to hold gifts valid if they can. This leads to a tendency to expand the legal definition of charity. On the other hand, jealousy of the tax concessions tends towards the opposite result. In other words, there is a tension between two conflicting tendencies, which to some extent explains the haphazard development of the law.

The jealousy over the tax position may also explain why the public benefit requirement for charitable status figures so largely. Lord Cross of Chelsea in *Dingle* v *Turner* [1972] AC 601 would have preferred different tests for validity on the one hand and tax concessions on the other. The law adopts the same test, however.

It is not only today that tensions between conflicting policies are felt, and it should be remembered that the legal definition of charity is the result of the development of several centuries. At certain periods, charity was viewed with extreme suspicion, particularly where, as in the case of the medieval church, the power of charitable donation could be seen in rivalry to the claims of the then nascent secular State, or where, as in the 17th and 18th centuries, charity was blamed for taking away the rightful expectations of heirs. It should not be forgotten that the mortmain legislation made testamentary gifts of land to charity void during this period (from 1736 to 1891), and this may paradoxically have resulted in a *wider* definition of charity being adopted, in order not to frustrate the claims of disappointed relatives (if the gift was held void, there was a resulting trust of the property for the estate).

Even at the height of philanthropic activity in the 19th century, middle-class social values of the time were strongly in evidence in an attempt to limit the distribution of charity to the 'deserving', and from the latter part of that century onwards, the fiscal authorities came to exercise a vigilance on behalf of the taxpayer.

It should come as no surprise, therefore, that the legal definition of charity has fluctuated over the centuries, depending on the prevailing social philosophies of the time, and that this, coupled with the conflicting policies of the present law, has resulted in a less than logical legal position obtaining today.

8.3   POLITICAL DIMENSION TO CHARITIES

Though this book is not intended to be a political treatise, and the author does not admit to holding any political views, nevertheless in this field the political dimension cannot be altogether avoided. The role adopted by charities 100 or so years ago has to some extent been superseded by State provision for the least fortunate in our society.

Some might even go so far as to argue that charities have no value alongside a State-funded system, but this is probably a minority viewpoint. Most people would probably hold that the freedom of individuals to decide whether to distribute any of their property to philanthropic purposes, and if so which purposes, is an important freedom, which is in no way in opposition to the Welfare State provision (in which, of course, individuals have very little direct say). At the very least, however, it is more difficult nowadays to justify tax concessions to charities, when at the same time many of the least fortunate are provided for by the Welfare State. Also, if the state has decided not to fund a particular purpose through the welfare scheme, it is odd that it should be required to fund it through the back door, by virtue of the tax concessions given to charitable enterprise.

Probably such an argument has indeed to some extent been taken on board by the courts and the legislature, the former by laying down more stringent conditions for charitable status, and excluding 'undesirable' forms of altruistic activity, the latter by requiring registration and to some extent supervision by a public body, namely, the Charity Commissioners (see section 8.4).

A more extreme argument is that the concept of charity itself takes for granted a society marked by disparities in wealth and influence, implies a decision as to which forms of positive discrimination are desirable and is antithetical to egalitarian ideologies which propound equal shares for all. Moreover, the possession of sufficient resources to allow for giving in favour of the less advantaged creates opportunities for controlling the behaviour of would-be recipients. Simply because charity is voluntary giving, the terms upon which it is given or withheld may be fixed by the intending donor. Even an apparently neutral criterion for giving, such as that of 'need', disguises a value judgment as to how much any member of society is entitled to expect, and how his wants should be met.

Such an argument is described (not actively advanced) by Chesterman in his book, *Charities, Trusts and Social Welfare* (1978).

This argument to some extent depends upon the acceptance of an egalitarian ideology, which probably most people do not hold. It is a view which is included partly for completeness, but also because whatever one's ideology there is no doubt that the terms of a gift are indeed controlled by the donor, and some might argue that at any rate where very large sums are concerned, the power that goes with such control is better administered by publicly controlled bodies than private individuals.

8.4   REGISTRATION OF CHARITIES

Though the definition of charitable status is at the end of the day a matter for the courts, the process of obtaining recognition as a charity today is primarily administrative and largely outside the direct control of the courts. The Charities Act 1960 provided for the comprehensive registration of charities, and an organisation seeking charitable status must normally apply for registration to the Charity Commissioners, who have power under the Act to grant or withhold registration according to their decision as to whether the proposed purposes are, in law, charitable.

The duty to maintain the register is placed on the Commissioners themselves by virtue of s. 4(1) of the Act but a duty to apply for registration is also placed on the charity trustees by virtue of s. 4(6). Registration is conclusive evidence of charitable status.

Therefore, though the importance of judicial decisions has not been diminished since 1960, some knowledge is also required of the work of the Commissioners, who exercise a quasi-judicial function in this area. In reaching their decisions, they may consult with other bodies, such as the Inland Revenue, which may also be called upon to judge the validity of claims to be treated as a charity. The overall effect of the procedure has been to reduce the number of reported court decisions on the boundaries of charity to a handful of test cases which raise significant issues of law.

Refusal by the Commissioners to register an organisation gives rise to a right of appeal, which is in the first instance an informal appeal to the Board of Charity Commissioners. Such appeals are rare, usually in single figures each year. Further appeal lies through the courts, initially the High Court, and thence to the Court of Appeal and House of Lords, but generally only the Inland Revenue is prepared to litigate to this level. The smooth functioning of the system is aided by the openness of the Commission's practices, which are made public through annual reports, and by the advice and assistance which is offered to applicants seeking to frame their trusts so as to meet the necessary criteria.

Viewed from the perspective of the saving thus effected in money and time, the registration process must be regarded as an improvement upon *ad hoc* litigation as a method of establishing charitable credentials. From the standpoint of the well-meaning donor or charity activist, however, the process of registration may appear as a system of gatekeeping, limiting the range of altruistic enterprises to settled and uncontentious fields already blessed by judicial decisions and the precedents of the Commission.

Further, although achieving charitable status carries numerous advantages, it also has the effect of bringing the organisation under the supervision of the Commissioners, who are given wide-reaching powers by the Act. Much of the routine work of the Commissioners consists of making schemes and orders to assist the efficiency of charity trustees, and in practice little use has been made of the powers to demand accounts, institute inquiries and, if necessary, to remove trustees. It is not, however, unknown for the Commissioners to warn organisations who engage in activities falling outside the legal definition of charitable purposes that they risk deregistration by so doing. This may be a serious curb, as we shall see in section 8.5.7.1, upon the actions of those charities which involve them in campaigns falling foul of the requirement that charities must not be political. Certain organisations therefore prefer to forgo the privileges of charitable status in favour of greater freedom of action, or seek registration only of branches which clearly limit themselves to charitable works such as education or the alleviation of poverty and distress.

8.5 LEGAL DEFINITION OF CHARITY

8.5.1 Introductory

8.5.1.1 Sources of law
There is no formal statutory definition of charity, despite occasional proposals. Nor does it appear likely that a statutory definition will appear in the near future. The courts in the past, however, used the preamble to the Statute of Charitable Uses 1601, sometimes referred to as the Statute of Elizabeth (which was part of a scheme intended to curb abuses), as a guideline to simplify their task of determining which purposes were charitable. The preamble listed those purposes which were regarded as charitable at the time. Purposes which fell within the 'spirit and intendment' of the preamble were accepted by the courts as being charitable. Those which did not were not, however much they may have been regarded as beneficial to the public.

By operation of the doctrine of precedent, what had originally been simply a convenient practice by the courts crystallised into rigid legal doctrine, and thus the preamble came, in effect, to have direct legal force. This is most unusual, because preambles to statutes usually have no legal force. Of course, the authority for the present law cannot be the preamble itself, but the cases which subsequently adopted it.

The purposes laid down in the preamble are many and diverse, but fortunately in the House of Lords in *Commissioners for Special Purposes of the Income Tax v Pemsel* [1891] AC 531, Lord Macnaghten categorised them under four main heads: relief of poverty, advancement of religion, advancement of education, and other purposes which are beneficial to the community. Any given charitable purpose may, of course, fall within more than one of these heads.

Generally, therefore, there is no need to go back before 1891 for a judicial definition of charity. As we shall see, however, for the fourth head the test still depends on the spirit and intendment of the preamble (*Scottish Burial Reform & Cremation Society v Glasgow Corporation* [1968] AC 138).

The Statute of Charitable Uses was repealed by subsequent legislation, so that for a time only the preamble remained (another very odd situation — a preamble without the rest of the statute). The preamble itself was repealed by the Charities Act 1960 and was not replaced. This repeal had no legal effect, however, because the cases which used the preamble as a guideline can still be taken to be authoritative. Indeed, Lord Wilberforce in the *Scottish Burial Reform* case, mentioned above, used the spirit and intendment of the preamble as a test of charitable status as late as 1968.

The main source of the modern law can therefore be taken to be Lord Macnaghten's classification in *Pemsel*. In addition to judge-made law, a body of precedent has now been built up by the Charity Commissioners in exercising their jurisdiction under s. 4 of the 1960 Act (see section 8.4). This body of precedent is not technically authority but may be assumed to govern the process of registration in practice, unless and until it is successfully challenged in a court.

Recreational charities are a special case, by virtue of the Recreational Charities Act 1958, which as we shall see provides a limited extension to the general law.

8.5.1.2 Requirement of public benefit

We have seen that charitable trusts are of a public nature, in that they are publicly enforced and controlled, and have certain tax concessions. There is also a requirement that to be charitable a purpose must, in addition to falling within the *Pemsel* heads outlined above, involve a public benefit. There are therefore two requirements for a purpose to be charitable. It must confer a benefit upon those who are directly the objects of the charity and it must also confer an additional benefit upon the public at large.

For example, if a charitable purpose such as education is to be advanced, it must not only confer a benefit on those in direct receipt of the education but must also be advanced in some way that benefits the public, or at least a substantial section thereof, rather than providing benefits for some artificially limited class of people. However, as we shall see, this requirement is not applied with the same rigour to each of the four heads of charity, and in the case of the relief of poverty its role is minimal. For this reason, the public benefit requirement will be dealt with separately under each head.

8.5.1.3 Overseas benefits

There is no rule of law which prevents the benefits of a charity being directed overseas, as opposed to being confined within the UK, or primarily directed within the UK. For example, in *Re Niyazi's WT* [1978] 1 WLR 910, a trust to construct a hostel for working men in Cyprus was held charitable as being for the relief of poverty. Missionary societies operating abroad always seem to have been regarded as religious charities and they often involve advancement of education also. There are, however, two qualifications concerning overseas benefits.

First, though the Charity Commissioners (Annual Report for 1963, paras 69–76) take the view that trusts to relieve poverty or to advance religion will be charitable wherever found, a trust which falls within the fourth head must involve a benefit, even if indirect, to persons within the UK.

Secondly, we shall see in section 8.5.7.1 that charity must not be tainted with political activity, and the large-scale charities which aim at assisting developing nations must avoid this pitfall. It seems that whereas it can be charitable to provide direct relief of observable poverty among a population, it is not charitable to seek to raise the total economy of an overseas country or to alter its laws in order to alleviate poverty.

8.5.1.4   Purposes must be exclusively charitable

A further point to be noted is that a trust must not merely be capable of application to charitable purposes, it must be exclusively so. If it is possible to benefit an object which is not charitable then the trust will not be exclusively charitable and will fail unless the courts feel able to sever the offending objects from the main corpus of the otherwise charitable purpose, or to declare that the non-charitable purposes are merely subsidiary.

So minor errors in drafting can have catastrophic consequences. For example, if a purpose is described as 'charitable *and* benevolent', 'benevolent' merely qualifies 'charitable' so only charitable purposes are included. But in *Chichester Diocesan Fund & Board of Finance* v *Simpson* [1944] AC 337, the words 'charitable *or* benevolent' would have permitted the trustees to devote all the funds to benevolent ends which were not also charitable. The trust therefore failed, leading to further litigation because funds had already been distributed by the trustees (*Ministry of Health* v *Simpson* [1951] AC 251). A gift to 'benevolent, charitable and religious' purposes was treated in *Williams* v *Kershaw* (1835) 5 Cl & F 111 n as allowing the trustees to select purposes which were benevolent but not necessarily charitable and religious. In other words, the comma was treated as allowing the trustees to select alternatives (i.e., as '*or*').

Though each case calls for independent construction, as a general guide it may be said that a comma, or the word 'or', is likely to lead to the listed purposes being interpreted disjunctively (i.e., as alternatives) while the word 'and' is usually read conjunctively. 'Charitable and . . .' succeeds; 'charitable or . . .' fails.

8.5.1.5   Profit-seeking

Generally speaking, it is incompatible with charitable status actively to seek profit as a primary objective, though incidental acquisition of profit should not be enough to disqualify.

8.5.2   Relief of poverty

8.5.2.1   What is poverty?

The concept of poverty is not capable of easy definition and the courts have not attempted to define it in precise terms (e.g., a particular level of income). It is not as extreme a concept as destitution (i.e., people can be poor who are not destitute) and, as we shall see, it varies depending upon one's status in life. People who are sufficiently well off to be able to live without State aid can be regarded as being poor for these purposes. Paradoxically, it is nowadays actually very difficult to relieve poverty among the poorest sections of society because a claimant of State benefit can suffer a reduction in that benefit if he receives more than a small donation from charity.

8.5.2.1.1   Relative nature of poverty   In *Re Coulthurst* [1951] Ch 661, Evershed MR said of poverty (at pp. 665–6):

> It is quite clearly established that poverty does not mean destitution; it is a word of wide and somewhat indefinite import; it may not unfairly be paraphrased for present purposes as meaning persons who have to 'go short' in the ordinary acception of that term, due regard being had to their status in life, and so forth.

Poverty, therefore, is a relative matter, depending on one's status in life, and the courts have been willing to allow trusts to assist such categories as 'distressed gentlefolk'. In *Re De Cartaret* [1933] Ch 103, a trust for annual allowances of £40 each to widows and spinsters 'whose income otherwise shall not be less than eighty or more than one hundred and twenty pounds per annum' was held charitable, even though there was a minimum income qualification and £80 a year in those days was a fairly substantial income.

8.5.2.1.2   Exclusively for the poor   Subject to the width of the definition of poverty, it is essential that poverty should be imposed as a qualification for benefit and that only the poor can benefit. Whereas a trust under any of the other four heads can be charitable even where affluent people can enjoy its benefits, a trust which may benefit rich persons as well as poor will fail under this head.

The rich must usually be expressly excluded, even where the nature of the benefit is unlikely to make it attractive except to the destitute. Thus in *Re Gwyon* [1930] 1 Ch 255, a clergyman had provided in his will for the distribution of trousers to the boys in the Farnham area. Though the trousers were described in such a way as to be unlikely to appeal to any but the very needy, because the rich were not expressly excluded, the provision was not charitable, and therefore failed (see section 8.2.2 on validity). Another case is *Re Drummond* [1914] 2 Ch 90, where a bequest of shares on trust to provide holidays for employees failed, even though the actual wages received by those employees were very low. This is also a reason why disaster fund appeals are often not charitable, but the organisers of recent appeals have sometimes preferred to forgo charitable status, and the consequent tax exemptions, rather than limit compensation expressly to the poor.

Sometimes the implication that the trust is to be limited to the poor can be drawn, however, even though the word 'poor' itself is not used. An old example is *Powell* v *Attorney-General* (1817) 3 Mer 48, where it was assumed that the widows and children of Liverpool seamen would necessarily be poor. More recently, in *Re Niyazi's WT* [1978] 1 WLR 910 considered in section 8.5.1.3, Megarry V-C accepted that persons requiring working men's hostel accommodation would be poor.

It would be inadvisable for settlors to rely too heavily on these decisions, however, and an express limitation is safer. For example, in *Re Sanders's WT* [1954] Ch 265, Harman J thought that the provision of dwellings for 'the working classes' was not sufficient to limit the benefit to poor persons. Nor will a gift for 'deserving' persons or 'those in need of financial assistance' suffice, but 'indigent' and 'needy' can be regarded as synonyms for poor. Poverty can also often be implied in the case of gifts to elderly or disabled recipients.

8.5.2.1.3 Methods of relieving poverty The measures must actually relieve poverty, so merely to provide amusement for the poor will not suffice under this head (though it might under the next head considered, if educational).

It used to be thought that relief of poverty had to be on-going, rather than by way of an immediate distribution of property. It was thought that an immediate distribution was indistinguishable from an ordinary private bequest. It is now clear from the Court of Appeal decision in *Re Scarisbrick* [1951] Ch 622 that this is no longer the case and that it is possible to relieve poverty by way of one-off payment or distribution. The question of whether or not a trust is perpetual in nature could, in the view of Jenkins LJ in that case, be relevant to the question of public benefit, considered in section 8.5.2.2, because an immediate gift would be less likely to be in favour of a class of persons, as opposed to individuals. But on the assumption that the public benefit test is satisfied, it is not fatal that the disposition is once and for all, rather than perpetual.

Relief need not even necessarily be in the form of direct hand-outs of money, goods or services, but could, for example, allow access to necessary amenities at reduced cost. So it was accepted in *Joseph Rowntree Memorial Trust Housing Association Ltd* v *Attorney-General* [1983] Ch 159 that the sale of homes to elderly persons at 70% of cost was charitable.

8.5.2.1.4 Modernising old charities Indeed, the growth in State welfare provision has reduced the attractiveness of hand-outs, for reasons explained at the beginning of section 8.5.2.1. Yet many old trusts to relieve poverty still bind trustees to distribute money or goods. One example required the trustees to spend the income in buying bread and linen for the poor of East Barning — in 1983, the fund available was £5.12! Obviously, a trust of this type serves little useful purpose today.

One of the major functions of the Charity Commissioners in recent years has been the making of schemes to modernise old and outmoded poverty charities. In addition, the Charities Act 1985 now allows trustees of charities more than 50 years old, by a simplified procedure, to change the objects to more suitable ones, so long as they are within the spirit of the original donor's intentions. Where the annual income of a charity is less than £200, the trustees may transfer its property to another charity having similar aims, or if its income is less than £5 a year, wind it up, by spending the capital as if it were income.

As long ago as 1967 the Annual Report of the Charity Commissioners (paras 17–20 and app. B) recognised the problem involved in cash hand-outs by commenting upon the undesirability of using charity funds to relieve the burdens of the DHSS and local authorities, and instead suggested other schemes (e.g., outings or home decoration). The comments were made in the context of cy pres schemes (see section 8.6) but are also useful guidance to trustees making applications under the 1985 Act.

8.5.2.2   Element of public benefit
It is unquestioned law that to relieve poverty is to confer a benefit upon the public at large, if only by mitigating the burden of support for the poor which would otherwise fall upon the community. In order for a trust to be charitable under this head it is, however, necessary that the trust should be intended to benefit a class of persons and not simply to make a gift to an individual, or group of individuals, who happen to be poor. In *Re Scarisbrick* [1951] Ch 622 Jenkins LJ stated the rule thus (at p. 655):

> I think the true question in each case has really been whether the gift was for the relief of poverty amongst a class of persons, or . . . a particular description of poor, or was merely a gift to individuals, albeit with relief of poverty amongst those individuals as the motive of the gift, or with a selective preference for the poor or poorest amongst those individuals.

This statement received the approval of Lord Cross of Chelsea in the leading case of *Dingle* v *Turner* [1972] AC 601, considered below. In *Re Scarisbrick* itself the class of potential recipients was sufficiently wide as to be incapable of exhaustive ascertainment ('such relations of my said son and daughters as shall be in needy circumstances . . .') so the trust was charitable.

Assuming that Jenkins LJ's test is satisfied, however, the public benefit requirements are less stringent under this head than under the others, and the class to be benefited can be quite small. We shall see that educational trusts, and probably those under the other heads also, can only be charitable if the beneficiaries are not linked by some personal nexus, such as the membership of a single family or company. The *Oppenheim* case [1951] AC 297, the leading House of Lords authority for this proposition, exempted 'poor relations' cases as anomalous and left open the position regarding them.

The poor relations anomaly stems from the practice of Chancery in the 19th century when faced with trusts expressed to be for poor relations; rather than allow these to fail for uncertainty or perpetuity under what was then the law, the courts rescued such trusts by holding them charitable. Since then the poor relations cases have been consistently followed (including, for example, in *Re Scarisbrick*), which is probably why the House of Lords left them alone in *Oppenheim*. Since then the House of Lords has considered them directly in *Dingle* v *Turner* [1972] AC 601 and expressly upheld them. In that case a trust for 'poor employees of E. Dingle & Co.' was held charitable, though it would have failed under the personal nexus test.

It is clear, therefore, that the personal nexus test does not apply to this head of charity.

8.5.3   Advancement of education

8.5.3.1   What constitutes education?

8.5.3.1.1   Wide range of activities covered   The preamble to the Act of 1601 speaks only of 'schools of learning, free schools, scholars in universities' and the 'education and preferment of orphans', but in modern times this category has grown to cover a very wide range of educational and cultural activities extending far beyond the administration of formal instruction.

Schools and universities are clearly charitable, and so now are nursery schools, adult education centres, and societies dedicated to promoting training and standards within a trade or profession. Education is not limited to teaching, however, and learned societies which bring together experts in a field to share and exchange knowledge may be charitable. Museums, zoos and public libraries may be educational to the public at large, quite apart from their research activities. Even cultural activities such as drama, music, literature and fine arts can come within this head, on the grounds that they have a role in the cultivation of knowledge and taste.

As with other heads of charity, it is essential that the organisation should not be profit-seeking and the purposes must be exclusively charitable. Thus a trust for 'artistic' purposes may be too wide (see *Associated Artists Ltd* v *IRC* [1956] 1 WLR 752).

It is also necessary that education be advanced, so that although research can be charitable, probably it will not be if, for example, it is carried on in secret. Scholarship for its own sake is also not charitable, and this is one of the reasons why researching the advantages of a new 40-letter alphabet was held non-charitable by Harman J in *Re Shaw* [1957] 1 WLR 729.

Learned societies are charitable, and professional and vocational bodies which advance education, such as the Royal College of Surgeons, are also charitable, even though one of the ancillary purposes is the protection and assistance of its members. Other examples include the Royal College of Nursing, the Institute of

Civil Engineers and the Incorporated Council of Law Reporting. Bodies whose chief purpose is to further the interests of the members and to promote the status of the profession will not, however, be charitable, for example, the General Nursing Council (see *General Nursing Council for England & Wales* v *St Marylebone Borough Council* [1959] AC 540).

8.5.3.1.2 Physical education   As we shall see in sections 8.5.5 and 8.5.6, physical activity which is of a purely recreational nature will not be charitable unless it falls within the provisions of the Recreational Charities Act 1958. Games and other leisure time pursuits can be charitable under this head, however, if educational. Thus in *Re Marriette* [1915] 2 Ch 284, a gift to provide squash courts at a public school was held charitable, Eve J remarking that the playing of games at boarding schools was as important as learning from books and that the proper education of young people can include a physical element. On the same principle, the provision of toys for small children can be charitable (the National Association of Toy Libraries is a registered charity) as are youth movements, such as the Boy Scout Movement, or trusts to provide school outings. In *Re Dupree's Deed Trusts* [1945] Ch 16, a chess contest for young men in the Portsmouth area was held to be charitable, though subject to the caveat that less intellectually demanding pursuits might not be. These cases have been approved and followed by the House of Lords in *IRC* v *McMullen* [1981] AC 1, a case involving the playing of football at schools and universities. The House also made it clear that the legal conception of charity was not static but changed with ideas about social values.

8.5.3.1.3 Value judgments   Inevitably, with a wide definition of educational purposes, the courts and Commissioners may be involved in subjective value judgments as to whether a particular purpose falls within or without the definition. The views of the donor will, of course, not be conclusive and expert evidence will be admitted in order to assist in evaluating the merit of artistic and cultural work.

In *Re Pinion* [1965] Ch 85, for example, the testator left his 'studio' for the purposes of a museum to display his collection of what were claimed to be 'fine arts'. However, expert witnesses thought that the paintings were 'atrociously bad', and one 'expresse[d] his surprise that so voracious a collector should not by hazard have picked up even one meritorious object'. The question arose as to the validity of the trust and this depended on whether it was charitable. Harman LJ described the collection as 'a mass of junk' and, reversing Wilberforce J, the Court of Appeal held the trust void. In *Re Hummeltenberg* [1923] 1 Ch 237 the court held void a trust to train spiritualistic mediums (though perhaps disciplined research into the paranormal, undertaken on scientific principles, could be charitable). On the other hand, in *Re Delius* [1957] Ch 299 a trust to promote appreciation of the works of the composer (the testatrix's late husband) was held charitable, but Roxburgh J made it clear that the undoubted merit of Delius's music was crucial and the same view would not be taken of a 'manifestly inadequate' composer.

While value judgments are inevitable in this area (or a school for pickpockets would be charitable), it is to be hoped that the courts do not take too stringent a view. *Pinion* is a fairly extreme case and should not, I would suggest, be extended too generally. In the first place, it is difficult to evaluate merit, particularly of artistic matters, objectively. Secondly, the requirements of public benefit (discussed in section 8.5.3.2), that education be advanced and that the object must not be political (see section 8.5.3.1.4) should provide largely adequate *research* safeguards against unmeritorious claims. Thirdly, especially in the area of research, it is often difficult to know in advance whether or not the results of research will be useful (after all, if you did know the conclusions, the research would be pointless).

Perhaps this last point was in the mind of Wilberforce J in *Re Hopkins* [1965] Ch 669, where he upheld as charitable a bequest to the Francis Bacon Society for the purposes of finding the Bacon-Shakespeare manuscripts. Though he observed that if found the discovery would be 'of the highest value to history and to literature', the search could equally have been futile, as not only were the manuscripts not known to exist but Wilberforce J thought their discovery unlikely. Value judgments are very difficult to operate when the outcome of the quest is uncertain, as will usually be the case where genuine research is concerned.

8.5.3.1.4   Political purposes   A trust for the advancement of policital purposes will not be charitable. Education, however, can undoubtedly cover political theory and philosophy. The borderline appears to fall at the point where partisan propaganda is seen to be masquerading in the guise of instruction. In *Re Hopkinson* [1949] 1 All ER 346, a trust for adult education in socialist principles fell foul of the line. The political angle was another reason why the trust in *Re Shaw* [1957] 1 WLR 729 failed. The Charity Commissioners commented on the problem in their Annual Report for 1967, para. 8, but seem to take a fairly generous view, regarding, for example, the promotion of racial harmony as charitable. For greater detail on the problem of political purposes generally, see section 8.5.7.1.

8.5.3.2   Element of public benefit
We saw in section 8.5.2.2 how, in the case of relief of poverty, even benefiting a small number of people may be regarded as conferring a public benefit. Yet whereas education is clearly a benefit to those in immediate receipt of it, it is not self-evident that educating a few people constitutes a benefit to the general public. Indeed, given that many of the cases under this head are in reality disputes over tax relief, it would be quite wrong if the education of a privileged few were to be regarded as charitable. Under this head it is therefore necessary that there is

some additional benefit to the general public or some appreciable sector thereof.

That is not to say that a particular form of education has to be capable of being enjoyed by everyone so long as access to it is reasonably open. Thus public schools may be charitable as long as they are not operated as profit-making ventures, although their fees may place them beyond the means of the majority. Even scholarships or endowed chairs, which can be enjoyed only by one person at a time, present no difficulty. The problems arise where it is sought to limit the range of the potential beneficiaries within a class which is insufficiently wide to constitute a section of the public.

It is clear that it may be charitable to provide, e.g., scholarships open to:

(a)   Persons following a common profession or calling, or their children and dependants.

(b)   People of common nationality, religion or sex.

(c)   The inhabitants of a given area, provided this is reasonably large, such as a town or county.

Special provisions for people suffering disability are also permissible, since they are a section of the public in a meaningful sense.

Nevertheless, the class must be able genuinely to be described as a section of the community, rather than simply a body of private individuals. Thus, for example, in *Davies* v *Perpetual Trustee Co. Ltd* [1959] AC 459, the Privy Council held non-charitable a trust which was confined to Presbyterian youths who were descended from settlors in New South Wales who had originated from the North of Ireland. Although quite large in number, this category of potential beneficiaries was held not to be a section of the public.

Under this head, and probably under all the heads except relief of poverty, it will also be fatal for the class of potential beneficiaries to be defined in terms of relation to particular individuals or companies. This approach originated in *Re Compton* [1945] Ch 123, where charitable status was denied to a trust to educate the children of three named families. It is understandable that the courts are reluctant to allow an essentially private arrangement to enjoy charitable privileges, especially tax advantages. The most authoritative statements, however, are those of Lord Simonds in *Oppenheim* v *Tobacco Securities Trust Co. Ltd* [1951] AC 297, where *Re Compton* was approved in the House of Lords:

Then the question is whether that class of persons can be regarded as such as a 'section of the community' as to satisfy the test of public benefit. The words 'section of the community' have no special sanctity, but they conveniently indicate first, that the possible (I emphasise the word 'possible') beneficiaries must not be numerically negligible, and secondly, that the quality which distinguishes them from other members of the community, so that they form by themselves a section of it, must be a quality which does not depend on their relationship to a particular individual.. . . . A group of persons may be numerous but, if the nexus between them is their personal relationship to a single propositus or to several propositi, they are neither the community nor a section of the community for charitable purposes.

In the trust with which the House of Lords was concerned, the number of potential beneficiaries was certainly not negligible. The income of the trust fund was directed to be applied 'in providing for . . . the education of children of employees or former employees of British-American Tobacco Co. Ltd . . . or any of its subsidiary or allied companies in such manner . . . as the acting trustees shall in their absolute discretion . . . think fit'. The number of present employees alone exceeded 110,000 so it was only the personal nexus rule which was fatal.

As Lord MacDermott pointed out in his dissenting speech, however, the rule is by no means easy to apply and produces odd results when the propositus is an employer. For example, a trust to educate the sons of railwaymen, not expressed as limited to a single company, would have been valid before the nationalisation of the railways, and void when British Rail became the sole employer. Nor is the personal link between employees as obvious as that between members of a family, among whom considerations of mutual interest might be considered to negate the altruistic status of the trust.

Nevertheless, the personal nexus rule is law, certainly for trusts under this head. There may, however, be loopholes, as, for example, in *Re Koettgen's WT* [1954] Ch 252, where an educational trust succeeded despite a direction that the trustees should give preference to the families of employees, up to a maximum of 75% of income. On the other hand, doubts have been expressed, e.g., in *IRC v Educational Grants Association Ltd* [1967] Ch 123, affirmed [1967] Ch 993, where in fact some 80% of the income of a fund was paid out for the education of persons connected with the Metal Box Co. Ltd. In a dispute with the Inland Revenue, it was held that the money had not been paid exclusively for charitable purposes.

Perhaps the real, if unstated, justification for the result in *Oppenheim* was the extent of the trustees' discretion in that case. The benefit to 110,000 or more people may in fact have been entirely theoretical — for example, if the trustees had used the funds to pay 15% of fees to those employees who sent their sons to boarding school, only the relatively small number who could afford the other 85% would actually have benefited. The problem is that the test in *Oppenheim* may not achieve the desired result in all cases; the House of Lords should have concentrated, I would suggest, on the extent of the trustees' discretion to limit the number of people who could in practice have benefited rather than on the nexus with the company.

8.5.4   Advancement of religion

8.5.4.1   What religion?
The law is remarkably tolerant as to which religions may be charitable and seems
reluctant to enter into value judgments in this area. As Cross J remarked in
Neville Estates v *Madden* [1962] Ch 832, 853, a case already considered in another
context in section 3.3, in which a trust for the members of the Catford Synagogue
was held charitable: 'As between different religions the law stands neutral, but it
assumes that any religion is at least likely to be better than none'. On the other
hand, it is important that religion be advanced. It is not charitable to save one's
own soul.

The preamble to the Statute of Charitable Uses 1601 gave little support for the
tolerant approach the law has taken, the only reference to religion within it
concerning the repair of churches. Nor has English law traditionally been
tolerant of religion outside the established church. It may be that the explanation
lies in the mortmain legislation in force from 1736 until the Mortmain and
Charitable Uses Act 1891, which, as we have seen, made many gifts to charity
void. Religious tolerance in this area, therefore, may have been used simply as a
device to strike down testamentary gifts, the authorities from that period still
having validity today.

In *Thornton* v *Howe* (1862) 31 Beav 14, for example, charitable status was
extended to a devise of land to promote the writings of Joanna Southcote, the
founder of a small but fervent sect in the West of England, who had proclaimed
that she was with child by the Holy Ghost and would give birth to a second
Messiah. The practical effect of the decision was to bring the trust within the
invalidating provisions of the mortmain legislation, but the case is still seen as a
landmark in establishing that any theistic belief, however obscure or remote, will
fall within the meaning of religion for the purposes of charity law. A recent
example to the same effect is *Re Watson* [1973] 1 WLR 1472, where Plowman J
held charitable a trust to publish the religious writings of a retired builder who
was virtually the sole remaining adherent of a small, fundamentalist group of
believers. Expert testimony regarded the theological merits of the works as very
small but confirmed the genuineness of the writer's beliefs.

It is not even necessary that the religious beliefs in question should be
Christian. Certainly the Jewish, Sikh, Hindu and Muslim faiths have been
accepted. The position of Buddhism was left open in *Re South Place Ethical
Society* [1980] 1 WLR 1565. In that case Dillon J remarked that religion is
concerned with man's relations with God, so it seems therefore that one
qualification is the need for a belief in some kind of God (or gods). In an old case
in the Privy Council, *Yeap Cheah Neo* v *Ong Cheng Neo* (1875) LR 6 PC 381, a
provision for the performance of ancestor worship was held non-charitable, and
this is a possible reason for that decision. High ethical principles or moral
philosophy, being concerned with man's relations with man, cannot amount to a

religion, though they may, or course, be educational and so charitable under that head. Plowman J also thought in *Re Watson*, considered above, that doctrines which were adverse to the foundations of all religion, and subversive of all morality, would not be charitable under this head.

It seems that the gift must be exclusively for religious purposes, so that a gift for 'missionary work' or 'parish work' will be too wide, since such work may involve elements not wholly religious. On the other hand, in *Re Simson* [1946] Ch 299, a gift to a named clergyman 'for his work in the parish' was held to be impliedly confined to his religious duties.

8.5.4.2 Advancement of religion

As with education, the means by which religion may be advanced may be many and various. Apart from the provision and maintenance of churches, and provision of or for the benefit of clergymen, such matters as church choirs, Sunday school prizes, and even exorcism, have all been held to advance religion.

Religion must be advanced, however. This seems to require some positive action. For example, in *United Grand Lodge of Ancient Free & Accepted Masons of England* v *Holborn Borough Council* [1957] 1 WLR 1080, Donovan J, in denying charitable status to freemasons (who attempted to claim rates advantages), commented that:

> There is no religious instruction, no programme for the persuasion of unbelievers, no religious supervision to see that its members remain active and constant in the various religions they may profess, no holding of religious services, no pastoral or missionary work of any kind.

Religion may have been a necessary qualification for membership of the lodge, as it might be for a church squash club, for example, but the lodge did not advance religion, any more than a church squash club would.

There must also be an element of public contact. Private salvation, however commendable, is not charitable. This is another explanation of *Yeap Cheah Neo* v *Ong Cheng Neo* (1875) LR 6 PC 381 (see section 8.5.4.1) because a provision for the performance of ancestor worship could benefit only the family group. The leading case is *Gilmour* v *Coats* [1949] AC 426, where the House of Lords had to consider a gift of £500 towards a Carmelite priory. The priory housed about 20 cloistered nuns who devoted themselves to intercessory prayer and had no contact at all with the outer world. This was held non-charitable on the grounds that there was no contact with the outside world. Arguments based on Catholic doctrine, to the effect that everyone benefited from the intercessory prayers, were rejected as being not susceptible to legal proof. Nor could any benefit be found merely in the example of the piety of the women, as it was too vague and intangible. The House of Lords also rejected the argument that, entry being open to all women, the priory should be treated on analogy with an educational institution offering scholarship entry, holding that an educational establishment which required its members to withdraw from the world and leave no record of their studies would not be charitable either.

The House also doubted *Re Caus* [1934] Ch 162, where Catholic masses for the dead were held charitable; however, these are open to the public at large even where a private function, such as a funerary rite, is incorporated into the celebration, so in principle the case is distinguishable from *Gilmour* v *Coats*.

There is authority that the requirement of public contact is not especially onerous. In *Neville Estates* v *Madden* [1962] Ch 832, Cross J, as we have seen, held charitable a trust for the members of Catford Synagogue. He thought that the rejection of example as a benefit in *Gilmour* v *Coats* would not apply to a restricted religious group if its members lived in the world and mixed with their fellow citizens, because they could thereby extend their example of religious living to the public at large. On this view religion can be advanced by example, so long as one mixes in the world in a *physical* sense. *Neville Estates* v *Madden* is authority that no more was required.

On the other hand, Harman J in *Re Warre* [1953] 1 WLR 725 had refused to allow charitable status to an Anglican house of retreat open to all members of the public wishing to retire from the world for a short period of meditation and spiritual renewal. On Cross J's reasoning one might have expected this to be charitable, because the meditators would return to the world after their spiritual renewal. It is not possible to state a clear conclusion, therefore, on the question of short-term private meditation since there are conflicting High Court views. Nevertheless, Cross J's view seems more in accord with recent High Court decisions and the recent practice of the Charity Commissioners.

8.5.4.3 *Public benefit*

There are dicta in *Oppenheim* v *Tobacco Securities Trust Co. Ltd* [1951] AC 297, considered in section 8.5.3.2, that the public benefit tests advanced in that case apply to all heads of charity except the relief of poverty. If these dicta are correct, the personal nexus rule must apply to religious charities. Certainly charitable status has been consistently denied to purely private devotions. We have also seen, above, how rites relating to ancestor worship were held non-charitable on the basis that they could benefit only the private family group.

I would suggest, however, that the true explanation of these cases is that there is no advancement of religion, rather than no public benefit, that so long as religion is genuinely advanced, there is no additional test of public benefit. On the personal nexus rule, two further comments are appropriate:

Todd's Rationale (a)   The rationale of the personal nexus rule, which is to deny tax and rates advantages to private educational schemes for elite family groups, does not apply as easily in the field of religion.

(b)   If a religious family group mixes actively in the community, arguably the benefit is to the community as a whole, rather than just to the family members. Therefore the *Oppenheim* test is satisfied unless the group shuts itself off from the rest of the community, as occurred in *Gilmour v Coats* [1949] AC 426.

8.5.5   Other purposes beneficial to the community

This provides a residual category of charitable purposes which it is almost impossible to define precisely. Not every purpose which might, by common consensus, be considered beneficial to the community can come within this head. What the law admits as charitable under this head is still governed, as we have seen (see section 8.5.1.1), by the general statement of charitable purposes which was set out in the preamble to the Statute of Charitable Uses 1601, for although this has itself been repealed, the cases which have relied upon its guidance over centuries are still themselves authority. If some wholly novel purpose appears, the question is not whether it is beneficial in some general sense, but whether it falls within the 'spirit and intendment' of the preamble, or can be held to do so by analogy with the principles developed through the cases.

It should therefore be obvious that it is not always possible to state whether a particular purpose is charitable under this head or not. Some cases are expressly mentioned in the preamble, however, and there are also classes of trust which have been specifically considered by the courts. About these, at least, it is possible to state conclusions.

8.5.5.1   Specifically included in the preamble

The preamble makes specific mention of the relief of aged, impotent (meaning disabled or handicapped) and poor people, and it has never been necessary to show that the recipients possess all three characteristics simultaneously. Trusts to assist the elderly are common, as are trusts for the handicapped, and no further requirement of poverty in the recipients is imposed. In other words, this head is wider than the relief of poverty head.

It must be the case, however, that the proposed purpose will offer some relief to the recipients. Since many of the disadvantages which accompany age or general disability can in fact be eased by material provision in the form of money or special equipment, this general requirement usually poses no problems. Probably, however, a gift of money which was wholly confined to such elderly or disabled people as are already wealthy could not be charitable, because it would fail to relieve the disadvantage of their condition. It is also likely that the class of recipients would not amount to a section of the public so as to satisfy the additional public benefit requirements.

Trusts to benefit the sick are prima facie charitable, and before the introduction of the National Health Service in 1946, charitable gifts were the main source of provision for those needing hospital care but unable either to afford it or to insure against illness or injury. Today, gifts to private hospitals will still be charitable since they help to ease the pressure upon the public services, as was noted in *Re Resch's WT* [1969] 1 AC 514. It is no objection that such hospitals tend to be of direct benefit to those who are relatively rich, though, as under other heads, a purely profit-making institution will not be charitable. There is no need to confine the benefits of the trust directly to the patients, and gifts which improve the efficiency of the service by providing homes for nurses or accommodation for visiting relatives are included under this head. Even organisations offering help with family planning, and those which seek to promote health by encouraging temperance, have been accepted for registration, but the Commissioners have found difficulty (see their Annual Report for 1975, para. 70) with fringe methods of healing not generally recognised by the medical profession. Methods which are widely recognised, such as acupuncture, osteopathy and faith healing, are acceptable, but in other cases some evidence of the method's effectiveness will be demanded.

Another category of benefits mentioned in the preamble was the 'setting out of soldiers', which has been extended to include the well-being and morale of the forces, or specific units thereof, charities for ex-servicemen, and the promotion of the efficiency of the police and the maintenance of law and order. Gifts to the Inland Revenue and for 'my country England' have been held charitable (*Re Smith* [1932] 1 Ch 153), but gifts expressed to be for 'public' or 'patriotic' purposes have failed as being too wide and not exclusively charitable.

Gifts for the 'repair of bridges, ports, havens, causeways, sea-banks and highways' were included in the preamble, and now that the State assumes responsibility for such matters, this category has grown to include such miscellaneous amenities as the National Trust, museums, art galleries, parks and community centres. In *Scottish Burial Reform & Cremation Society* v *Glasgow Corporation* [1968] AC 138, a crematorium was held charitable. And while it is not charitable to erect a monument to oneself, the commemoration of significant people or events (e.g., war memorials) will qualify. The Earl Mountbatten of Burma Statue Appeal Trust has been registered as being 'likely to foster patriotism and good citizenship' (Charity Commissioners' Annual Report 1981, paras 68–70).

The 'preferment of orphans' mentioned in the preamble has its modern counterpart in the provision of orphanages and local authority homes, but in *Re Cole* [1958] Ch 888 a majority of the Court of Appeal held non-charitable a trust for the general welfare and benefit of children in such a home out of fear that this might permit the provision of amenities not of an educational nature, such as radios or television sets, and this decision was followed in *Re Sahal* [1958] 1 WLR 1243. In this respect, therefore, purposes are unlikely to succeed under this head unless they will also succeed under the educational head.

Trusts to aid the rehabilitation and reform of prisoners have been accepted as charitable since the 19th century, but it is not easy to envisage circumstance in which the reference in the preamble to the ransom of captives has any application today.

A gift for the benefit of a locality such as a town, county or parish, or for its inhabitants will be charitable, although one might have expected it to fail either because of failure to specify exclusively charitable purposes or on the ground that there is an insufficient public benefit. The explanation may lie in an analogy with gifts to local authorities. They have long acted in the capacity of trustees of various charities and so such gifts may be *impliedly* confined to charitable purposes. In any event, gifts to localities were probably within the spirit of the reforms of 1601 historically, as these reforms were largely directed towards easing the burden of local poor rates. The trust must, it seems, be cast in terms of benefit for an area or its residents for the time being (not, for example, a trust for expatriate Welshmen, unless the purposes were charitable for some other reason).

8.5.5.2 *Animal charities*

Animal charities are among the most popular with the public, but their inclusion within this head of charity owes nothing to the preamble and rests upon a process of reasoning by analogy. As with religious toleration, the motive may well have lain in the mortmain legislation, but precedents of that period are of course still followed today.

In *London University* v *Yarrow* (1857) 1 De G & J 72, a trust to study the diseases of animals useful to mankind was held charitable but this would probably have been a valid educational charity anyway. A more general authority, creating a wider precedent still valid today, was *Tatham* v *Drummond* (1864) 4 De G J & S 484, where a bequest for the relief and protection of animals taken to be slaughtered was held charitable, so that the gift failed under the mortmain legislation. (M.L. made gifts to ch void)

It is not, however, the benefit to the animals themselves which has been fastened onto, to provide principled justification for the inclusion of animal charities under this head (though in this respect the Irish are more logical: in Ireland, the good of animals requires no further justification). Rather, the assumed benefit is to humans, by encouraging them in 'feelings of humanity and morality generally' (see the judgment of Swinfen Eady LJ in *Re Wedgwood* [1915] 1 Ch 113, 122).

To consider for the moment examples of valid animal charities, taking a broad view, Romer J held a gift to a named lady to aid her work in caring for cats and kittens to be charitable in *Re Moss* [1949] 1 All ER 495, and homes for lost dogs, needy horses, donkeys etc. have been accepted, along with well-known organisations such as the RSPCA and the PDSA. On the other hand, the need to benefit humans leads to the conclusion that the protection of creatures harmful to man could not be charitable under this head, nor, according the Court of Appeal in *Re Grove-Grady* [1929] 1 Ch 557, would be the creation of a sanctuary where animals would be protected from all human intrusion. No doubt, however, both these could, in the case of trusts appropriately drafted, be valid as educational charities, for example by the inclusion of a provision that the wildlife be studied. Nor presumably would it matter in that event that the animals might be free to molest and harry one another, since the required benefit is to humans, not to the animals themselves.

Sometimes the courts will unavoidably be faced with value judgments as to the relative merits of competing benefits. On the issue of whether the abolition of vivisection might be a public benefit, for example, the House of Lords held in *National Anti-Vivisection Society* v *IRC* [1948] AC 31 that its suppression was not beneficial, since vivisection is a vital element in medical research, which is itself of undoubted public benefit. We shall see in section 8.5.7.1, however, that there is an alternative reason for this decision.

Private trusts for pet animals are not charitable because there is no public benefit but, as we saw in section 3.2.1, they may nevertheless be valid as private purpose trusts of an anomalous type.

8.5.5.3 Trusts for recreational purposes

Until the 1950s it was assumed that while some recreational purposes, such as boys' clubs, women's institutes and parish halls, were potentially charitable, sporting facilities were not, unless they were either educational or promoted efficiency in the armed forces. A series of cases in the 1950s, however, suggested that no recreational purpose will be charitable at common law. As we shall see in section 8.5.6, however, a fifth (limited) head of recreational charities has now been added by statute.

In *IRC* v *Glasgow Police Athletic Association* [1953] AC 380 the encouragement and promotion of all forms of athletic sport and general pastimes was held non-charitable, although it might have been allowed had the purpose been merely incidental to improving police efficiency. In *Williams's Trustees* v *IRC* [1947] AC 447, a trust to promote social and recreational purposes among Welsh people living in London had also been held non-charitable, partly on the basis that purely social activities could not be charitable within the spirit of the preamble to the Statute of Charitable Uses 1601. Thus, in *IRC* v *Baddeley* [1955] AC 572, a reduction in stamp duty on a conveyance of land was refused because the purposes of the conveyance were not charitable. The conveyance was to a Methodist mission, and the purposes were essentially those of promoting the 'religious, social and physical well-being' of residents of an area by providing facilities for 'religious services and instruction; and for the social and physical training and recreation' of such people. The inclusion of purely social purposes prevented these purposes from being exclusively charitable.

8.5.5.4   Element of public benefit under the fourth head

If the purpose itself is one which qualifies under this head, it may not be fatal that only a limited number of persons will benefit in practice, so long as the benefits are, in theory, generally available. Where, however, the benefit is expressly limited to a restricted class, such a class must be a section of the public. Certainly the personal nexus test applies, and though Lord Reid thought otherwise in his dissenting speech in *IRC v Baddeley* [1955] AC 572, it may even be that the courts adopt a more stringent approach to public benefit under this head than under the other three heads.

For example, in *Williams's Trustees v IRC* [1947] AC 447, doubt was expressed by Lord Simonds as to whether the Welsh people, as defined in the trust instrument, could be a section of the public. In *IRC v Baddeley* it was said that the persons to be benefited must either be the whole community or the inhabitants of a particular area. If some further restriction is imposed, thus creating in effect a class within a class, the test of public benefit will not be satisfied. It is possible that what constitutes a section of the public depends on the purposes of the particular trust, and the courts are more likely to strike down arbitrary restrictions which are irrelevant to those purposes but which simply serve to exclude other sections of the public. This may be the real reason for the decision in *IRC v Baddeley*. The limitation was to Methodists living in West Ham and Leyton, and the trust (which was not exclusively religious, as we have seen, but included social purposes and the provision of playing fields) was held not to be charitable. As Lord Simonds observed (at p. 592): 'Who has ever heard of a bridge to be crossed only by impecunious Methodists?' He went on to say that what is true of a bridge for Methodists is equally true of any other public purpose falling within the fourth head, and of the adherents of any other creed.

8.5.6   Recreational Charities Act 1958

We have seen in section 8.5.5.3 how doubt was cast by a number of decisions about 30 years ago, on the charitable status of a number of social trusts which had always been assumed to be charitable. The Recreational Trusts Act 1958 was enacted to restore the status quo ante in respect of those trusts.

Section 1 states that it shall be, and be deemed always to have been, charitable to provide, or assist in the provision of, facilities for recreation or other leisure-time occupation if the facilities are provided in the interests of social welfare. A proviso adds that nothing in the section shall be taken to derogate from the principle that a trust or institution to be charitable must be for the public benefit. The requirement that the facilities are provided in the interests of social welfare is not to be satisfied unless the facilities are provided with the object of improving the conditions of life for the persons for whom the facilities are primarily intended, and either:

(a)   Those persons have need of such facilities as aforesaid by reason of their youth, age, infirmity or disablement, poverty or social and economic circumstances, or

(b)   The facilities are to be available to the members or female members of the public at large.

Subject to the requirement of social welfare, there is specific reference to the provision of facilities at village halls, community centres and women's institutes, and to the provision and maintenance of grounds and buildings to be used for the purposes of recreation or leisure-time occupation, extending to the provision of facilities for these purposes by the organising of any activity.

There is also express provision (in s. 2) for miners' welfare trusts.

The result of none of the cases mentioned in section 8.5.5.3 is affected, as the recipients of benefits under those trusts do not fall within the Act. But where the Act applies, the spirit of the preamble to the Statute of Charitable Uses 1601 seems no longer to be relevant, and it must therefore be taken that the statute has added a fresh head of charity.

The requirement of social welfare, although by no means unique to this Act, has raised problems. In *IRC* v *McMullen* [1979] 1 WLR 130 the Court of Appeal split on the issue of whether the recipients must by implication be 'deprived', the majority holding that the class to be benefited must be disadvantaged in such a way as to have a special need for the facilities. Bridge LJ, however, dissented, and preferred a wider view that social welfare may be promoted by benefits which extend to the better off as well as the socially deprived. The House of Lords ([1981] AC 1) left the issue open, holding, as we have seen (section 8.5.3.1.2), that the trust was valid as an educational charity. Indeed, all their lordships expressly refused to decide which of the approaches adopted in the Court of Appeal was correct, and no conclusion can therefore be reached.

Presumably, social welfare indicates some element of provision for others, so that a group acting purely to benefit themselves would fail to qualify. In any event, such an enterprise would lack the necessary element of public benefit preserved by the Act.

8.5.7   Purposes which create problems under any head

8.5.7.1   *Political purposes*
A trust cannot be charitable under any head if its purposes are, directly or indirectly, political. A trust to promote the aims of a particular political party is clearly not capable of being charitable, and attempts to disguise such objectives as educational trusts have generally failed.

Wider instances of the propagation of some broad political doctrine independent of any political party are also outside the ambit of charity. In *Re*

Bushnell [1975] 1 WLR 1596, money was left to advance awareness of the benefits of socialised medicine and to show that its realisation was fully possible only in a socialist state. The testator had died in 1941, before the introduction of the National Health Service. One of the grounds upon which the trust was held void was its political bias in favour of socialism.

A political taint will also be fatal to trusts seeking to promote aims which most civilised nations hold to be high aspirations. In *Re Strakosch* [1949] Ch 529, the promotion of racial harmony between English and Afrikaans communities in South Africa was held non-charitable, and registration of community councils is refused where their principal aims are the promotion of interracial accord. The same will apply where the aims are harmony and peace if such movements overtly or covertly call upon governments to promote specific policies, such as disarmament. One reason sometimes given for denying charitable status to attempts to promote moral objectives is that they necessarily involve a propagandist element biased in favour of only one side of the argument. Such trusts may sometimes succeed if educational, however. In *Re Women's Service Trusts* (1976, unreported), for example, a trust to promote equal opportunities for women in the economic and political spheres was accepted as educational and therefore charitable.

Where the objectives involve attempting to bring about a change in the law, they will be considered political and therefore non-charitable. This was another ground for the failure of the trust in *Re Bushnell*, above, since in 1941 legislation would have been needed (and was of course later enacted) to introduce socialised medicine. It was also an additional reason for the failures of the National Anti-Vivisection Society, and Shaw's 40-letter alphabet, considered earlier in this chapter, and accounts for the inability of, e.g., Amnesty International, the Campaign against Racial Discrimination and the National Council for Civil Liberties to be registered. The ostensible rationale is that it is for Parliament, not the courts, to decide whether any change would be in the public benefit. Charities may, however, campaign against changes in the law, which may enable some political purposes of a generally conservative nature to obtain registration.

The Charity Commissioners, as we saw in section 8.4, exercise supervisory control over charities and one area is the permissible limits to political involvement by charities. Their Annual Reports of 1969 and 1981 point out that charity trustees who engage in political activities risk personal liability to repay trust funds expended in breach, and that charities whose purposes are found to be wide enough to permit political action may be deregistered. Charities may aid governments on particular issues by giving information and by rational persuasion, but must avoid seeking to remedy the causes of poverty which lie in social, economic and political structures or to eliminate other social injustice.

In *McGovern* v *Attorney-General* [1982] Ch 321, Amnesty International tried to procure charitable status for some of its activities by creating a trust of those parts which were thought most likely to be accepted as charitable. The objectives of the trust were the relief of needy persons who were prisoners of conscience and their relatives; seeking the release of such prisoners; seeking abolition of torture and inhuman punishment, and research into human rights and dissemination of the findings. The objectives were not confined to the United Kingdom. It was held that the first and fourth objectives might be charitable but that the trust as a whole failed because of the political aspects involved in seeking release of prisoners of conscience and the abolition of torture. The court could not judge whether these aims would be for the benefit of the public here or abroad, nor could the aim of reversing the policies of foreign governments be charitable. To grant this status might prejudice the relations of the British government with foreign countries, and this consideration of policy could not be overlooked by the court.

The Charity Commissioners have frequently expressed their willingness to advise those seeking charitable status or doubtful as to whether proposed activities might conflict with the charitable status of existing trusts.

8.5.7.2 Self-help

Though self-help organisations may possibly have been regarded as charitable in the 19th century, when, for example, friendly societies contributed considerably to the then limited provisions for welfare, Hall V-C held in *Re Clark* (1875) 1 Ch D 497 that a friendly society was not charitable because of the absence of any stipulation that benefits should be restricted to those members who were poor as well as old, disabled or sick.

Since that decision it has been possible to state safely that self-help organisations are not charitable. If they are not poverty charities they clearly fail on the *Oppenheim* personal nexus test. Hall V-C envisaged that they may succeed as poverty charities, where, as we have seen, public benefit tests are less stringent, but this also must be regarded as doubtful because a second principle has developed that the benefits of charity must be provided by bounty and not bargain. Where, as is the case with many friendly societies, the beneficiaries have, in effect, bought their entitlement in a contractual arrangement, the element of altruism essential to charity is lacking.

Thus in *Re Hobourn Aero Components Ltd's Air Raid Disaster Fund* [1946] Ch 194, a case to which we have referred in another context in section 5.4, a fund established by employees to relieve members suffering in consequence of air raids on Coventry was held non-charitable on the grounds first, that the employees among whom benefit was confined could not be a section of the public, and secondly, that the fund represented a self-help arrangement in which the members' entitlement to benefit turned upon the fact of their having subscribed to the fund. In other words, even if this had been an otherwise valid poverty trust (and one wonders why the court did not take the point that the claimants would almost certainly be needy after losing their possessions in an air raid), the trust would still have been refused charitable status on the second ground, as indeed would almost any self-help organisation.

One can see why profit-making self-help organisations should not be charitable. One can also see why charitable status should be restricted, as Hall V-C thought, to those self-help organisations which relieve poverty; after all, it is unlikely that many would argue that the collective purchases of racehorses or private yachts or aircraft should be subsidised by the taxpayer. But the bounty-not-bargain argument seems harsh, even anomalous. It is, after all, accepted that some payment for benefits received from bodies which are undoubtedly charitable may legitimately be demanded; no one expects to be admitted to a public school, or the Victoria and Albert Museum, free of charge. Nor, I would suggest, is the element of altruism necessarily absent from the *Hobourn Aero* type of arrangement; a commitment to support one another where need arises is surely different from an investment made in the hope of profit or an insurance policy purchased to protect oneself against calculable risks. It is still open for the courts to accept the first ground in *Hobourn Aero* while rejecting the second.

8.5.7.3 Disaster appeals

These will be valid if for the relief of poverty, otherwise, like self-help organisations, will fail on the grounds of public benefit. This leaves the organisers of such funds with two alternatives. One possibility is that they can apply a means-test criterion to the receipt of benefit, which they may regard as invidious. For example, in the Aberfan coal-tip disaster of 1966, the majority of victims were children and, far from it being easy to show that their deaths produced material deprivation among the relatives, one could actually argue that the cost of rearing the children has been saved. In fact, the Commissioners eventually held that the fund was charitable, when money was paid to enable people to move away from the area altogether. Chesterman, *Charities, Trusts and Social Welfare*, gives an extremely comprehensive coverage of this appeal (pp. 339ff).

The other possibility, often favoured by fund organisers (e.g., the Penlee lifeboat disaster fund in 1982), is to avoid the means test and draft the appeal in such a way as to avoid charitable status altogether. In that event, the tax concessions will also be forgone. Perhaps more importantly, the cy pres doctrine described in section 8.6 will not apply and there may be difficulties over distribution of any surplus left over after the purposes have been achieved (see section 5.4). It may even be, as we have seen, that the Crown will take some or all of the surplus as *bona vacantia*, not perhaps the most fitting consequence of the altruism of the donors.

8.6   CY PRES

This Anglo-Norman phrase meant something like 'as near as possible', and the doctrine of cy pres in charity law lays down that where property given on trust for charitable purposes cannot be used in the precise manner intended by the donor, the court (and since about 130 years ago the Charity Commissioners) may make a scheme for the application of the property to purposes resembling as closely as possible the donor's original intention. The idea, in other words, is not to frustrate the intention of the donor (who cannot be consulted if the gift is testamentary) any more than necessary. The doctrine dates back at least as far as the 17th century. It only applies to charities — if private purposes fail, the results are as discussed in chapter 5.

The application of the doctrine has been significantly widened by the Charities Act 1960. This may reflect a difference of emphasis. The equitable doctrine was probably based on the presumed intention of the donor and could in some circumstances militate against the efficient operation of charitable enterprises (see, e.g., section 8.6.1.3). The 1960 Act, on the other hand, is concerned more with the efficient running of charities, even at the expense of the donor's intentions.

8.6.1   Position apart from the 1960 Act: inherent jurisdiction of the courts

The question whether cy pres can be applied can arise either because it is clear from the outset that the donor's intention cannot be fulfilled, as where the organisation which he has singled out for benefit has already ceased to exist, or because, at some later time, during the continuance of the trust, it turns out that the purposes cannot be achieved. Cy pres is more easily invoked in the latter case, for once property has been dedicated to charity, there is no possibility of a resulting trust to the donor. Where, however, a gift fails from the start, the courts have, since the early 19th century, insisted that before the property can be applied cy pres, a general or 'paramount' charitable intention must be shown.

8.6.1.1   Initial failure

The question turns on whether the intention of the donor was specific or general. If it was to further some specific purpose which cannot be carried out, or benefit some specific institution no longer in existence, then the gift fails and the property will return to the settlor, or his estate, on a resulting trust, as discussed in chapter 5. If, however, the intention is a more general one, which might be satisfied by applying the property to a purpose or institution similar to that specified, a cy pres scheme may be ordered. Each case turns upon the meaning attributed by the court to the instrument creating the gift.

In *Re Rymer* [1895] 1 Ch 19, a gift was held to be for a specific seminary which had ceased to exist, and so failed. This is the general position where no paramount general intention can be found.

It is possible for there to be an initial failure even where the institution to whom the donation is made exists, but where there is a condition in the gift that makes it impossible for that body to accept the gift. In _Re Lysaght_ [1966] Ch 191, there was a condition (which would have disqualified Jews and Catholics) which led the Royal College of Surgeons to decline the gift. The gift was saved because the court found a general charitable intention on the part of the testatrix, to establish medical studentships. The cy pres doctrine therefore operated; the condition could be deleted as not being essential to the fulfilment of the general intention. A scheme was ordered on the terms of the will as it stood without the condition. Recently, in _Re Woodhams_ [1981] 1 WLR 493, a general charitable intention to foster musical education was found, allowing the court to remove the restriction which would have limited scholarships to boys from two named children's homes and which would have prevented the donees from accepting the gift.

Sometimes the charity specified by the donor has never existed at all. There is some authority that if so, it is easier to discover a general charitable intention than in the _Re Rymer_ situation, presumably on the basis that only a general intention can be attributed to the donor who fails correctly to specify the beneficiary.

In _Re Harwood_ [1936] Ch 285, for example, a gift was made to the Peace Society in Belfast, which could not be shown ever to have existed. Farwell J found that there was an intention to benefit societies aimed at promoting peace, and the gift was therefore applied cy pres. A second gift in the will, in favour of the Wisbech Peace Society, which had once existed but had ceased to do so prior to the testatrix's death, was held, however, to have lapsed. Though the case is still authority on this issue, doubt may perhaps be cast on the assumption that the promotion of peace is in fact capable of being charitable. We saw in section 8.5.7.1 how there may be difficulties with purposes regarded as political, and this may be such a purpose. Interestingly, some military purposes may, as we have seen in section 8.5.5.1, be covered by the preamble to the Statute of Charitable Uses!

A similar construction was adopted in _Re Satterthwaite's WT_ [1966] 1 WLR 277, where the will listed a number of organisations concerned with animal welfare. It appeared that the list had been thoughtlessly compiled, the testatrix's chief concern being to divert her residuary estate away from human beneficiaries, of whom she held a low opinion. One of the named institutions, the London Animal Hospital, had never existed as a charity, although a private veterinary surgeon had practised under that description prior to the date of the will. The gift was interpreted as a gift to a non-existent charity and applied cy pres, there being ample evidence of a general charitable intention in favour of animal welfare.

Suppose there is a gift to an existing non-charity included among a series of gifts to charities. It seems that this will not be taken as an indication of general charitable intent. In *Re Jenkins's WT* [1966] Ch 249 Buckley J declined to hold that a gift to the British Union for the Abolition of Vivisection could be taken as charitable simply by being included in a list of gifts to unquestionably charitable organisations.

8.6.1.1.1   *Non-existent body, but no initial failure*   It may be possible to save the gift if the institution can be said to continue to exist in some other form. In recent years many small charities have amalgamated, and it is sometimes possible to regard the new body thus formed as being the same as the old. In *Re Faraker* [1912] 2 Ch 488, a gift to 'Mrs Bailey's Charity, Rotherhithe' (which was assumed to be a reference to Hannah Bayly's Charity) passed to the new charity formed by an amalgamation of the Bayly charity with several others. It will be otherwise, of course, where a charity has been terminated under a power in its trust deed and so cannot be said to continue in its new guise. Many charities have no such power of self-destruction, and a moribund charity may be found to be still in existence and so capable of taking a gift. It should be noted, in parentheses (and see section 8.5.2.1.4), that the Charities Act 1985 grants powers of termination where the income has fallen below £5 a year.

Another approach is to find that the gift was made for the *purpose* of the named charity, rather than for the body itself. This is much easier if the body concerned is unincorporated.

If the body is unincorporated then by definition the gift cannot be to it but must be to its purposes, and those purposes can still be fulfilled by making a cy pres scheme. Where the body is a corporation, however, a gift to it will prima facie lapse if the corporation has ceased to exist, just as a gift to a human individual would lapse if the person concerned had died before the gift was made. The gift may be rescued only on the cy pres principles already outlined, i.e., if the court is able to find a general charitable intention going beyond the specific aim of benefiting the named corporate charity.

Re Finger's WT [1972] Ch 286, a decision of Goff J, provides a convenient illustration. There was a gift to the National Radium Commission, an unincorporated association, and a gift also to the National Council for Maternity and Child Welfare, which was a corporate charity. Both had ceased to exist by the time the testatrix died. The gift to the National Radium Commission was interpreted as a gift to its purposes, and since these still continued, the gift did not fail. All the court needed to do was to settle a scheme to apply the property elsewhere. This is not a cy pres scheme, but rather an instance of finding a substitute trustee to carry out the purpose of the trust and it would not have been necessary to look for any general charitable intention above and beyond those purposes. The gift to the National Council for Maternity and Child Welfare, on the other hand, would have failed, except that in the case it was possible to discern a general charitable intention which allowed for the application of the gift cy pres.

Another example is the Court of Appeal's decision in *Re Koeppler's WT* [1985] 2 All ER 869, where Slade LJ, giving the main judgment, construed a gift to a non-existent body as a valid trust for educational purposes, on similar principles to those adopted in *Re Finger's WT*.

8.6.1.2 Subsequent failure

Cy pres has a much wider application here, and none of the difficulties which arise in the event of an initial failure arise here.

Once property has been dedicated to charitable purposes it remains so, and if those purposes cease to be capable of achievement there can be no resulting trust to the settlor or his estate unless the terms on which the gift was originally made provide for this to happen. It is not necessary to search for a general charitable intention on the part of the settlor. The only relevant consideration is whether there was an outright disposition in favour of charity. Where this is so, funds which cannot be applied to the original purpose, whether because that purpose is impossible or because there is a surplus left over after the purpose has been achieved, may be applied cy pres.

In *Re Slevin* [1891] 2 Ch 236, a legacy had been left to the Orphanage of St Dominics, Newcastle-upon-Tyne. The orphanage ceased to exist after the date of the donor's death, but before the legacy could be paid over. Since the orphanage had survived its benefactor, by however short a time, the gift was effective in favour of charity and could be applied cy pres. In *Re King* [1923] 1 Ch 243, a surplus was left after the purpose (the setting of a stained-glass window in a church) was carried out. Finding that the whole fund, and not just the sum sufficient for the window, had been dedicated to charity, Romer J applied the surplus cy pres (to the setting of a second window).

Nor will it matter that the gift to charity was intended to be postponed until some future date under the terms of the will or gift. In other words, the relevant date is that of the original donation, even though the charity may only at that time obtain a future interest in the property. If A dies leaving property to B for his life, thereafter to C (a charity), and C ceases to exist after A's death but before B's, this is regarded as a subsequent, not an initial, failure.

Thus, in *Re Moon* [1948] 1 All ER 300, the testator directed that a legacy should be paid to the trustees of a Methodist church for the purposes of missionary work after the death of his widow. The purposes were no longer practicable by the time of the widow's death and Roxburgh J held that the question of whether the gift had lapsed must be resolved in relation to the time when the gift was made, that is, at the death of the testator. Since the purposes would have been practical then, there was an effective gift to charity at that time and the failure was subsequent and not initial. A similar result was reached in *Re Wright* [1954] Ch 347, where a testamentary gift for the founding of a convalescent home was to take effect after a life interest, at the end of which time the property was insufficient for the purpose. The date of the testatrix's death was taken to be crucial in determining the question of whether the gift was practicable.

at pt of death

8.6.1.3 *Modernisation of moribund charities*

The difficulties before 1960 were not so much in the case of a clear failure, for example, a charitable body ceasing to exist, but rather the opposite, where a charitable body refused to die, in spite of becoming outdated and obsolete. There was no effective system whereby moribund charities could be modernised.

Until the reforms introduced by the Charities Act 1960, the courts' inherent jurisdiction was confined to rather narrow limits, being available only where it was 'impossible' or 'impracticable' to carry out the terms of the trust. Some very peculiar trusts were kept on foot by the limits of the cy pres doctrine before 1960, obliging trustees to distribute bread, linen, stockings, boots etc. among the poor. One old trust specified the distribution of green waistcoats in memory of the testator's surname. Nevertheless, some old trusts were reformed under the doctrine, for example, *Attorney-General* v *City of London* (1790) 3 Bro CC 121, a trust to propagate Christianity among the infidels of Virginia.

The test is stated in *Re Weir Hospital* [1910] 2 Ch 124. A testator left two houses to be used as a hospital. The premises were not suitable and the Charity Commissioners approved a scheme to use them as a nurses' home instead, perpetuating the testator's name by renaming a hospital in his honour. The Court of Appeal held that the scheme was *ultra vires*, since the original purpose was not impossible to fulfil, merely difficult. No doubt the court was anxious not to depart too far from the original wishes of the testator, and the scheme at issue was a significant departure.

Occasionally, however, the doctrine has been used to eradicate a condition of the trust which was inimical to its main purpose, as in *Re Robinson* [1923] 2 Ch 332, where a condition requiring a preacher to wear a black gown was thought likely to offend the congregation and reduce attendance, or *Re Dominion Students' Hall Trust* [1947] Ch 183, where a colour bar was removed from a trust intended to promote community of citizenship among members of the Commonwealth.

The court has also an inherent jurisdiction to approve alteration of terms relating to the administration of a trust where this is necessary to carry out the trust effectively. In *Re J.W. Laing Trust* [1984] Ch 143, this was employed to delete a term requiring trustees to distribute, within 10 years of the settlor's death, a fund which by then had risen to over £24 million.

8.6.2   Charities Act 1960

The policy of the Act is to modernise outmoded trusts; as we have seen this was difficult using only the inherent jurisdiction of the courts. Section 13(5) places a duty upon trustees to seek the application of property cy pres if and when appropriate circumstances arise. Much of the work of the Commissioners consists in settling and approving schemes of this kind.

Section 13 also extends the circumstances in which property may be applied cy pres. No longer is it necessary to show that it is 'impossible' or 'impracticable' to carry out the terms of the trust. It is enough that the original purpose has been fulfilled as far as possible, or cannot be carried out according to the directions given and the spirit of the gift, or if there is a surplus left over, or if the purposes have been adequately provided for by other means, or become useless or harmful to the community. Cy pres may also apply where the original purposes relate to an area, or class of persons, which has ceased to have any relevance, having regard to the spirit of the gift. There are also provisions for the amalgamation of small charities if that is more efficient. It should be noted that s. 13 only affects the definition of when failure occurs for cy pres purposes, and all the other requirements of the doctrine remain. Thus, for example, it is still necessary to show a paramount charitable intention in the case of an initial failure.

In interpreting the section, the Commissioners attempt, so far as possible, to effect the intentions of the donor, these being understood in the context of modern conditions (see their Annual Report 1970, para. 41).

Section 14 provides reform to cope with the problems which may arise if property is given for charitable purposes which fail and where it is difficult to find the donors. In the case of private trusts, as we saw in chapter 5, the operation of the resulting trust doctrine frequently results in the funds passing to the Crown as *bona vacantia*. Section 14 is intended to prevent this result where money is given for charitable purposes. The section has application only in the case of initial failure, as in the case of subsequent failure no question of returning the gifts to the donors would arise.

Section 14 allows the application of such property cy pres, regardless of charitable intention, when the property has been given either by a donor who cannot be found after reasonable advertisements or inquiries, or who has executed a written disclaimer of his rights. There is a conclusive presumption that property raised by cash collections by way of collecting boxes, or other methods which make it hard to tell one gift from another is within the section. Such methods might include lotteries, competitions, sales etc.

9

Trustees I: Commencement, Nature and Termination of Office

9.1 INTRODUCTION, AND OVERVIEW OF THE NATURE OF TRUSTEESHIP

9.1.1 Layout of the chapters on trustees

Up to now we have been concerned largely with different types of trust and requirements for their validity. Chapters 9, 10 and 11 are about trusteeship and the actual administration of trusts. This chapter is of a general nature: how trustees are appointed and removed (or retire), and the general nature of their office. Chapter 10 takes a much more detailed look at their main powers and duties. Chapter 11 is about what happens when something goes wrong — what can the beneficiaries do about it?

There are a number of general points to appreciate before embarking on the topic:

(a) It will soon become clear how onerous the office of trusteeship is. Legal ownership without its equitable counterpart is by no means a privilege. It is no wonder that the courts require very clear evidence, for example, that a settlor has constituted himself trustee (see section 2.2). Nor will it come as a surprise that trusteeship is often undertaken on a professional basis and that the charges can be very high.

(b) Whereas some of what follows in chapters 9 and 10 is inherent in the nature of any trust, many of the powers and duties described represent simply a fall-back position where nothing to the contrary is provided in the trust instrument. In fact, however, the precise scope of such powers and duties will, in the case of most express trusts, be governed by the terms of the trust instrument, and not by the fall-back legal position.

Modern trusts created by deed of settlement or will, prepared under expert legal advice, generally seek to give the trustees the widest possible powers, being almost invariably drafted with tax saving in mind. Frequently also provision is made for the remuneration of trustees, on which see section 9.5, and it is usual to include clauses designed to limit the trustees' liability for breach of trust. The trust instrument may therefore contemplate considerable deviation from the rules to be considered in this and the next chapter.

Also, it is less certain how far these rules apply to constructive trustees, whose powers and obligations may depend upon the circumstances in which the trust arises.

It therefore follows that much of the material in chapters 9 and 10 is of greater theoretical than practical importance. Partly for this reason, less extensive coverage is given than in many textbooks. Also, the intention has been to concentrate on principle rather than detail: this is after all an introductory book, not a practitioners' encyclopaedia, and some intricacies are deliberately omitted.

(c)   Quite a lot of the material is statutory, but usually the relevant sections only consolidate the previous law, or re-enact, either exactly or with slight differences, earlier provisions. It should not be a shock, therefore, occasionally to find cases cited as authority on the interpretation of a section where the cases actually predate the section now in force.

9.1.2   Overview of the functions of trustees

9.1.2.1   Creation of the trust
Upon creation of the trust, the trustees become the legal owners of the trust property. Where the trust is created *inter vivos*, they will normally be parties to the deed which creates it and which has the effect of vesting the trust property in them. In the case of a testamentary trust, it is usual to appoint the same persons to be both executors and trustees, so the acquisition of the legal title to the testator's property is automatic inasmuch as it vests in his personal representatives from the moment of death. Upon completion of the administration of the estate, it may be necessary, depending on the nature of the property, to execute additional formalities signifying that they now hold in the capacity of trustees or, if other persons are to act as trustees, to vest the property in them (see section 9.3).

In any event, it is the duty of those who take property as trustees to familiarise themselves with the nature of the property and the terms of the trusts upon which it is held. They must also ensure that all formalities necessary to vest the property have been complied with, such as procuring registration as shareholders etc. At this stage, it may also be necessary to consider the conversion and disposal of any unproductive assets and the settling of any liabilities outstanding against the trust estate. Trustees appointed to an existing trust, for example, in replacement of a retiring trustee, must satisfy themselves that the affairs of the trust are in order and that no breach of trust has occurred: if it has, steps must be taken as soon as possible to put matters right and recoup any loss.

9.1.2.2   Day-to-day running of the trust
The duty of the trustees in the day-to-day running of the trust is to manage the property so as to preserve the value of the capital and produce an income for the beneficiaries. In effecting administrative functions, they may employ the services of agents such as solicitors, accountants and stockbrokers. There are, however, some discretions which must be exercised personally, such as distributions to be

made under a discretionary trust. Details on powers of delegation are given in section 9.4.

In managing the affairs of the trust, the trustees must act honestly and must take (according to Lord Blackburn in *Speight* v *Gaunt* (1883) 9 App Cas 1, 19) 'all those precautions which an ordinary prudent man of business would take in managing similar affairs of his own'. The selection of investments involves additional considerations, for although ordinary business prudence may sometimes involve accepting a degree of risk or speculation, trustees must confine themselves to those securities which are authorised by the trust instrument or by statute and avoid hazardous investments.

A somewhat higher standard of care is required of paid trustees than of unpaid, non-professional trustees, in that the former will be held to the standards of skill and expertise which they claim to possess. In *Bartlett* v *Barclays Bank Trust Co. Ltd (No. 1)* [1980] Ch 515, at p. 534, Brightman J said:

> A trust corporation holds itself out in its advertising literature as being above ordinary mortals . . . so I think that a professional corporate trustee is liable for breach of trust if loss is caused to the trust fund because it neglects to exercise the special care and skill which it professes to have.

All trustees (if more than one) are required to be active in the management of the trust, and equity makes no concession to any notion of a 'sleeping trustee'. A trustee who concurs in the decisions of the rest is treated as having acted in the same degree as the rest, and is equally liable if a breach is committed since he might have prevented it by exercising his independent judgment. However, a trustee who, after giving proper consideration to the matter, reasonably defers to the knowledge of his fellow trustees may be excused from liability, as we shall see in chapter 11.

Trustees of private trusts must act unanimously and not by majority vote, unless the trust instrument authorises them to act upon a majority decision. This rule in effect gives each trustee a veto in the exercise of powers and discretions arising under the trust. The veto does not apply to duties because there is, of course, no question of deciding whether or not to comply with a duty since to do otherwise will be a breach. As we have already seen, for example, in section 2.7, in the case of trusts for sale, where there is normally a power to postpone sale, the power to postpone has to be exercised unanimously, or the trust to sell will prevail.

9.1.2.3 Termination of the trust

Sooner or later a private trust will come to an end and the trustees will be required to distribute the property among the beneficiaries. Needless to say, they must distribute it to those who are properly entitled and failure in this regard will be a breach for which they may be liable.

9.1.2.3.1 Standard of care The onus is heavy. Trustees have been held liable where they made payment on the strength of a forged marriage certificate (*Eaves v Hickson* (1861) 30 Beav 136) or in the erroneous belief that a valid charitable trust was created (*Ministry of Health v Simpson* [1951] AC 251). They may even be liable where they acted upon legal advice (*National Trustee Co. of Australia Ltd v General Finance Co. of Australasia Ltd* [1905] AC 373) although, as we shall see (section 11.2), this may be a factor which would induce the court to exercise its discretion under s. 61 of the Trustee Act 1925 to excuse the trustees from liability.

The problems of wrongful payment are dealt with more fully in chapter 11, but it may be noted here that trustees may apply to court for directions in doubtful cases or, in the last resort, protect themselves by paying money into court.

Section 27 of the Trustee Act 1925 gives trustees power to advertise for claimants, in accordance with certain formalities, and to distribute the whole of the fund to those who come forward. By this procedure they obtain the same protection as if they had administered the trust under a court order. The rights of those properly entitled to follow the property (see chapter 11) are not thereby prejudiced. Other potential liabilities can be met by setting aside a fund, distributing under a court order, or obtaining an indemnity from the beneficiaries before distributing.

9.1.2.3.2 Discovery of all those entitled A special problem may arise by virtue of the statutory reforms made by the Family Law Reform Act 1969, the Adoption Act 1976 and the Legitimacy Act 1976, which give new rights to children in some circumstances. These may be persons of whose existence the trustees or personal representatives have no notice, and these Acts therefore provide protection for the trustees without diminishing the rights of the persons entitled to recover their property.

9.2 APPOINTMENT OF TRUSTEES

In the normal case, trustees will be appointed by the document which brings the trust into existence, and the Trustee Act 1925 makes provision for any additional appointments which may be necessary during the continuance of the trust. The settlor will usually name those whom he wishes to act as trustees, and where the settlement is *inter vivos* the trustees themselves will normally be parties to the deed of settlement since the purpose is both to declare the trusts and to vest the property in the trustees. In the uncommon case where the settlor simply declares his intention henceforth to hold some of his property on trust, he will himself be the sole trustee. Alternatively, he may decide to appoint other trustees as well and take steps to vest the property in himself and his co-trustees jointly.

Where trusts are created by will, it is usual to appoint the same persons to be both executors and trustees. The fiduciary duties of executors are very similar to those of trustees, but they are not identical, and it may be important to know at what point an executor has ceased to act as such and become a trustee. Generally, this will occur when the executors assent to the vesting of property in themselves as trustees, although in the case of personalty this assent may be implied since no formalities are necessary. In the case of land, an assent in writing is required since this is an essential document of title.

9.2.1 No trustee available

It may happen that for some reason a trust comes into existence without there being anyone able or willing to act a trustee, for example, if the trustee appointed by the will have predeceased the testator or if the trust arises by operation of law. An instance of the latter is where an outright bequest of property is made to a minor who cannot give a good receipt for the property until he comes of age. The absence of trustees will not invalidate the trust. If the trust is *inter vivos*, the settlor himself will be the trustee. If it arises by will, the personal representatives of the testator will hold the property on trust. Where an instrument creating the trust names someone as having power to appoint trustees, he may use that power to fill the gap. If all else fails, the court will appoint trustees.

9.2.2 Acceptance once and for all

No one can be compelled to accept office as a trustee under an express trust, although a person may find himself a trustee against his will by operation of law, e.g., a constructive trustee. Once the office is accepted, it cannot later be renounced, although retirement is possible under certain conditions. In theory, the office of trustee is lifelong, and where a trustee dies in office any liabilities which he has incurred will persist against his estate. Should the trustee wish to disclaim, he should do so as soon as possible and preferably by deed, for failure to disclaim may lead to a presumption that he has accepted. Acceptance will also be presumed once the trustee has started to act in relation to the property.

9.2.3 Who may be trustee?

Anyone who has the legal capacity to hold the legal title to property may be appointed a trustee of that property. A corporation may thus be a trustee provided its constitution authorises it so to act. An infant may become a resulting or constructive trustee of personalty (*Re Vinogradoff* [1935] WN 68) although not of land, but s. 20 of the Law of Property Act 1925 declares the express appointment of an infant trustee void, and s. 36(1) of the Trustee Act 1925 permits his replacement by a person of full age. These restrictions apart, the settlor may appoint as he pleases. Traditionally, certain appointments, such as that of a beneficiary or one of his relatives, or the solicitor to the trust, have been regarded as undesirable by the courts, but they are not invalid and are commonly made in practice.

Certain special categories of trustee exist, the most important in practice being the trust corporation, usually but not always the executor and trustee company of a bank. The main advantages of appointing a trust corporation are its longevity, financial stability and expertise, and the fact that it may act alone in circumstances where two private trustees would be necessary. The chief disadvantage is that its fees are likely to be high. The qualifications necessary for a company to be a trust corporation are contained in the Public Trustee Rules 1912 as amended.

Other special trustees include custodian trustees, the Public Trustee, and judicial trustees. They perform specialist functions which in practice are rare.

9.2.4 Appointment of new trustees during continuance of the trust

If an occasion for the appointment of new trustees arises during the continuance of the trust, rather different considerations apply than those governing the initial appointments.

9.2.4.1 Role of the settlor

It should be recalled that once a settlor has completed the steps necessary to create a trust, he has no further interest in the trust property. It follows that he retains no rights in regard to the appointment of trustees in the future. If he wishes to control future appointments, he must nominate himself in the trust instrument as being the person having power to appoint new trustees, and any appointments that he makes will be in this capacity and not by virtue of his being settlor.

Alternatively, he may prefer to nominate some other person to exercise the power of appointing trustees, particularly where the trust is intended to extend beyond his lifetime. A well-drafted trust instrument will be required for this, because the terms of any power to appoint will be strictly construed. It is usual nowadays, when nominating a person in the trust instrument to exercise the power of appointing new trustees, to draft the power in very simple terms, since in the event of any inconsistency between the terms of the trust instrument and the statutory power considered in section 9.2.4.2, the latter will prevail.

9.2.4.2 Trustee Act 1925, section 36

It is obviously desirable that there should always be some person having power to appoint new trustees, and s. 36(1) of the Trustee Act 1925 makes provision for this. The effect of this complex section is to create a hierarchy of categories of persons having power to appoint. There is an order. Those persons falling into the first category have the first right to make the appointment, and only if there is no one in that category, or no one able and willing to act, will the power become exercisable by the persons within the next category. By virtue of the section, the following persons, in this order, may appoint:

(a) The person(s), if any, nominated in the trust instrument.

(b)　The existing trustees, if any.

(c)　The personal representatives of the last, or only surviving trustee.

If there is no one in any of these categories who is able and willing to act then the power given by s. 36(1) cannot be exercised at all.

That is not the end of the matter, however, because the court may have jurisdiction to appoint under s. 41 of the Act, considered in section 9.2.4.3.

The circumstances which give rise to a power on the part of the appropriate person to appoint fresh trustees in replacement for the original trustees are also specified in s. 36(1) and are as follows:

(a)　Where a trustee has died. This covers not only the situation of a trustee dying while in office, but also that of a trustee dying before assuming office, as where a trustee named in a will predeceases the testator. The Act makes no provision for the perhaps unlikely case of all trustees dying before the will comes into effect, as noted above.

(b)　Where a trustee remains out of the United Kingdom for more than 12 months. The absence must be for a continuous period, so that a trustee who occasionally returns for short visits cannot be removed under this head (*Re Walker (Summers* v *Barrow*) [1910] 1 Ch 259. So long as the absence is continuous, its cause is immaterial, so that a trustee who remains abroad involuntarily by reason of illness or imprisonment abroad may be replaced. Where it is intended that the trust should operate in another jurisdiction, care should be taken expressly to exclude the operation of this part of s. 36(1) to protect the tenure of foreign residents who have been specifically selected as trustees.

(c)　Where a trustee desires to be discharged from all or any of the trusts or powers reposed in or conferred on him. Although it is not permitted to disclaim in relation to part only of the trust before assuming office, a trustee who accepts office and later seeks to be discharged may be relieved of his duties with regard to a part only of the trust, while retaining a say in the management of those parts in which he has an interest.

(d)　Where a trustee refuses. This seems apt to permit an appointment to be made in replacement of a trustee who disclaims, although strictly, of course, such a person never becomes a trustee. Old authorities on the predecessor of s. 36 favour this interpretation.

(e)　Where a trustee is unfit to act. This appears to refer to defects of character, and although no precise description can be given of the circumstances in which a trustee can be described as unfit for the purposes of s. 36(1), the courts will remove a trustee as unfit where he has been convicted of a crime of dishonesty, or he has become bankrupt and his continuation in office is opposed by the beneficiaries, or he has been imprudent in the management of his own affairs. A bankrupt trustee who is free from moral blame may, however, be permitted to remain in office.

(f)   Where a trustee is incapable of acting. This covers the case where a trustee is unfit due to mental or physical incapacity and also where some legal incapacity is imposed, as where wartime regulations forbid certain foreign nationals to hold property in this country. Special provisions apply where a trustee has also a beneficial interest under the trust and is a patient under the Mental Health Act 1983. In this case, the leave of the authority having jurisdiction over him under Part VII of the Act will be required before a new trustee can be appointed in his place.

(g)   Where the trustee is an infant. The express appointment of an infant trustee is void, but a trust could be deprived of an active trustee because of the infancy of a person named as a trustee and the section appears to cover this contingency.

(h)   By virtue of s. 36(3), where a corporate body acting as trustee has been dissolved. It is deemed to be incapable of acting from the date of dissolution.

In addition to the power of appointing new trustees by way of replacement, there is also power to appoint additional trustees, the existing trustees remaining in office. Where there are currently three or fewer trustees, none of whom is a trust corporation, and it is thought desirable to have more, appointment may be made by the person nominated in the trust instrument for the purposes of appointing new trustees or by the existing trustee or trustees, in that order. The total number of trustees must not be raised beyond four, although more than one at a time may be appointed. The power is contained in s. 36(6), and is independent of the power to appoint replacement trustees under s. 36(1) above.

An appointment under s. 36 must be in writing, and in practice it will be made by deed, to take advantage of the vesting provisions of s. 40 (see section 9.3).

9.2.4.3   Appointment by the court under Trustee Act 1925, section 41

The court has an inherent power to appoint trustees as part of its supervisory jurisdiction over trusts, which is supplemented by s. 41 of the Trustee Act 1925. Under this section, the court may appoint whenever it is expedient that an appointment should be made and it is inexpedient, difficult or impracticable to bring this about without the assistance of the court.

Application to the court may be made by a beneficiary or by a trustee, but if it is possible to appoint under a power in the trust instrument or under s. 36, this should be done in preference. If there is some person having power to appoint and seeking to exercise that power in good faith, the court will not interfere even if the proposed appointment is not one which it would itself have made.

Where allegations of misconduct against a trustee are being made, it may act under its inherent jurisdiction, but the proper course is to begin the action by writ so that the trustee knows what accusations he has to meet.

The court's assistance may properly be sought when no one has power to appoint, or no one is willing and able to exercise it, or where there is some doubt as to whether the power has become exercisable. Recourse to the court may be the only way of replacing elderly or sick trustees who have become incapable of acting for the trust, as in *Re Phelp's ST* (1885) 31 ChD 351, where the sole trustee was 85 years old, deaf and failing in intellect, or of meeting the case where the only person having power to appoint is too old or ill, or too young, to be able to exercise it. In practice, application is sometimes made by trustees who wish to avoid later argument over the propriety of a particular appointment.

Certain principles govern the court's selection in appointing trustees. At one time, a beneficiary, or even one of his relations, would have been unsuitable because of the possibility of a conflict between duty and self-interest. Nor would the family solicitor be chosen, ostensibly to avoid the indelicate task of assessing the probity of a member of the legal profession. Both kinds of appointment are commonly made out of court, however, and the attitude of the courts appears to be changing.

The court will not, however, make an appointment which favours the interests of certain beneficiaries above others, nor will it willingly appoint against the known wishes of the settlor. For example, in *Re Tempest* (1866) LR 1 Ch App 485 a trustee had predeceased the testator and there was strong disagreement between the surviving trustee and a faction among the beneficiaries over who should replace him. It was clear that the surviving trustee would be unwilling to act with the person appointed by the court at first instance. Turner LJ considered that it would be going too far to say that a court would refuse to appoint a person with whom the existing trustees refuse to act, since that would amount to giving them a veto. The court should inquire whether the objection is well-founded and act accordingly. Regard will be had to whether a proposed appointment will promote or impede the execution of the trust.

Persons permanently resident abroad will not normally be suitable, but where the beneficiaries have emigrated and the trust property is situated abroad, the court may make such an appointment (*Re Windeatt's WT* [1969] 1 WLR 692).

9.2.4.4 Role of the beneficiaries

Where a sole beneficiary is absolutely entitled to the entirety of the trust property, or where all the beneficiaries are *sui juris* (i.e., not children or people who used to be called lunatics until that term became unfashionable) and together so entitled, the rule in *Saunders* v *Vautier* (1841) 10 LJ Ch 354, considered in greater detail in section 12.1.2, permits the beneficiaries to terminate the trust. They may then, if they so wish, set up a new trust to which they, now as settlors, have the right to appoint the trustees. This course of action, however, will require transfers of title attracting *ad valorem* stamp duty, and may well give rise to liability for capital transfer (to be called inheritance tax) or other tax upon the dissolution and fresh settlement.

There seems no reason in principle why, if the beneficiaries may appoint in this roundabout fashion, they may not do so directly, but the courts have taken a contrary view. Thus, it seems that those who have the right to appoint under a statutory power (considered in sections 9.2.4.2 and 9.2.4.3) may do so regardless of the wishes of the beneficiaries. In *Re Higginbottom* [1892] 3 Ch 132, an illiterate lady of no means, and having no interest in the trust, became executrix of the last survivor among the trustees, and therefore was entitled by virtue of the statute to appoint new trustees. The majority of the beneficiaries opposed this and requested the court to appoint trustees of their choosing, but Kekewich J refused to interfere with the lady's right to make the appointment herself. More recently, in *Re Brockbank* [1948] Ch 206, a trustee wished to retire and the beneficiaries sought to have a trust corporation appointed in place of the remaining trustees, who opposed the change on the ground of the cost to the trust of the trust corporation's fees. The beneficiaries argued that since they were all *sui juris* and collectively entitled, the trustees were obliged to appoint in accordance with their wishes. Vaisey J rejected this argument. The beneficiaries might terminate the trust if they so wished but they were not entitled to control the trustees' exercise of their statutory power to appoint while the trust subsisted.

9.3 FORMALITIES FOR VESTING OF TRUST PROPERTY IN NEW TRUSTEES

As we saw in Chapter 2, where a settlement is created *inter vivos*, the trust property will be vested in the trustees as part of the transaction. If the settlor declares himself sole trustee there is, of course, nothing more to be done. In a testamentary trust, where the same persons are appointed as executors and trustees, the change of role involves the executors investing the property in themselves as trustees, which is notional in the case of most kinds of personalty but requires a formal assent in the case of land. If other persons are to take over as trustees, the property must be vested in them with whatever degree of formality is appropriate to that property. Similarly, when new trustees are appointed to an existing trust, the property must be vested in them so that they hold it jointly with the existing trustees.

9.3.1 The formalities themselves

In brief, formalities are required as follows (all those relating to land are dealt with in greater detail in land law textbooks):

(a) Unregistered freehold land — a conveyance must be executed.

(b) Unregistered leasehold land — the lease must be assigned.

(c) Registered land, either freehold or leasehold — the appropriate transfer, and its registration at the Land Registry must be completed.

(d) Stocks and shares — these must be formally transferred, and the transfer registered in the books of the company or other body issuing the shares.

(e) Where the property is a debt, it must be formally assigned and notice given to the debtor, to secure priority over future assignees.

(f)   Negotiable instruments (e.g., cheques) payable to order — these must be delivered and endorsed.

(g)   Personal chattels (i.e., ordinary goods) — these may be physically handed over unless there are specific documents of title to be transferred, e.g., for a car or an aeroplane.

9.3.2   Consequences of improper vesting

Proper vesting is vital since the trustees may be held personally liable for any loss arising from failure in this regard. A newly appointed trustee must satisfy himself that all is in order, and cannot say that it should have been attended to by the other trustees. However, in the case of a newly appointed trustee, some of the formalities of vesting are obviated by s. 40 of the Trustee Act 1925. The effect of this section is that where he is appointed by deed containing a declaration in appropriate terms, the trust property vests automatically in the new trustee and his co-trustees as joint tenants.

Unfortunately, certain types of property are excluded from the operation of s. 40. This is inconvenient, since they include the most common types of property held in trust, but there are good reasons for the exclusion. The types of property excluded are:

(a)   Land held by way of mortgage. This is partly so that the mortgagor knows who to pay, but does not need to know all the details of the trusts, which ought in principle to be kept secret from him. Another reason concerns the rules for the priority of mortgages in certain circumstances, for which reference to land law textbooks is recommended.

(b)   Land held under a lease which contains a covenant against assignment (i.e., transfer of the lease to any but the original lessor) unless permission to assign was obtained prior to executing the deed of appointment. This is because if vesting was automatic upon appointment of new trustees, there would necessarily be a breach of the covenant against assignment, and this might render the lease liable to forfeiture (i.e., termination by the landlord).

(c)   Stocks and shares must be formally transferred and registered in the company's books. This is because under the Companies Acts, legal title to stocks and shares depends upon registration, and companies can recognise as shareholders only those who appear in their books. For greater detail, refer to company law textbooks.

It should also be noted that, notwithstanding any of the above, where land is registered, s. 47 of the Land Registration Act 1925 requires trustees to supply the Land Registry with a certified copy of the deed of appointment.

9.4 PERSONAL NATURE OF TRUSTEESHIP

We have seen how the duty of trustees regarding the exercise of their discretions is essentially of a personal nature. Yet since trustees need not be experts in finance etc., it is obviously very important for trustees to be able to employ others to carry out the more specialised aspects of trust management.

Equity has therefore always allowed the employment of agents in effecting specialised administrative functions, for example, solicitors, accountants and stockbrokers. Prior to the intervention of the Trustee Act 1925 two principles had been established by the House of Lords in *Speight* v *Gaunt* (1884) 9 App Cas 727. First, it was permissible to employ an agent where this was reasonably necessary or in accord with normal business practices. Secondly, where such an agent was employed, trustees would not be liable for losses attributable to the agent so long as they took proper care in his selection, employed him within his proper sphere and exercised reasonable general supervision over his work.

9.4.1 Power to delegate and the 1925 legislation

The Trustee Act 1925 considerably widened the scope of the power of delegation. First, as to the question of when it is permissible, by virtue of s. 23 of the Act, it is no longer necessary to justify the employment of an agent by reference to the needs of the trust or normal business practice. Instead, s. 23(1) provides:

> Trustees or personal representatives may, instead of acting personally, employ and pay an agent, whether a solicitor, banker, stockbroker, or other person, to transact any business or do any act required to be transacted or done in the execution of the trust, or the administration of the testator's or intestate's estate, including the receipt and payment of money, and shall be entitled to be allowed and paid all charges and expenses so incurred, and shall not be responsible for the default of any such agent if employed in good faith.

Clearly, the effect of s. 23(1) is considerably to reduce the burdens of trusteeship by permitting trustees to reduce their own workload at the expense of the trust.

The section applies only to executive or administrative functions, and does not alter the fundamental principle, at least where the property is within the UK, that trustees may not delegate the powers and discretions which belong to them alone by virtue of their office. These discretions are not of a purely executive nature but involve real choices, for example, deciding how to distribute under a discretionary trust. They may, and sometimes must, take expert advice before exercising these discretions, but the decision must be theirs alone.

In respect of property outside the UK, however, s. 23(2) allows trustees to delegate not only their powers of sale, management etc., but also their discretions. Such delegation had been accepted as justified since the middle of the

19th century where property had to be administered abroad.

Section 23(3) permits the delegation to a limited class of professional agents certain functions which are most conveniently performed by such agents but which would not otherwise be permissible. They sanction practices that have now become normal. Section 23(3)(a) meets the case where a receipt for money is contained in the body of a deed, a common practice in conveyances of land. The solicitor acting for the vendor will typically hold the deed until completion when he will hand it over to the purchaser in exchange for the purchase price. Were it not for this section, it would probably be improper for trustees to employ an agent to hold a receipt, in case he absconds with the purchase money. Because of the Act trustees who engage in this normal (and usually harmless) practice will not be liable merely because they appointed the solicitor. Similar protection is conferred by s. 23(3)(c) where solicitors or bankers employed to receive money under insurance policies are granted custody of the policy and the trustees' signed receipt.

9.4.2   Liability for agents since 1925

A second question then arises, which is whether trustees can be held liable in the event of the agent defaulting and causing loss to the trust. It is clear that trustees will be liable for the default of an agent whose appointment is not proper. It also seems clear that if the trustees purport to delegate their own discretions, any purported exercise of those discretions by the agent will be void and the trustees will be liable for any resulting loss.

What is less clear is the extent to which trustees who properly appoint an agent may be liable for the default of that agent. Is it sufficient that the appointment itself should be a valid exercise of the power to employ an agent, or must the trustees also use special care in selecting the agent and perhaps exercise supervision over his actions?

A failure to take reasonable care in selecting the agent, or delegation of that choice to someone else, will render the trustees liable for loss arising from his default. This follows from the fact that the choice of agent is within the trustees' own, non-delegable discretion, so that to select without proper care or to shuffle off that choice is a default on the part of the trustees.

Since 1925, however, s. 30(1) of the Trustee Act 1925 provides that:

> A trustee . . . shall be answerable and accountable only for his own acts, receipts, neglects, or defaults, and not for those of any other trustee, nor for any banker, broker, or other person with whom any trust money or securities may be deposited . . . nor for any other loss, unless the same happens through his own wilful default.

This provision substantially reproduces provisions of the Law of Property Amendment Act 1859, and under those provisions, 'wilful default' was treated as a failure to do what was reasonable, so that failure to supervise an agent might render a trustee liable. Section 23(1), however, states that trustees 'shall not be responsible for the default of any such agent if employed in good faith', which suggests that so long as the appointment was made in good faith, liability will not arise where loss is due to inadequate supervision.

In *Re Vickery* [1931] 1 Ch 572, Maugham J attempted to resolve the issue where the executor of a will had employed a solicitor to wind up the estate, giving the solicitor signed authority to collect money on deposit with the Post Office. About six months later, a beneficiary under the will informed the executor that the solicitor had previously been suspended from practice and objected to his being employed in connection with the estate. The executor pressed the solicitor for settlement, finally placing the matter with another solicitor, but by this time the original solicitor, and the money, had disappeared. Maugham J held the executor not liable, finding that the appointment had been made validly and in good faith. In interpreting the meaning of 'wilful default' within s. 30(1), he relied upon the construction reached by Romer J in *Re City Equitable Fire Insurance Co. Ltd* [1925] Ch 407. In that case it was said that a person guilty of wilful default 'knows that he is committing and intends to commit a breach of his duty, or is recklessly careless in the sense of not caring whether his act or omission is a breach of duty'. In other words, it is virtually necessary to show that the trustee is fraudulent, unless the original appointment was wrongful.

Not everybody to whom money is entrusted comes within s. 30, however. Cross J did not apply the section in *Re Lucking's WT* [1968] 1 WLR 866, where large sums of money were entrusted to a managing director who was an old friend of the trustee, and who went bankrupt having spent the money. Where the section does not apply, the standards applied in *Speight* v *Gaunt* (1884) 9 App Cas 727, considered at the beginning of section 9.4 still do.

The decision in *Re Vickery* has been much criticised on the grounds, among others, that it imported the common law meaning of 'wilful default' into equity, and that it so widens the protection of trustees under s. 23(1) as to make the rest of that section redundant. It is only a decision at first instance, of course, and so could be wrong. Nonetheless it may be suggested that, since the whole tenor of s. 23 is to allow trustees to repose confidence in their properly appointed agents, it would be a strange interpretation which required them to supervise activities which they have properly chosen to delegate as being beyond their own competence to perform.

The Law Reform Committee, in its 23rd Report on the Powers and Duties of Trustees (Cmnd 8733, 1982), approved the construction given to 'wilful default' but recommended that the reference to good faith in s. 23 should be replaced with a provision that trustees should not be liable if it was reasonable to employ an agent and if reasonable steps were taken to ensure that the agent was competent and that the work was competently done. On the whole, the Committee recognised the extent to which trusteeship is undertaken professionally today and considered that the problem lay more with the power to delegate in the first place being presently too easily available. It therefore recommended that trustees should only be able to charge the trust with the expenses of employing agents where those charges are reasonably incurred, taking into account the trustees' knowledge, qualifications, experience and level of remuneration.

9.5   FIDUCIARY NATURE OF TRUSTEESHIP

9.5.1   What relationships are fiduciary and what is their nature?

The nature of a trustee's duty towards a beneficiary is fiduciary. We are concerned in this book primarily with the duties of trustees, but it should be noted that the law also recognises other fiduciary relationships. Many of the cases considered in this section relate to other fiduciary relationships, but these cases are authoritative on trustees also.

Examples of other fiduciary relationships are those of agent and principal, company director and company, and partner and copartner. Additionally, the duties owed by solicitors, accountants, guardians and receivers are sometimes regarded as fiduciary. As will appear, the term may also encompass wider relationships and its precise extent it not entirely clear.

It is of the essence of any fiduciary relationship that the fiduciary has no personal interest in the way the duty is performed. In other words, where a fiduciary has a discretion, he must not have a personal interest in exercising the discretion in a particular way. A trustee, for example, must be motivated to benefit the trust, not himself. That is not to say that fiduciaries are not entitled to receive any benefit for their services; banks, accountants and solicitors are after all unaccustomed to working for nothing, and it will be apparent by now that trusteeship is an onerous business. The amount of their reward must not depend, however, on the manner in which their discretion is exercised.

9.5.2   Payment of trustees

In many parts of the United States, statutory rates of payment are established but in this country only the Public Trustee and a number of other trustees acting in an official capacity have any statutory entitlement to charge fees.

There are a number of ways in which trustees and other fiduciaries may be entitled to payment, but these should be regarded as exhaustive. If a trustee does not come within one of the following heads, he is not entitled to any money for the performance of his duties:

(a)   The right to remuneration may be fixed by contract between settlor and trustee at the outset: banks' charging clauses are an example of this.

(b)   Section 30(2) of the Trustee Act 1925 entitles a trustee to reimbursement for expenses from trust funds.

(c)   The courts have a jurisdiction to authorise payment. In one of the cases involving a breach of fiduciary duty considered below, *Boardman v Phipps* [1967] 2 AC 46, though a solicitor as fiduciary to a family trust was not entitled to keep profits received as a result of his position, he was held to be entitled to liberal remuneration on a *quantum meruit* basis, which is to say, on a reasonable basis for work done for the benefit of the trust, including work that had been performed gratuitously. The Court of Appeal took a similar view in *O'Sullivan v Management Agency & Music Ltd* [1985] 3 All ER 351, another case involving a breach of fiduciary duty. The remuneration included even a reasonable profit element but was not related to the actual profits obtained in breach of fiduciary duty, which had to be accounted.

In *Re Duke of Norfolk's ST* [1982] Ch 61, the Court of Appeal was prepared to exercise this jurisdiction to increase the remuneration of a trustee over the amount agreed in the original settlement. The quantity of work had increased because new property had been added to the settlement, and the tax position had been substantially altered by the introduction of capital transfer tax in 1975. The trustee was held entitled to extra remuneration for the increase in work.

In none of the above cases, however, is the amount of remuneration dependent on the manner in which the discretion (if any) of the trustee is exercised. Thus there can be no conflict between the interests of the trust and the personal interests of the trustee. Otherwise, trustees must not benefit in any way from their position as trustees. The courts refuse to allow *any possibility* that a conflict of interest may occur. Whether any conflict occurs in fact is not relevant. In other words, it is immaterial that the trust does not suffer, or even that it gains, from the activities of the trustee. The trustee has to show that there is no possible causal connection between his position and any profit made by him (outside the categories outlined above).

It will be seen, therefore, that the law is extremely strict. Some argue that it is too strict, and can stifle entrepreneurial spirit; in some of the cases below such stifling appears indeed to have occurred. This is inevitable if the law insists that a trustee is to exercise truly independent judgment, but it is arguable that the law accords too high a value to the principle of independence, and too little to the encouragement of initiative by trustees. It should be remembered that many equitable principles developed in the days when family settlements were the main variety of trust, and initiative was not therefore an especially valued asset in a trustee. Some would argue that to apply similar principles today is inapposite.

On the other hand, trustees are frequently in a position where they can defraud the beneficiaries, especially with testamentary gifts where the settlor is dead, and rigid rules may be the only way in which abuse can be prevented. It is, after all, very difficult to show that a fraud has occurred in a particular case, and perhaps the law should not require it. Furthermore, the law has the advantage of certainty. It is fairly clear what trustees may and may not do, and it is possible to negotiate terms freely before accepting appointment.

There are three main situations where a conflict of interest may arise between the trust and the personal interest of the trustee, which the law therefore prevents from arising. First, a trustee may not purchase trust property (or sell property to a trust). Secondly, he must not set himself up in competition with the trust. Thirdly, he must not make any profit by virtue of his position.

So far as remedies are concerned, any property or money acquired which can be regarded as being trust property (as in sections 9.5.3 and 9.5.5.1) will be held on constructive trust by the trustee for the beneficiaries. Where a trustee has obtained incidental profits from his office, to which he is not entitled on the basis of the principles discussed below, he can be required to 'account' (i.e., pay over to the trust) those profits. In many of the cases either remedy would be available, but in the case of the remedy of account it is unnecessary to show that the profits obtained by the trustee have ever been the property of the trust. Thus it is often a more appropriate remedy in the cases described in sections 9.5.4, 9.5.5.2 and 9.5.5.3.

9.5.3   A trustee may not purchase trust property

The principle here is that if a trustee purchases trust property, he can abuse his position and buy at less than the best price obtainable. Similarly if he sells to the trust, he may be able to demand too high a price. This principle is by no means limited to trustees, or even fiduciaries, but is applicable to any situation where the same person is effectively both seller and purchaser simultaneously. For example, when a mortgagee (who is not in a fiduciary position) exercises his powers of sale if a mortgagor defaults, there are stringent limits on selling to himself or to a company in which he has an interest — see, for example, the safeguards demanded by the Privy Council in *Tse Kwong Lam* v *Wong Chit Sen* [1983] 3 All ER 54, to ensure that if this occurs, the sale is in good faith and the best price is obtained, by taking independent advice on the method of sale and the amount of the reserve.

The rule is very strict where trustees are concerned, so that there must be no possibility of the trustee taking advantage of his position, whether he does so in fact or not. The lengths to which the law goes is shown by *Wright* v *Morgan* [1926] AC 788, where a trustee who had resigned his trusteeship purchased trust property at a price that had been fixed by independent valuers. One may have thought that not even a possibility of conflict arose here. The arrangements had been made while he was still trustee, however, and the Privy Council held that this sale must be set aside.

It is possible for purchases by trustees to be valid, but only in very exceptional circumstances. It is essential not only that the trustee paid a fair price, as he had in *Wright* v *Morgan*, but also that he took no advantage of his position and made full disclosure of his interest. For example, in *Holder* v *Holder* [1968] Ch 353 an executor (Victor) purchased two farms that were part of the estate at a fair price at an auction. It was clear, however, that Victor had not been active in his role as executor and had acquired no information as a result of it. Additionally, the plaintiff beneficiary had accepted his share of the purchase money in full knowledge of the facts, and so was disentitled from taking the action on the grounds of acquiescence.

Holder v *Holder* should not be regarded as laying down more than the narrowest of exceptions, however. The rigour of the general rule was restated by Vinelott J in *Re Thompson's Settlement* [1985] 2 All ER 720, where *Holder* v *Holder* was distinguished and almost limited to its own facts.

The same principles apply to sales of property to trusts by trustees.

9.5.4 A trustee must not set himself up in competition with the trust

Similar principles apply here, because the trustee may gain for himself the benefit of any goodwill acquired by the trust and possibly also useful information. It is not necessary to show that he has in fact done so, however.

In *Re Thomson* [1930] 1 Ch 203 an executor was restrained from carrying out a yacht-broking business in competition with the estate. The substantive issue did not come before Clauson J because the executor had, as a consequence of an earlier interlocutory injunction granted by the Court of Appeal, transferred the business to the sole beneficiary. The question of costs was still outstanding, however, and depended on whether the original action was justified. The point of interest about the case is that Clauson J, in finding against the executor, did not think it would have made any difference if he had resigned his executorship so long as he had contemplated starting a competing business while still an executor. There is a logic in this approach, because such contemplation may have affected the manner in which his duties as executor were performed. It has been argued that Clauson J's view depends on the specialist nature of the business, but it is difficult to see why this should make any difference.

9.5.5 A trustee must not make any profit by virtue of his position

9.5.5.1 Keech v Sandford

In *Keech* v *Sandford* (1726) Sel Cas Ch 61, the trustee took over the benefit of a lease which had been devised to the trust when that lease expired. Presumably he would not have been in a position to do so had he not been trustee. The lessor had refused to renew the lease for the trust, on the grounds that the beneficiary was an infant, against whom it would be difficult to recover rent. The trustee thereupon took the lease for his personal benefit, and profited from it.

There cannot have been any actual conflict of interest, because the trust itself could not have benefited, given the views of the lessor. Nor would King LC say that there was any fraud in the case, but the trustee had to assign the benefit of the lease to the infant, and account for profits received. The trustee was the one person in the world who could not take the lease for his own benefit, because by so doing he would be profiting from his position. The same principle applies where a trustee of a lease purchases for himself the freehold reversion (*Protheroe* v *Protheroe* [1968] 1 WLR 519, CA).

9.5.5.2   Other cases

The principle extends to any profits made by virtue of a fiduciary position, and if the profits are to be retained, the fiduciary must show that there is no causal connection between the position and the profit. The remedy against the fiduciary is an account of profits; in effect, the profits received are held by him as constructive trustee. It is of no moment that the trust has suffered no loss; the remedy is not compensatory in nature. It is necessary that the fiduciary accounts for all profits received in order to ensure that his duty and interest can never conflict.

For example, in *Re Macadam* [1946] Ch 73 trustees who used their position to appoint themselves to directorships of a company were held liable to account to the trust for all the fees they received as directors. This type of situation can commonly arise in private companies, because eligibility for appointment to directorships can depend on the legal ownership of a minimum number of shares, and indeed trustees may be under a duty to procure their representation on the board if it is necessary in order to safeguard the value of the trust shares.

Similar principles apply to anyone in a fiduciary position, an extreme example, where the term 'fiduciary' was used in a very wide sense, being the House of Lords decision in *Reading* v *Attorney-General* [1951] AC 507. Reading had been a sergeant in the British Army, and had made at least £19,000 illegally by helping smugglers to transport smuggled goods by riding in the lorries in his uniform. Unfortunately for Reading, the £19,000 was confiscated and he was forced into the role of plaintiff, petitioning for its return. He failed because as a fiduciary he was liable to account for his profits to the Crown. It is not easy to appreciate why an army sergeant is employed in a fiduciary capacity, but the use of the uniform to deceive the authorities may be the decisive factor.

The causal connection between position and profit must be established, however. It was not in *Re Dover Coalfield Extension Ltd* [1908] 1 Ch 65, a case similar to *Re Macadam*, but where a trustee had already become a director before becoming trustee. Similarly, in *Re Gee* [1948] Ch 284, although a trustee became a director after refraining from using a vote, exercisable by virtue of his holding trust shares, he would have been elected anyway, however he had voted (even if he had voted against himself), by virtue of the votes of the other shareholders. Harman J held that the remuneration received as director was not accountable to the trust. In neither of these cases could it be said that the trustees had made any profit by virtue of their position.

9.5.5.3   Cases involving information received as fiduciary

Cases where profits are made from information acquired in a fiduciary position are really only a specific application of the general principles enunciated in the previous section. An example is *Industrial Development Consultants Ltd* v *Cooley* [1972] 1 WLR 443. The defendant, a managing director for the plaintiff company, had been negotiating on their behalf a contract with the Eastern Gas Board. The negotiations failed and it was clear that the Eastern Gas Board objected to the plaintiff company particularly. In other words, it appeared that whatever the defendant had done, the negotiations would have failed, and so the plaintiff company suffered no loss as a result of the defendant's subsequent action.

The Eastern Gas Board then began negotiations with the defendant personally, and the end result was that he terminated his contract with the plaintiff company, and contracted with the Eastern Gas Board himself, on similar terms to those originally proposed on behalf of the plaintiff company. Roskill J held that the defendant was constructive trustee of the benefit of the contract for the plaintiff company. It is a similar case to *Re Macadam*, except that the causal factor here was not the voting power of a trustee, but information acquired in a fiduciary capacity.

A case which has given rise to much greater controversy is that of *Boardman* v *Phipps* [1967] 2 AC 46. Boardman was solicitor to a trust, whose property included a large (but not majority) holding in a public company. He became worried about the competence of the management of the company and tried to persuade the managing trustee of the trust to acquire a majority holding in the company. His attempts at persuasion were unsuccessful, so Boardman decided to make the acquisition himself. He did so and then, by selling off some of the assets of the newly acquired company, Boardman made a large profit for himself. Additionally, however, because the trust still had a large share in the same company, his activities resulted in a large profit for the trust as well. The fact that the trust benefited is one of the reasons for the controversy surrounding the case, but surely it is in fact irrelevant.

In most respects this was simply a personal transaction by Boardman, resulting in a personal profit to him. Unfortunately, however, it appeared that in negotiating for the majority shareholding he had, in good faith, obtained information in his capacity as solicitor to the trust, which he would not otherwise have obtained. The House of Lords therefore held (by a 3–2 majority) that he held the shares acquired as constructive trustee for the trust, and that he must account for the profit made. It was immaterial that he acted in good faith. He was, however, entitled to generous remuneration on a *quantum meruit* basis, on the principles discussed in section 9.5.2.

One view of the case, adopted by Lords Hodson and Guest, was that the information obtained was trust property. This view is open to criticism (e.g., Gareth Jones (1968) 84 LQR 472) but it is not in fact a necessary step in the reasoning, at least so far as an account of profits remedy is concerned. The case is surely an application of the principle that one must not profit from a fiduciary position. The problem really is whether a causal relationship is established, and the dissenting judges, Viscount Dilhorne and Lord Upjohn, seemed to take the view that it was not because the trustees never had any intention of purchasing the shares for the trust. This may not, however, be the relevant question; arguably the question should have been: 'Would Boardman have gone ahead anyway even without the information acquired by virtue of his fiduciary position?'

If so, there is no causal connection between the position and the profit, and the case is like *Re Gee*. If not, it is an application of *Re Macadam*, and Boardman should have been held to account.

Oakley argues (*Constructive Trusts*, pp. 48–9) that an intermediate course could have been taken, based on the Court of Appeal decision in *Seager* v *Copydex Ltd* [1967] 1 WLR 923, where confidential information was effectively given a value, and damages awarded on the basis of that value. The argument as applied to *Boardman* v *Phipps* would allow Boardman to keep his profit, but subject to a damages claim for wrongful use of confidential information. The solution has the merit of rewarding Boardman for his enterprise, while nonetheless recognising that he may have acted wrongfully in relation to the trust.

I am not convinced that a middle course is desirable, however, and wonder whether the outcry about the case does not derive from the undoubted but irrelevant fact that the trust greatly benefited from Boardman's activities. Boardman was liberally rewarded for benefiting the trust, and claimed to be allowed to keep speculative profits. There is no reason why private speculators should not be allowed to do so, but those who are acting as fiduciaries accept by taking on fiduciary positions that their remuneration is limited to the categories described above, however much they benefit the other party. All the cases point to this conclusion, and as a result trustees, discretion can be exercised in an independent manner. The real issue surely is which category Boardman fell into.

9.6   TERMINATION OF TRUSTEESHIP

9.6.1   Retirement

We saw in section 9.2.2, how in principle the office of trustee is lifelong. Nevertheless, a trustee may voluntarily retire in one of several ways:

(a)   He may take advantage of any power to retire contained in the trust instrument, although such a power is nowadays uncommon.

(b)   If someone can be found to replace him, he may retire under the provisions of s. 36(1) of the Trustee Act 1925 (see section 9.2.4.2).

(c)   He may retire under the provisions of s.39 of the Act even without replacement, under the following conditions:

(i)   his retirement must leave the trust with not less than two private trustees or a trust corporation to act for it; and

(ii)   the remaining trustees must consent to his retirement; and

(iii)   anyone empowered to appoint trustees must consent.

Retirement, and any necessary consents, must be in the form of a deed. Unlike s. 36(1), s. 39 does not permit retirement from part only of a trust.

(d) The beneficiaries may consent to his retirement, so as to debar themselves from holding the trustee accountable for any event arising after the date of such consent. This is only an aspect of the rule that a beneficiary who consents to a breach of trust has no right of action in respect of that breach (see section 11.2) and, unless all are *sui juris* (i.e., suffering from no incapacities, such as infancy or mental handicap) and collectively entitled to the entire trust property, the trustee will not obtain his discharge from the trust. It will also be prudent to obtain the consents of the other trustees, to avert any claim by them to an indemnity.

(e) The court may discharge a trustee without replacing him under its inherent jurisdiction, but will not do so if this would leave the trust without a trustee. In such a case it may make an order for administration of the trust by the court, so that the trustee remains in office but is relieved of responsibility. Alternatively, if the trustee pays the entire trust fund into court, he thereby loses the right to exercise any of his discretionary powers in the trust, which amounts to virtual retirement. He remains in office for the purpose of receiving notices of dealings with the trust property, however, and may be made a party to any action brought by the fund.

Though the once-and-for-all nature of trusteeship looks harsh in theory, in practice the statutory provisions for retirement are almost always sufficient.

9.6.2 Death of a trustee

Trustees hold their office, and the trust property, jointly. There is a right of survivorship with joint tenancies so that, upon the death of a trustee, his office and the trust estate devolve on the survivors. As we saw in section 1.2.6, one of the attractions of the early use was its ability to allow estates to pass from generation to generation with few conveyances of legal titles. This was achieved in part by vesting the legal title in a number of feoffees to uses jointly and relying on the right of survivorship on the death of any one of them. Trusts today operate in the same way and for essentially similar reasons.

The equitable rule was codified in s. 18(1) of the Trustee Act 1925, which provides:

Where a power or trust is given to or imposed on two or more trustees jointly, the same may be exercised or performed by the survivors or survivor of them for the time being.

If one trustee dies, then, the rest may carry on the trust without interruption, subject to the possible need to appoint a replacement if the numbers have been reduced below what is required for effective management.

Although the trust property vests automatically in the survivors, due steps should be taken to ensure that any register or document of title is brought up to date.

When a sole surviving trustee dies, the trust property devolves on his personal representatives and is held by them on the terms of the trust. Section 18(2) enables the personal representatives to exercise all the powers of the former trustee, although they are not obliged to do so. The personal representatives can only act until new trustees are appointed. Often, they will themselves be the persons having the power to appoint (see section 9.2.4.2).

9.6.3 Removal of a trustee

A trustee may be removed against his will in any of the following ways:

(a)   Under an express power in the trust instrument. Such power is almost never inserted in a domestic trust, and if it exists it will be strictly construed. More commonly it is found in certain commercial transactions. A common example is an equitable mortgage effected by depositing the title deeds with the lender, where the mortgagor may declare himself a trustee of the legal estate for the lender. In turn, the lender is likely to reserve a power to remove and replace the mortgagor as trustee — simply a means of protecting himself.

(b)   He may be removed, under s. 36(1) of the Trustee Act 1925 if he remains out of the United Kingdom for more than 12 months, refuses or is unfit to act or is incapable of acting, by the appointment of some other person to act in his place.

(c)   He may be removed by the court either in the exercise of its jurisdiction under s. 41 of the Trustee Act 1925, where the appointment of a new trustee may involve removing an existing trustee, or under its inherent jurisdiction where an action for the administration of the trust is brought.

Removal is not a step to be taken lightly, but it is not necessary to show misconduct. Friction between trustees may be a ground for removing one (*Re Henderson* [1940] Ch 764). A mere dispute between the trustee and the beneficiaries over the manner in which the trustee exercises his discretions will not generally suffice, but it may be proper to take this into account. The main consideration will always be the welfare of the beneficiaries (*Letterstedt* v *Broers* (1884) 9 App Cas 371, PC).

Unless removal is urgently necessary, however, the court is reluctant to worsen the position of the trustee by so doing, as where he may lose security for costs payable to him in the event of a successful appeal (*Re Pauling's ST (No. 2)* [1963] Ch 576).

10

Trustees II: Powers, Discretions and Duties

10.1 GENERAL DESCRIPTION AND OVERVIEW

10.1.1 Powers and duties

Equity equips trustees with a number of powers, and imposes also a range of duties, most of which may be modified or excluded by the express terms of the particular trust. *(directly)*   *depends on S'ors intention*

The distinction between trusts and powers has been considered in section 2.5. A similar distinction exists between the duties of the trustee's office on the one hand, and his powers or discretions on the other. Trustees have a discretion as to whether or not they will exercise a power, and if after proper consideration they decide in good faith not to exercise it, the beneficiaries have no ground for complaint. Generally speaking, however, there will be a duty to undertake such consideration where it would be appropriate. There is, of course, no discretion as to whether to fulfil a duty, but there may be an element of discretion as to how precisely a duty is fulfilled, as in the selection of investments.

10.1.2 What are the powers and duties?

In view of the different types of situation in which trusts come into being, it is only to be expected that powers and duties will vary according to the character of the trust, for example, whether the trustees are required to accumulate or distribute income and so on.

However, it will be seen that some kinds of power are in principle widely available to trustees. Most of these are now statutory and they are chiefly concerned with facilitating the management of the trust.

Generally, therefore, trustees will be under an obligation to invest the funds in authorised securities according to the powers given to them by the trust instrument or under the Trustee Investments Act 1961, discussed in section 10.6. In so doing, they must take expert advice where necessary, and make any adjustments required by the equitable rules of apportionment, which, as we shall see in section 10.7.2, are designed to preserve a fair balance between capital and income. They must also ensure the proper payment of tax. At some stage, they may have to consider matters such as the sale of trust property, provision for infant beneficiaries and the exercise of any powers of appointment. Accounts must be kept and copies of these supplied to the beneficiaries. It is usual and desirable for trustees to meet at appropriate intervals to transact the trust business, and minutes of these meetings, and a trust diary or minute-book, will be kept.

The trust instrument itself will usually give additional powers appropriate to the particular trust, which in the case of the modern tax-saving trust may be very wide indeed. Older trusts are somewhat less likely to grant extensive additional powers, and here the statutory powers are more important. They are nevertheless also of relevance in the modern style of trust, for they will be incorporated into the trust to the extent that they are not expressly excluded by the trust instrument, and may be useful if for any reason it proves impossible to rely upon a specially given power.

The duties of trustees will similarly vary, depending on the nature of the trust. Here, it is possible to state that there are certain fundamental duties arising from the fiduciary nature of the trustee, and these affect all trustees. The duty of loyalty, i.e., the duty not to make a personal profit from the trust, considered in section 9.5, is an example.

Other duties relate to the safe keeping of the trust property, and include the duty to maintain proper custody of documents of title, the duty to invest etc. The extent to which these apply depends upon the character of the trust property. Trustees also have duties towards the beneficiaries (see section 10.7), such as the duty to inform them of their rights and to provide them with information regarding the affairs of the trust, and the duty to distribute the property in accordance with their entitlements. They must also consider the need to maintain fairness between the beneficiaries, and select investments which preserve a balance between the interests of the income beneficiaries and those interested in the capital of the fund.

Some duties may be, and frequently are, modified by the trust instrument: the insertion of a charging clause, also considered in section 9.5 is an example. Others, such as the duty to make proper distribution, are inherent in the nature of any trust, although even here the trust instrument may limit the personal liability of the trustees in the event of a breach.

It will be apparent that the administration of all but the simplest trusts calls for a considerable degree of business competence, and nowadays most trusts of any size will have a professional trustee such as a bank or trust corporation to act for them. The professional may act either as sole trustee, or in conjunction with one or more individuals. This sort of mixture can be useful in family settlements, combining the expertise of the professional with the more intimate knowledge of family circumstances supplied by the private trustee.

A recent illustration of the difficulties which can arise where private trustees lack professional guidance arose in *Turner* v *Turner* [1984] Ch 100, where private trustees exercised powers of appointment at the behest of the settlor, not appreciating the duty to consider the exercise of the power which attached to their office (the nature of which is discussed in chapter 2). They thus acted in breach of trust and most of the appointments so made were held void.

10.1.3   Constructive trusts

This chapter is about express trusts. Constructive trustees are in a peculiar position, for they hold under a trust imposed by operation of law, and although the circumstances may be such that it is perfectly obvious to the constructive trustee that he is holding the legal estate in the property on trust for someone else (as might occur, for example, on facts similar to those in *Hodgson* v *Marks* [1971] Ch 892, see section 3.5), it is equally possible that the constructive trustee may be entirely ignorant of the fact that he holds on trust until such time as the issue is determined by a court. Such may be the case, for example, where he takes property as a purchaser with constructive notice of a trust or takes as a volunteer (i.e., not giving value) with no notice at all.

It is improbable that a constructive trustee is under comparable duties to those of an express trustee in the matter of investing trust property, and it would certainly be harsh to hold him liable for, e.g., non-investment or non-apportionment when he may be entirely unaware of the beneficiaries' claims.

The duties of constructive trustees are uncertain, and it may be that the only duty is that of holding the property or its proceeds (and perhaps any profits) on behalf of the beneficiaries. But much may turn upon the conduct of the trustee, and a constructive trustee who fraudulently misapplies property subject to a trust may be placed under a more onerous liability than one who has acted innocently.

10.2   SALE OF TRUST PROPERTY

A power to sell some or all of the trust property is usually given by the trust instrument, either expressly or by implication, and even in the absence of such power, trustees will often be permitted to sell by statute or, as a last resort, by order of the court. Some specific cases require consideration.

10.2.1   Settled land

The powers and duties which derive from the Settled Land Act 1925 are unique, and quite different from those which operate under any other trust.

As was explained in section 1.6.4, settled land today is very rare (though land is sometimes accidentally settled, especially by people who make wills without taking legal advice). We saw in that section how the Settled Land Act 1925 creates in effect a statutory trust of the land. It is most unusual, however, because virtually the sole function of the trustees of the settlement is to take the proceeds if the land is sold, so as to protect the (overreached) interests of the beneficiaries under the trusts of the settlement. The legal estate (fee simple absolute in possession) and the powers of sale are vested not in them but in the tenant for life. Further, very little limit is placed on the power of the tenant for life to sell the land—he has far more extensive powers than a normal trustee in this regard.

10.2.2 Trusts for sale of land

The nature of the trustees' powers to sell in this case have been covered in section 2.7.2.

10.2.3 Other trusts of land

It is possible to have a trust of land which involves neither a strict settlement nor a trust for sale, e.g., a sole trustee holding the land on a simple bare trust. An example is *Hodgson* v *Marks* [1971] Ch 892 (see section 3.5.1.3.2), which is a very unusual case. Indeed, from a land law perspective, one of the difficulties of that case was precisely that it was so unconventional, and did not therefore fall within the overreaching or registration provisions of the 1925 legislation.

Even with this type of trust, the trustee will have a power to sell under s. 1(1) of the Trustee Investments Act 1961 (considered below) unless the trust instrument, assuming there is one (there was not in *Hodgson* v *Marks*), specifically prohibits sale.

Trustees (except of settled land) are given further powers to sell or mortgage property, where they are required to pay out or apply capital, by the Trustee Act 1925, s. 16.

10.2.4 Personal property

Section 16, or s. 1(1) of the Trustee Investments Act 1961 will generally be wide enough to enable trustees to raise money from the sale of chattels where necessary, even if no such power is expressly or impliedly given by the trust instrument itself.

Chattels which are heirlooms, i.e., intended to devolve with land subject to a settlement through successive generations, are governed by the Settled Land Act 1925, and may be sold only by the tenant for life upon obtaining a court order.

Section 57 of the Trustee Act 1925 empowers the court to authorise the sale, lease, mortgage, surrender, release or other disposition of property subject to a trust whenever it considers such a transaction expedient but where the trustees lack the necessary power. Again, the section does not apply to a strict settlement.

10.2.5 Standard of care

In exercising their powers of sale, trustees have an overriding duty to obtain the best price they can on behalf of the beneficiaries, and while there may be circumstances in which it will be proper to reject the highest offer if it is suspect, the trustees will be in breach of their duty if they permit ethical considerations to entice them into accepting a lower price. This may require trustees to resile from an agreement on later receiving a better offer.

Trustees may thus be faced with a difficult choice between a quick and sure sale on the one hand, and holding on for a better price on the other. For example, in *Fry* v *Fry* (1859) 28 LJ Ch 591 the testator, owner of an inn, directed that it should be sold 'as soon as convenient'. His executors refused an offer of £900 and held on in the hope of a better one. Meantime, the coming of the railway took away the inn's trade, and the inn was finally sold at a much lower price, leaving the executors liable to make up the difference between the actual selling price and the offer of £900 out of their own pockets.

10.2.6 Power to give receipts

The power to sell or otherwise deal with trust property is of little value unless the purchaser can obtain a valid receipt for his money, and so s. 14(1) of the Trustee Act 1925 gives a power, notwithstanding anything to the contrary in the trust instrument, to give an effective receipt. The receipt in writing of a trustee is thus effective to exonerate a purchaser from any obligation to see that the trustees apply the money in accordance with the trust—a necessary provision since a purchaser who was aware that the property was held on trust might otherwise be taken to hold it as constructive trustee under the bona fide purchaser doctrine (see section 1.4.6).

It is likely that nothing in the section affects the principle that if there is more than one trustee, a receipt to be valid must be given by all jointly. Also, in the case of settled land or trusts for sale of land, the purchase money must be paid to two trustees in order effectively to overreach the beneficial interests.

10.3 POWER TO INSURE

In the absence of any express provision in the trust instrument, trustees are under no duty to insure the trust property, and will not be liable for failure to insure if subsequent loss or damage occurs. Nor, in general, does the trustee have any power to insure, unless given expressly by the trust instrument.

An exception is s. 19 of the Trustee Act 1925, which gives trustees a limited power to insure against loss or damage by fire (but not against other insurable risks) any building or other insurable property, up to three-quarters of its value, and pay the premiums out of the trust income. The section does not apply where property is held on a bare trust.

The rationale, it seems, for the absence of any implied duty or power to insure, is to guard against the possibility that the premiums will make significant inroads into the trust income. It should be remembered that the principles developed before the introduction of modern forms of insurance, and many prudent commercial men today would regard insurance as a most elementary precaution. The Law Reform Committee, in its 23rd Report, on the Powers and Duties of Trustees (Cmnd 8733, 1982), recommends that trustees should be under a positive duty to insure whenever a prudent man of business would do so, up to the full value of the property if necessary.

All the above applies only to first-party insurance of the trust property. There is nothing to stop the trustees insuring *themselves* for third-party liability towards the trust in the event of their own breach, though they cannot reimburse themselves from the trust property for the premiums they pay on insuring themselves.

10.4   POWER TO COMPOUND LIABILITIES

As legal owner, a trustee has the right to maintain an action with regard to the trust property. Where the claim is itself a legal claim, only the trustee as legal owner will be able to sue. This is of importance where debts are owed to the trust. It may be the duty of the trustee, for example, to pursue the claims of the trust by proving in the bankruptcy of a debtor.

The pursuit of legal claims, and the possibility of compromise, are not easily amenable to absolute duties, but require a discretionary element. Litigation is, after all, a risky business. Even in an apparently cut-and-dried situation like the bankruptcy of a debtor, the costs of proving in bankruptcy may outweigh any likely benefits to the trust, in which case a trustee should not pursue the matter.

Section 15 of the Trustee Act 1925 therefore provides trustees with an element of discretion in dealing with persons who are involved in contention with the trust, who in practice will usually be persons who owe it money. As they think fit, trustees may enter into a range of transactions of the sort which businessmen would often enter, for example, accepting compositions of debts, allowing time for payment of debts and so on. Provided the trustees act in good faith, they will not be responsible for any loss arising from the exercise of these powers.

In exercising their discretion, the trustees should consider the wishes of the beneficiaries, but are not bound to act in accordance with them. The section also applies to personal representatives.

10.5   MAINTENANCE AND ADVANCEMENT

The powers of maintenance and advancement are appropriate to family-type settlements, which are described in section 2.1. They have the object of providing for infant beneficiaries (under 18) who are not as yet entitled to any of the income or capital but who require financial support during their minority.

Payments by way of maintenance are payments out of income, in theory to provide for routine necessities such as education or board and lodging, while payments by way of advancement are sums advanced from capital, in theory to cover major costs such as setting up the infant in his profession.

Originally such payments were made for their theoretical purposes but in recent decades, significant use has also been made of these powers in reducing the tax liability of trusts (see chapter 13). For example, early advancements of capital could until 1975 be effective to avoid liability to estate duty entirely, and even now can be used to reduce capital transfer tax (or from 1986, inheritance tax) liability, while the purpose of maintenance payments is often to reduce liability for income tax. The real (but often hidden) issues arising in this section are the extent to which schemes intended purely to save tax can be valid.

10.5.1 Maintenance

A power to maintain is not implied into the trust instrument. Therefore it must be expressly given, or advantage may be taken of the power contained in s. 31 of the Trustee Act 1925. The statutory power operates provided no contrary intention is expressed. But where the statutory power is expressly excluded it cannot be used, even if an express power turns out to be useless. In *Re Erskine's ST* [1971] 1 WLR 162, a settlement contained a provision for accumulation which was void for perpetuity. But since the statutory power to maintain was excluded by the provisions of the trust instrument, the income which the trustees had accumulated could not be applied for the beneficiary, and resulted to the settlor's estate.

10.5.1.1 Statutory power
The power to maintain under s. 31(1) can only arise where the beneficiary is entitled to receive intermediate income under the trust. This will be the case either where his interest is vested (unless a contrary intention is shown, as by a specific grant of that income to someone other than the beneficiary) or where it is a contingent interest which carries the intermediate income. If there are prior interests, or if the beneficiary's interest is as a member of a class of discretionary beneficiaries, the power will not be available at all.

The question of whether contingent gifts carry the intermediate income is dealt with by complex rules, which seem to reflect no coherent policy and are beyond the scope of an introductory book. These rules derive from a combination of case law, s. 175 of the Law of Property Act 1925, and s. 31(3) of the Trustee Act 1925.

Assuming income to be available, the trustees have a discretion as to whether to maintain the beneficiary. Section 31 directs them to have regard to the age and requirements of the infant, whether any other income is available for his maintenance, and generally to the circumstances of the case. The money may be paid to the parent or guardian of the infant or directly for his benefit, e.g., school fees. If the infant is married, they may pay it directly to him.

Subject to contrary intention in the trust instrument, the power to maintain ceases when the beneficiary reaches the age of majority. Even if by then his interest is still contingent, the trustees must pay the whole of the income to him until he obtains a vested interest or dies.

10.5.1.2   Court's inherent jurisdiction
The court has inherent jurisdiction to approve the use of income or even capital for the maintenance of infant beneficiaries, but in practice this is rarely necessary.

10.5.2   Advancement

The power of advancement permits trustees to pay capital sums to or on behalf of a beneficiary some time before he is entitled to claim the fund. The power may be given by the trust instrument or, subject to contrary intention, the power contained in s. 32 of the Trustee Act 1925 may be used.

Section 32 allows trustees at any time to pay or apply capital money for the 'advancement or benefit' of any person entitled to that capital or a share thereof. Subject to that limitation, the powers are wide, applying, for example, whether the interest is vested or contingent, or whether in possession, remainder or reversion. Up to one-half of the beneficiary's share may be advanced.

The trustees' discretion whether to make an advancement is absolute, so long as it is for the 'advancement or benefit' of the beneficiary. The ambit of the power is very wide, and it appears to be possible to use it for schemes which are frankly intended only to save taxation.

The House of Lords decision in *Pilkington* v *IRC* [1964] AC 612 is the leading case. The trustees proposed to advance one-half of the share of a two-year-old girl (Penelope) and resettle it. The child was in no need of the moneys advanced, and too young for the traditional purposes of advancement to be relevant. The only benefit to her would be the effect of saving estate duty which would otherwise have been payable on the death of her father, the life tenant of the trust, and one of the issues was whether this was a sufficient 'benefit'. The resettlement was also actually disadvantageous to her, inasmuch as her entitlement to the capital on the advanced funds was postponed until she reached 30. Others apart from Penelope stood to benefit, however, if Penelope died before reaching 30, in addition to which the other income beneficiaries necessarily benefited from the postponement of her entitlement to the capital.

The House of Lords held that none of these factors rendered the proposed exercise of the power objectionable. There was no need to show that the advancement was to meet some personal need of the beneficiary, and the saving of estate duty was itself a sufficient benefit. Nor was it relevant that other persons might benefit if the provision as a whole would benefit Penelope.

In fact, however, the resettlement in *Pilkington* infringed the rule against perpetuities as it then stood. Thus, although the advancement was valid, the resettlement was not.

The trustees must be satisfied that an advancement will be for the benefit of the beneficiary, and also that it will in fact be applied for the purpose. In *Re Pauling's ST* [1964] Ch 303, the Court of Appeal held that the trustees could pay the money to the beneficiary for his use only if they considered that he could be trusted. If they decide to make him an advancement for a particular purpose, they must ask themselves whether he will carry it out: they should not make a payment for a purpose and then leave him free to do with it as he pleases. The question was left open as to whether trustees can recover money which the beneficiary requests but then applies for some quite different purpose.

10.6 DUTY TO PROTECT THE TRUST ASSETS: INVESTMENT

This is a continuing duty which begins with the collection of the assets upon assuming office, and ends only with the final distribution of the property among those entitled to it.

10.6.1 Initial duties

From the outset, trustees must acquaint themselves with the terms of the trust and the state of the property they are to hold, ensure that funds are appropriately invested, and see that all securities and chattels are in proper custody. If there is property outstanding, all proper steps must be taken to gather it in.

In *Re Brogden* (1888) 38 ChD 546, trustees were held liable where they refrained from suing to enforce a covenant to pay £10,000 into the settlement, although their motive was their reluctance to endanger the family business, of which the covenantor's estate formed the major part. In *Ward* v *Ward* (1843) 2 HL Cas 777 n, trustees were not liable for failure to sue a beneficiary who might have been ruined by the action, along with his family who were also beneficiaries, but this is probably an extreme case. In *Re Brogden*, the Court of Appeal held that the only excuse for failure to enforce payments due to trust was the well-founded belief that action would be fruitless.

As we saw in section 10.4, however, trustees have power by s. 15 of the Trustee Act 1925 to compromise actions, compound liabilities and allow time for payment of debts, and will not be liable for the exercise of these powers in good faith.

10.6.2 Protection of assets by investment

10.6.2.1 *General principles*

Once the assets are in, they must be protected, and an important aspect of this is the selection of proper investments. Investment is today more than ever a field for experts, and only a broad outline of trustees' duties in this regard can be given here. Two main principles operate, however. First, trustees have a general duty to act fairly as between the beneficiaries, and secondly there are limitations on risky investments.

The first principle dictates, for example, that investments must be selected which produce income for the income beneficiaries while at the same time preserving the capital for those ultimately entitled to it. This rules out certain popular forms of investment such as antiques or a wine cellar, since these produce only capital appreciation and no income.

There is also a general duty to diversify, that is, to spread the risks of investment by spreading the funds between different investments.

So far as the second principle is concerned, the law is extremely cautious. Nowadays it is therefore usual to give trustees extremely wide powers expressly, and further authority to amend if necessary. The general law is therefore of rather limited practical application, save where the express power fails to cover all the property in the trust. Wherever possible, it is usual to exclude the operation of the Trustee Investments Act 1961, which after a quarter of a century is somewhat out of touch with contemporary investment practice. If all else fails, the court may be persuaded to extend the trustees' investment powers under the Variation of Trusts Act 1958 (see section 12.2.4).

10.6.2.2   Trustee Investments Act 1961

This section is concerned with the unusual position where no express provisions are made in the trust instrument.

Until 1961, there was no general power to invest in equities (ordinary shares) at all. The Trustee Investments Act 1961, which repealed and replaced s. 1 of the Trustee Act 1925, was designed to give trustees the power to invest a portion of the trust fund in equities (i.e., the purchase of ordinary shares in companies), which otherwise would have required express power in the trust instrument.

Trustees who wish to take advantage of the Act are required to divide the fund into two parts, equal at the time of division and called the narrower-range part and the wider-range part. Only the wider-range part can be invested in ordinary shares, so the provision limits the proportion of the fund that can be invested in that way. For the purpose of this division, they should obtain a valuation, which if made in writing by a person believed by the trustees to be qualified will be conclusive. After the initial division, there is no need to ensure that both parts remain equally valuable, but any additions to the fund must be equally split between the two parts.

A list of authorised investments is provided in the First Schedule to the Act, and Parts I and II of the Schedule both deal with narrower-range investments. Those in Part I are fixed-interest investments where the capital value does not fluctuate, and trustees may select these without taking any expert advice. They include such things as National Savings Certificates and National Savings Indexed-Income Bonds. Those listed in Part II may fluctuate, and expert advice must be obtained before selecting these investments, which include government securities, deposits with building societies and mortgages of freeholds or long leaseholds.

Part III deals with wider-range investments, in which the trustees may invest the wider-range part of their fund. There is no obligation to do so, and even after making a division they may decide to keep all investments within the narrower range. If they decide to invest the wider-range part in ordinary shares, they must select shares which are quoted on the UK Stock Exchange, are fully paid up (or required to be so within nine months of issue), and are issued by a company whose issued and paid-up capital is at least £1 million and which has paid a dividend on all its shares which rank for dividend within each of the immediately preceding five years.

If property accrues to either part of the fund, such as a bonus issue of shares accruing to the wider-range part, the accrual remains with that part. Any other addition to the trust fund, however, such as where the trustees choose to purchase under a rights issue, must be apportioned between the two parts so that each is increased in value by the same amount. This can be done directly, or by making a compensating transfer from one part to the other.

If the trustees decide to withdraw property from the trust fund in the exercise of any of their powers or duties, they have a discretion as to which part they will use, and no compensating transfer is necessary. They may wish to do this, for example, to set up a separate fund by way of provision for an infant beneficiary. If they set up a separate fund out of a fund which is already divided into the narrower-range and wider-range parts, the new fund must also be divided, either into equal halves, or into the same proportions as the two parts of the original fund bore to each other when the separate fund was removed, or in some proportion intermediate between these two, if the trustees wish to use the powers of the Act in relation to the new separate fund.

10.6.2.3   Investment outside the 1961 Act

Express powers to invest outside the Act are known as 'special powers', usually given to allow trustees to invest in private companies, which would not otherwise be authorised investments, or in the purchase of land. If the whole property of the trust is encompassed by these special powers, then the Act will be irrelevant, but if not, the trustees must, if they wish to use the investment powers of the Act, divide the trust property into three parts. The special-range part will consist of such property as is encompassed by the express powers, and the rest will be split into equal narrower-range and wider-range parts, to which the rules mentioned in section 10.6.2.2 will then apply. Accruals to special-range property join the special-range part of the fund, but if any special-range property is to be converted out of the special range, it must be apportioned equally between the narrower-range and wider-range parts of the fund, or a compensating transfer must be made.

10.6.2.4   Criteria for choice of investment

Trustees must not, of course, make unauthorised investments, but even in selecting those which are authorised they must exercise the usual standard of care, bearing in mind that the trustees are not acting for themselves but for others. This standard of care applies to investments under express powers as well as those granted under the 1961 Act.

In this context, the usual standard of care is that which 'an ordinary prudent man would take if he were minded to make an investment for the benefit of other people for whom he felt morally bound to provide' (see the judgment of Lindley MR in *Re Whitely* (1886) 33 ChD 347, 355, adopted by Brightman J in *Bartlett* v *Barclay's Bank Trust Co. Ltd (No. 1)* [1980] Ch 515).

This may require the trustees to set aside their personal views as to the desirability of particular investments. They must not refuse to invest in, e.g., armaments, if such investment is in the best financial interests of the beneficiaries, although if all the beneficiaries were adult they might take into account their views on the impropriety of a proposed investment (see *Cowan* v *Scargill* [1984] 3 WLR 501).

By s. 6(1) trustees are required to have regard both to the need for diversification and the suitability of the proposed investment to the trust. Presumably, then, trustees might reasonably refrain from investments which are at odds with the purposes of a charitable trust.

Any investment in Part II or Part III of the First Schedule must be made on the basis of advice, even if the power to invest in these Parts derives from an express special power. The advice must be in writing, and must come from someone whom the trustee reasonably believes is qualified to advise, unless the advice is being given by a trustee to his fellow trustees, or where, as in the case of a trust corporation, the decisions on investment are in the hands of servants competent to advise.

Obtaining advice does not permit the trustee to place blind faith in his adviser, because the final decision cannot be delegated. He must consider the advice, and reach his own decision as a prudent man of business. Where advice was initially required, trustees must also consider at what intervals further advice should be sought upon the retention of the investment, and may incur liability if failure to exercise due consideration results in a loss.

Special considerations apply where an investment by way of mortgage is proposed.

Trusts which comprise a controlling interest in a company also require brief mention, since shares in a private company are a fairly common form of trust property. Since the trustees as legal owners of the shares may be in a position to control the activities of the directors, the question arises as to whether their duty to safeguard trust assets extends to attempting to direct the policy of a commercial enterprise.

In *Re Lucking's WT* [1968] 1 WLR 866, Cross J suggested that a controlling shareholder should insist upon representation on the board, and in any event, the trustees must avail themselves of the fullest possible information as to the state of the company in order to safeguard the beneficiaries. In *Bartlett* v *Barclays Bank Trust Co. Ltd (No. 1)* [1980] Ch 515, a series of speculations led to a large overall loss to the trust, and Brightman J was of the view that the trustees should, if necessary, be prepared to remove the board. The principle seems clear: trustees in this situation must, if necessary, curb possible beneficial speculations to avoid the risk of their going wrong. They cannot shelter behind the acts of the directors where they themselves are in a position to control those acts.

Trustees are obliged to invest within a reasonable time, and in the meantime the fund should be placed on deposit with a bank, so as to produce at least some interest. If the trustees unreasonably fail to find an investment for the trust funds, they will be liable themselves to pay interest to the fund.

10.6.2.5 Retaining an investment

Liability may arise not only through the making of unauthorised investments, but also from the improper retention of an investment.

The retention of even an authorised investment may in certain circumstances be improper. Where the 1961 Act applies, and the trustees have made investments for which advice is required (i.e., those within Parts II and III of Schedule 1 to the Act) they must also determine at what intervals advice should be sought on the question of retaining the investment (s. 6(3)).

By s. 4 of the Trustee Act 1925, trustees are protected from liability for breach arising only of continuing to hold an investment which has ceased to be authorised. There will still be a duty to consider the propriety of retaining the investment, however, for the section does not confer protection when a duty to realise the investment has arisen on some other ground than the investment having become unauthorised.

These provisions apart, the standard of care is as before, so the trustees will not be liable, according to Lindley LJ in *Re Chapman* [1896] 2 Ch 763, 776, if they have acted 'honestly and prudently, in the belief that [retention] was the best course to take in the interests of all the parties'. A mere error of business judgment will not therefore amount to a breach of trust in these circumstances.

In order to meet the standards of the prudent man of business, of course, it may be necessary to take advice and periodically to review the trust investments, quite apart from the requirements of s. 6(3) of the 1961 Act.

In the unusual case of the trustees being restricted by the trust instrument to a single investment (as in the case, perhaps, of a private company or a pension fund limited to investment in a single industry), the lack of power to switch investments could in theory pose serious problems for the trustees. It seems unlikely that they must passively watch the funds deteriorate: business prudence would appear to require that they should apply to the court under s. 57 of the Trustee Act 1925 for any necessary additional powers to preserve the funds.

10.7 DUTIES OF TRUSTEES TOWARDS BENEFICIARIES

10.7.1 General principles of control by beneficiaries

Though the ultimate benefit under a trust goes to the beneficiaries, the trustees are concerned not only with their wishes, but also those expressed by the settlor on creation of the trust. There is therefore no general principle which permits the beneficiaries to control the way in which trustees exercise their discretions. Were it otherwise, the trustees would be hopelessly handicapped in fulfilling their overriding duty towards the trust as a whole, and the court will never compel the trustees to act under orders from the beneficiaries where a power or discretion has been entrusted to the trustees alone. This will hold as long as the trust continues, but as we have seen the beneficiaries collectively can sometimes dissolve the trust and resettle the property on any terms they wish, under the *Saunders* v *Vautier* doctrine.

During the continuance of the trust, however, in *Tempest* v *Lord Camoys* (1882) 21 ChD 571, the beneficiaries desired the trust to purchase an estate, but one of the trustees objected. Jessel MR refused to interfere with that trustee's bona fide decision. Strictly, the trustees are under no obligation even to consult with the beneficiaries as to how a power or discretion should be exercised, although of course they will often do so in practice.

An exception arises by virtue of s. 26(3) of the Law of Property Act 1925, which requires trustees of land under a statutory trust for sale to consult beneficiaries in possession, and to give effect to their wishes so far as is consistent with the general intentions of the trust. The reason is, as we saw in section 2.7, that these are fictitious trusts for sale, whose main purpose is to simplify the conveyancing of shared land, but even in this limited case there is no overriding obligation to follow the beneficiaries' directions.

10.7.1.1   Disclosure of reasons for decisions

The need to protect trustees from importuning beneficiaries is evident. However, the courts have gone further, and established that trustees will not be compelled to disclose the reasons behind the exercise of a discretion. In *Re Beloved Wilkes's Charity* (1851) 3 Mac & G 440, charity trustees were required to select a boy to be educated for the ministry, preference to be given to boys from four named parishes if a fit candidate could be found. The trustees, without giving reasons, selected a boy who did not come from one of the named parishes, but whose brother had put forward his merits to the trustees. It was held that in the absence of evidence that the trustees had exercised their discretion unfairly or dishonestly, the court would not interfere.

This poses an obvious problem for any beneficiary wishing to challenge a decision made by trustees. If trustees are not required to give reasons for their decisions, it will generally be impossible to know whether they have exercised their discretions in a proper manner.

If on the other hand the trustees choose to disclose their reasons, then the court may consider their adequacy. In *Klug* v *Klug* [1918] 2 Ch 67, a trustee whose daughter was a beneficiary refused to consider the exercise of a power of appointment in her favour, and from the correspondence it appeared that her reason was annoyance that the daughter had married without her consent.

Neville J held that the trustee had not exercised her discretion at all and that it was the duty of the court to interfere. Where the trustees take steps to keep the basis of their decisions private, however, there appears to be little that a beneficiary can do if the decision is not obviously unreasonable or fraudulent.

This leads to the question of whether the beneficiaries are entitled to have access to any written records of how the trustees have conducted the trust business. It is usual practice for trustees to keep a trust diary or minute book in which decisions affecting the trust are kept, but there is no requirement that the reasons for trustees' decisions should be recorded. The beneficiaries are, however, entitled to access to documents connected with the trust, known as 'trust documents', and indeed, have a proprietary interest in such documents. If those documents disclose the reasons for a decision, this would seem to offer the beneficiaries a way round the difficulty that trustees will not be compelled to disclose reasons.

The Court of Appeal, however, in *Re Londonderry's Settlement* [1965] Ch 918, effectively closed this door. In that case a beneficiary, dissatisfied with the sums appointed to her by trustees, pressed them to disclose various documents connected with the settlement. The trustees sought directions from the court. The Court of Appeal found that the category of 'trust documents' had not previously been defined with any degree of clarity, but concluded that all documents, held by trustees *qua* trustees are prima facie trust documents, but that documents containing confidential matters which a beneficiary is not entitled to know about should not be disclosed, either (in the view of Harman J) because they are protected by analogy with the rule that trustees need not disclose reasons, or (according to Salmon LJ) because a document which a beneficiary is not entitled to see cannot be a trust document.

It would appear, then, that the only way in which a beneficiary can gain sight of documents disclosing the trustees' reasons is to bring a hostile action against the trustees, as a preliminary to which an order for discovery of documents can be sought from the court. Unless the beneficiary already has substantial evidence of misconduct, this course will be fraught with difficulties.

10.7.1.2 Trust accounts

There is no argument here: beneficiaries are entitled to be informed of the condition of the trust property, and trustees must be ready at all times to produce trust accounts. Normally, the beneficiaries will be supplied with copies, perhaps in a simplified form, although strictly they are entitled to see the original accounts and to have copies made at their own expense. Income beneficiaries (e.g. life tenants under a family settlement) are entitled to see the accounts relating to the entire property of the trust, but remaindermen are entitled only to those accounts which relate to capital transactions and may therefore affect their interests.

It is not obligatory or even usual to have trust accounts subjected to an audit, but this may be done, at the absolute discretion of the trustees, who may employ an independent accountant and charge the costs to the trust fund. By s. 22(4) of the Trustee Act 1925, an audit is not to be carried out more frequently than once every three years, unless the nature of the property or other special difficulties so require. Any trustee or beneficiary may apply for an investigation and audit of the trust accounts by virtue of s. 13 of the Public Trustee Act 1906. A copy of the auditor's report is supplied to the applicant and to each trustee.

10.7.2 Apportionment

The general duty of trustees to act even-handedly as between the beneficiaries entails the necessity, where there are successive interests under a trust, to take certain steps to ensure that a fair balance is maintained between the capital and income of the trust, so that the former is preserved for those entitled in the future while at the same time allowing a reasonable income to those currently entitled. The rules relating to apportionment are an instance of this principle, and although it is nowadays usual practice to exclude their operation where possible, they are by no means without relevance, particularly in their application to accretions to the trust fund. It has been said that in special circumstances the court itself may direct an apportionment (*Re Kleinwort's Settlements* [1951] Ch 860), but this does not appear to have been done in practice.

10.7.2.1 *Howe* v *Earl of Dartmouth*

Some types of property are inherently unsuited to being held for successive interests. A wasting asset, which will soon be used up, provides no benefit to the remaindermen, while a reversionary interest which may not accrue for many years will provide no present income for the life tenant. The obvious way to achieve fairness as between the beneficiaries is therefore to sell the property and invest the proceeds so as to produce an income for the life tenant and an addition to capital for the benefit of the remainderman.

Obviously no problem arises if the trust instrument so directs, e.g., in the case of a trust for sale, but *Howe* v *Earl of Dartmouth* (1802) 7 Ves Jr 137 compels trustees to sell in other circumstances, even if there is no express direction, in some testamentary trusts of personal property (not land). The principle in the case only applies to settlements of the types of property considered in the preceding paragraph, and where there is no contrary intention expressed in the will.

Where a duty to convert (i.e., sell) arises under this principle, the normal date at which the property should be converted is one year from the death of the testator, that is, at the end of the 'executors' year' allowed for the administration of the estate to be carried out. If there is power to postpone the sale and conversion, however, this cannot apply, and the valuation for the purposes of apportionment is taken to be the date of the death.

It will usually not be possible to convert and reinvest on either of these specific dates, so some principle is needed for apportioning the income from the asset, until actual conversion. This is unnecessary if there is a clear intention that the tenant for life should have the actual income, or if the property is realty (and so not subject to the rule in *Howe* v *Earl of Dartmouth*) and no contrary intention appears, in which event the life tenant will receive the actual income.

Otherwise complex actuarial calculations are required, which turn on the precise nature of the property. For property which produces no present income, such as a reversionary interest, the principles deriving from the decision in *Re Earl of Chesterfield's Trusts* (1883) 24 ChD 643 apply, and apportionment between capital and income is calculated by a formula. In effect, an assumption is made of 4% interest, compounded annually. Thus, suppose the property produces £1,000 at sale. The capital element will be the amount which if invested at 4% compound interest would have produced £1,000. This will be less than £1,000, and the income will be the rest.

Where the asset produces income, the life tenant is entitled to 4% of its value as interest, and if extra income is actually produced, it accrues to capital.

There is also a formula, based on an assumption of 4% compound interest, for apportioning the payments of liabilities out of the fund (e.g., funeral expenses, debts of the testator) to capital and income. This formula derives from *Allhusen* v *Whittell* (1887) LR 4 Eq 295. *(see p/c)*

It seems likely that none of these formulae could easily be applied without employing the services of an accountant, to the obvious detriment of the fund. Perhaps for this reason, they are in fact frequently ignored. Another difficulty is that 4% is a very low rate of return today, and it is possible that if the issue were to come again before a court, a higher rate would be considered appropriate on the principles discussed in chapter 11. This in turn gives rise to a third problem, which is that until that occurs, trustees do not know which interest rate to apply.

It is no surprise, therefore, that the Law Reform Committee, reviewing these principles in its 23rd Report (1982), advocated their replacement with a statutory duty of a more general nature, to hold a fair balance between beneficiaries, with express power to trustees to convert capital to income and vice versa, and a duty to have overall regard to the investments of the trust. The effect of this if enacted would simplify the actuarial calculations required in these situations.

10.7.3 Duty to distribute

This has already been mentioned in section 9.2. The remedies available to those who suffer as a result of wrongful distribution are considered in chapter 11.

11

Trustees III: Breach of Trust

11.1 LIABILITY

11.1.1 What is breach of trust?

Generally speaking, any failure to comply with the duties laid upon the trustee by the trust instrument, if there is one, and of the obligations laid upon him by equity, as described in chapters 9 and 10, will be a breach of trust. Such failure may take the form of some positive action, such as investing in unauthorised securities, or an omission, such as neglecting to have the trust property placed in the name of the trustee. Even a merely technical act of maladministration may result in liability if in fact it causes a loss to the trust estate.

Nor, at least in the case of an express trust, does it matter how the trust was created (though the duties imposed on constructive trustees, as we saw in section 10.1, may be less). Volunteer beneficiaries are entitled to have their interests protected to the same extent as those who have given consideration, and it is of no relevance either that the trust was created voluntarily by the same person who, in his capacity as trustee, is now charged with breach of trust. In other words, a settlor-trustee is liable to the same extent as any other trustee.

11.1.2 Basis of liability

The basis of a trustee's liability is compensation to the beneficiaries for whatever loss may have resulted from the breach or, if an unauthorised profit has been made, the restoration to the beneficiaries of property rightfully belonging to the trust. The objective is not to punish the trustee, and so his personal fault is immaterial once a breach is established. Of course, fault in an objective sense may be relevant to the question whether there has in fact been a breach, there being, as we have seen, a general standard of care based on normal business practice.

There are no degrees of breach, however. Liability can attach to a trustee who has acted honestly in the beneficiaries' interests, just as it can to a trustee who has acted fraudulently for his own ends. Further, since the standard of care is objective (i.e., measured against the level of competence of an ordinary prudent man of business rather than that of the particular trustee), liability can attach to a trustee who lacks the knowledge or skills to avoid the breach, and is doing his incompetent best, if that best is not up to the objective standard required.

Protection of the beneficiaries, and not the nature of the wrongdoing, is the crucial element.

The court may, however, take into account degrees of culpability in exercising its discretion to grant relief from liability (see next section) or in fixing the amount of interest which the trustee may be liable to pay on the sum lost to the trust estate (see section 11.3).

11.1.3   Personal nature of trustee's liability

A trustee is liable personally for his own breach of trust, and not vicariously for breaches committed by his fellow trustees. However, a trustee who passively permits a breach to occur may thereby put himself in breach of his own duties because, though trustees are not required to police each other's conduct, they are expected, as we have seen, to be active in the administration of the trust. Thus, a trustee who leaves funds under the control of a fellow trustee without enquiry, or fails to take steps to obtain redress if he discovers a breach, will be in dereliction of his own duty to the beneficiaries.

We saw in section 9.4 how s. 30 of the Trustee Act 1925 provides that:

A trustee . . . shall be answerable and accountable only for his own acts, receipts, neglects, or defaults, and not for those of any other trustee . . . nor for any other loss, unless the same happens through his own wilful default.

Arguably this section, like its predecessor, s. 31 of the Trustee Act 1859, does no more than restate the pre-existing law, because it does not alter the principle that a trustee remains liable for his own acts, upon which the liability considered in the preceding paragraph is based.

On the other hand, in *Re Vickery* [1931] 1 Ch 572, discussed in section 9.4.2, Maugham J assumed that s. 30 had altered the law, at least in relation to liability for agents, for he interpreted the phrase 'wilful default' as meaning 'a consciousness of negligence or breach of duty, or recklessness in the performance of duty'. If this meaning is applied in relation to co-trustees, the section clearly confers extra protection. But *Re Vickery* concerned the liability of an executor for the default of an agent, not a fellow trustee. As we saw in section 9.4.2 the decision has been criticised, so it is unlikely that it will be extended so as to affect what is after all the personal liability of a trustee.

Apart from *Re Vickery*, it had generally been accepted that s. 30 did not alter the previous law, under which liability was incurred where a trustee handed over money without securing its proper application, or permitted a fellow trustee to recover money without inquiring what he did with it, or refrained from taking steps to obtain redress for a breach of which he was aware. It has yet to be decided whether, in these circumstances also, it will be necessary to prove that a passive trustee was guilty of 'wilful default' as defined in *Re Vickery*, but I would suggest that this is unlikely.

A trustee will not, upon accepting office, become liable for breaches committed prior to his appointment. His first steps upon taking office, however, should be to examine the documents and accounts of the trust, and if he discovers that a breach has occurred, he should take action against the former trustees to recover the loss. Failure to do so may itself amount to a breach for which he will be liable, save perhaps in the rare case where he can show that action would have been futile (because there would then be no causal relationship between the breach and the loss).

A trustee cannot escape liability for his own breach of trust by retiring from office, for even after his retirement he remains liable for breaches committed while he was in office, and his estate remains liable after his death. He will not be liable for breaches committed after the date of his retirement, unless it can be shown that he retired in order to facilitate a breach of trust (*Head* v *Gould* [1898] 2 Ch 250).

11.1.4   Liability as between trustees

The liability of trustees is said to be joint and several, which means that if two or more trustees are liable, a beneficiary may choose to sue some or all of them, or perhaps only one, and recoup the entire loss from those against whom he chooses to proceed. Similarly, he may levy execution against any one of them for the whole amount.

As between themselves, however, the trustees were until 1978 regarded by equity as being equally liable, so that a trustee who was compelled to pay more than his fair share of the loss could in turn enforce a contribution from the others. In enforcing equal contribution, equity disregarded any differing degrees of involvement in the breach. Thus in *Bahin* v *Hughes* (1886) 31 ChD 390 a passive trustee was liable to the same extent as an active one.

There were exceptions to the principle of equal contribution, however, which still apply after 1978:

(a)   Where there has been fraud. A fraudulent trustee is solely liable, and can claim no contribution from the honest trustees.

(b)   Where a trustee has got money into his hands and made use of it, he will be liable to indemnify a co-trustee who is obliged to replace the funds.

(c)   Where one trustee was a solicitor and the rest relied on his judgment (*Re Partington* (1887) 57 LT 654). The mere fact that a trustee happens also to be a solicitor will not make him liable to indemnify the other trustees, for it is necessary also that the others rely on his judgment. Thus, he will not be liable if it is shown that the other trustees were active participators in the breach, and did not participate merely in consequence of the advice and control of the solicitor

see p164

(*Head* v *Gould* [1898] 2 Ch 250).

(d)   Where a trustee is also a beneficiary he will be required to indemnify his co-trustees to the extent of his beneficial interest, and not merely to the extent that he has personally received some benefit from the breach (*Chillingworth* v *Chambers* [1896] 1 Ch 685). Only after that interest is exhausted will further liability be shared equally. The principle seems to be that a beneficiary may not claim any share of the trust estate until he has discharged his liabilities towards it.

The equitable position has been affected by the Civil Liability (Contribution) Act 1978. Under this Act, any person liable in respect of damage suffered by another person, including damage arising from breach of trust, may recover contribution from any other person in respect of the same damage. By s. 2(1) the amount of the contribution is:

such as may be found by the court to be just and equitable having regard to the extent of that person's responsibility for the damage in question

and may by virtue of s. 2(2) amount to a total indemnity. The Act therefore gives the court a discretion (but not a mandatory duty) to depart from the rule of equal distribution and have regard to degrees of fault.

The Act does not apply to the limited number of exceptions to the general equitable principle described above, and may indeed not affect the equitable position at all, since it is left to the court to determine what is 'just and equitable'. One other situation is clearly unaffected by the 1978 Act. If all the trustees were involved in a fraud, equity would not allow those who paid the damages to claim any contribution from the rest, on the ground that a plaintiff could not base a claim upon his own wrongdoing. The 1978 Act makes no special provision for such a case, but though the court is theoretically free to exercise its discretion in allocating liability to contribute, it is inconceivable that a fraudulent trustee would be allowed to sue. Where some but not all of the trustees are excused from liability under s. 61 of the Trustee Act 1925 (see section 11.2.5), it would seem to follow that those who are not excused can claim no contribution from them. Under the 1978 Act, the excused trustees would seem not to be persons who are liable in respect of any damage, so presumably the court cannot direct them to make contribution.

11.1.5   Criminal liability of trustees

In the course of a breach of trust, criminal offences may be committed, but breach of trust is not of itself a criminal offence. There used to be a difficulty about theft, because the trustee as legal owner of the trust property, could not be guilty of stealing it, and a special offence of conversion by a trustee had to be created in order to make him punishable. Under the Theft Act 1968, he may now be guilty of ordinary theft, however, because of s. 5(2).

11.1.6 Bankruptcy of a defaulting trustee

If a trustee who is liable for a breach becomes bankrupt, the claim in respect of the breach is provable in his bankruptcy. His duties towards the trust are not affected by his bankruptcy, so the odd situation arises whereby he has a duty (as trustee) to prove in his own bankruptcy (as debtor). If he fails to do this, he commits a further breach of trust which is not affected by any subsequent discharge from bankruptcy, and he will be liable to the trust for the resulting loss (i.e., dividend that he would have received in the bankruptcy).

If the original breach of trust was fraudulent, the trustee also remains liable for it even after his discharge from bankruptcy.

11.2 QUALIFICATIONS TO LIABILITY, AND DEFENCES

11.2.1 Consent or participation by beneficiaries

A beneficiary who consents to or participates in a breach of trust will not usually be able to succeed in a claim against the trustees, even if he has obtained no personal benefit from the breach. The consent or participation of one beneficiary will not, of course, prevent those who did not consent from claiming, and if it is uncertain which beneficiaries have consented, the court may order an inquiry. No particular form of consent is required.

To be effective, consent must be that of an adult who is *sui juris* and not acting under an undue influence which prevents him from making an independent judgment. In *Re Pauling's ST* [1964] Ch 303, the trustees of a marriage settlement had made a series of advances to the children of the life tenant, but in the case of each of the four children, not until after they had reached majority. As we saw in section 10.5, the advances were made in breach of trust because the trustees did not ensure that the moneys advanced were used for their proper purpose. They were actually used partly to reduce the life tenant, Mrs Younghusband's overdraft; a conflict of interest arose also, therefore, because the trustees were the life tenant's bankers. A wide range of defences was argued, both before Wilberforce J and in the Court of Appeal, but on this issue several of the payments which went to benefit the parents were presumed to have been the result of undue influence over the children. Whether undue influence has been exercised is a question of fact, depending on circumstances. The trustees will not be liable if it cannot be shown that they knew, or ought to have known, that the beneficiary was acting under such influence.

Consent involves more than mere awareness of what the trustees are proposing to do. Otherwise, trustees could protect themselves by simply telling the beneficiaries beforehand. In *Re Pauling's ST* [1962] 1 WLR 86 Wilberforce J explained (at p. 108) that:

> [T]he court has to consider all the circumstances in which the concurrence of the cestui que trust was given with a view to seeing whether it is fair and equitable that, having given his concurrence, he should afterwards turn round and sue the trustees.

He went on to say that it is not necessary that the beneficiary should know that what he is concurring in is a breach of trust, provided that he fully understands what he is concurring in. Nor is it necessary that he should personally benefit from the breach. This statement of the law was approved by the Court of Appeal in *Holder* v *Holder* [1968] Ch 353, where a beneficiary was held unable to set aside a sale after affirming it and accepting part of the purchase money.

11.2.2 Release or acquiescence by beneficiaries

A beneficiary will also be unable to succeed in his claim if, on becoming aware of the breach, he acquiesced in the breach or released the trustee from liability arising therefrom.

Release suggests some active waiver by the beneficiary of his rights. A waiver requires a positive act which is intended to be irrevocable. It is like making a gift and, as with gifts, no consideration need move from the donee (in this case the trustee). As with consent, there need not be any particular formalities and release may even be inferred from conduct.

If a release cannot be shown, it may still be possible to show that the beneficiary acquiesced in the breach. It is usually accepted that the acquiescence doctrine is based on an implied contract, whereby the beneficiary is taken to have agreed not to rely on his rights. The evidence required for this intention to be inferred is less than in the case of release and the doctrine is often applied where a beneficiary has done nothing to pursue his claim.

Delay in making the claim is not in itself evidence of acquiescence, but where the length of time between the breach and the claim is very great, slight additional evidence will suffice. As in the case of consent, the release or acquiescence must be that of an adult who is *sui juris*.

Undue influence or lack of full knowledge will prevent the trustee from relying upon these defences, the test being as in the consent doctrine, above.

11.2.3 Impounding the beneficiary's interest

The court has an inherent power to impound the interest of a beneficiary, thus providing the trustee with an indemnity to the extent that the beneficiary's interest will suffice to replace the loss of the trust.

The power can arise where a beneficiary has merely consented to the breach, but only if some benefit to him can be proved, and then only to the extent of that benefit. If the beneficiary has gone further, and actually requested or instigated a breach, the power can be exercised whether or not he has received a personal benefit from the breach.

Needless to say, the trustee has to show that the beneficiary acted in full knowledge of the facts but it is not necessary to show that he knew that the acts he was instigating or consenting to amounted to a breach.

There is also a statutory discretion to impound, but the courts seem to have treated it as consolidating rather than extending their powers. Section 62(1) of the Trustee Act 1925 (replacing an earlier section) provides:

> Where a trustee commits a breach of trust at the instigation or request or with the consent in writing of a beneficiary, the court may, if it thinks fit, make such order as to the court seems just, for impounding all or any part of the interest of the beneficiary in the trust estate by way of indemnity to the trustee or persons claiming through him.

The effect of the court making such an order is that the beneficiary is not only debarred from pursuing his own claim against the trustee, but also liable to replace the losses suffered by the other beneficiaries, to the extent ordered by the court, and perhaps up to the full value of his own interest. To this extent, the trustee is protected at the beneficiary's expense.

The discretion is a judicial discretion, and though the section appears to extend the inherent power of the court by giving a discretion to impound a beneficiary's interest regardless of whether he obtained a benefit, it has received a restrictive interpretation. It seems that the court will make an impounding order in any case where it would have done so before the Act; generally speaking, in any case where the beneficiary has actively induced the breach (for which it has never been necessary to show benefit).

It must, of course, be shown that the beneficiary was fully aware of what was being done. In *Re Somerset* [1894] 1 Ch 231, a beneficiary had urged the trustees to invest in a mortgage of a particular property, but had left them to decide how much money they were prepared to invest. Lindley MR said (at p. 265):

> In order to bring a case within this section the cestui que trust must instigate, or request, or consent in writing to some act or omission which is itself a breach of trust, and not to some act or omission which only becomes a breach of trust by reason of want of care on the part of the trustees.

The words 'in writing' have been held to apply only to consent, and not to instigation or request (*Griffith* v *Hughes* [1892] 3 Ch 105). So it is necessary only for a request or instigation to be oral.

The power to impound will not be lost upon an assignment of the beneficial interest. Nor is it lost when the court replaces the trustees in consequence of the breach. In *Re Pauling's ST* [1962] 1 WLR 86 the trustees resisted removal because they were claiming an indemnity out of the interests of the parents. Wilberforce J at first instance held that they were entitled to such indemnity and that this would be unaffected by their replacement.

Apart from statute, it is the practice, where trustees have, under an honest mistake, overpaid a beneficiary, for the court to make allowance for the mistake in order to allow the trustee to recoup as far as possible (*Re Musgrave* [1916] 2 Ch 417). An overpaid beneficiary is not compelled to return the excess, but further payment may be withheld until the accounts are adjusted.

If a payment is made by mistake to someone who is not entitled, the trustee may recover on an action for money had and received if the mistake was one of fact, but not if it was a mistake of law (*Re Diplock* [1947] Ch 716). It is also certain that the error must be corrected where trustee-beneficiaries overpay themselves.

11.2.4   Lapse of time

Lapse of time may protect a trustee in one of two ways. By the Limitation Act 1980, limits are set upon the time within which certain actions for recovery may be brought, while in cases not covered by statutory limitation, a defendant may rely upon the doctrine of laches.

11.2.4.1   Limitation Act 1980

By s. 21(3), any action by a beneficiary to recover trust property or in respect of any breach of trust (other than situations covered by self-dealing and fair dealing rules) must be brought within six years from the date on which the right of action accrued. A right of action in respect of future interests is not treated as having accrued until the interest falls into possession.

Under s. 21(1), no period of limitation applies where the action is in respect of any fraud to which the trustee was a party, or privy, or where (in summary) it is sought to recover from the trustee trust property still in his possession or the proceeds of sale of such property. Protection is also lost where the trustee converts trust property to his own use. Conversion to the trustee's own use, however, implies application in his own favour, so that if the funds have been used to maintain an infant beneficiary, or dissipated by a fellow trustee, the protection of limitation remains available.

Where fraud is the issue, this must be fraud by the trustee himself. In *Thorne* v *Heard* [1894] 1 Ch 599 a trustee was protected by a section in similar terms of an earlier Act, where he had left trust funds with a solicitor who had embezzled them, the trustee himself being no more than negligent. Where the trustee is in possession of trust property or its proceeds, no dishonesty need be shown.

Section 22 prescribes a limitation period of 12 years for actions in respect of any claim to the personal estate of a deceased person. It is often hard to determine at what point executors have completed the administration of an estate and become trustees, but it is thought that the 12-year period will apply although for all other purposes the executors would be regarded as trustees.

Plaintiffs under disability are permitted an extended period in which to bring an action by s. 28, and by s. 32, where fraud, concealment or mistake is alleged, time runs only from the point when the plaintiff discovers the fraud or mistake, or could with reasonable diligence have discovered it.

It should be noted that a person other than a bona fide purchaser for value without notice who receives property from a trustee also falls within these rules.

11.2.4.2 Laches

Where no statutory limitation period applies, the defendant may rely on the equitable doctrine of laches, that is, he may show that it would be unjust to allow the plaintiff to pursue his claim in view of the time that has elapsed since it accrued. The court has a discretion to allow or refuse the defence, and mere delay may suffice, but where possible, the courts have preferred to regard delay as furnishing evidence of acquiescence by the plaintiff.

11.2.5 Section 61 of the Trustee Act 1925

This section gives the court a wide discretion to excuse honest and reasonable trustees from liability for breach of trust. It applies also to executors. The section provides:

> If it appears to the court that a trustee . . . is or may be personally liable for any breach of trust, whether the transaction alleged to be a breach of trust occurred before or after the commencement of this Act, but has acted honestly and reasonably, and ought fairly to be excused for the breach of trust and for omitting to obtain the directions of the court in the matter in which he committed such breach, then the court may relieve him either wholly or partly from personal liability for the same.

Dishonesty will obviously disqualify a trustee from obtaining relief, but opinions may vary as to whether a trustee has acted 'reasonably'. The usual standard, as we have seen, is that of the prudent man of business in relation to his own affairs. Failure to obtain directions might be thought to fall below this standard, but the section implies that relief may nonetheless be granted.

Unauthorised investments appear to be the most common circumstances in which applications are made, and it may not be easy to show that this sort of risk-taking meets with the standard of the prudent businessman. Reasonable conduct may be more easily shown where the breach consists in some error made in the course of a complex administration. Professional trustees may claim the protection of the section, but the courts have been less ready to excuse failure where a high standard of expertise is professed by the trustee.

It may be that, even if the trustee is shown to have acted honestly and reasonably, the question of whether he ought fairly to be excused will be separately considered.

11.3 PERSONAL REMEDIES AGAINST TRUSTEES

All the usual equitable remedies are available to guard against breach of trust, so it is possible, for example, to prevent such a breach by injunction. This section deals with the problems where a financial remedy, for example, an account of profits, is sought once a breach has been committed.

11.3.1 Measure of liability

This is the actual loss to the trust estate which arises, directly or indirectly, from the breach, usually with interest. Where an unauthorised profit has been made, the trustees must account for this profit, but this will be the limit of their liability. It should also be noted that the trustees are liable only for losses which arise causally from a breach of trust. They are not required to act as insurers for the beneficiaries, and any losses which arise despite the exercise of due diligence on the part of the trustees must be borne by the trust estate.

Subject to the above limitations, assuming the plaintiff can establish a causal connection between the breach and the loss, there are no rules governing remoteness of damage such as apply in tort or contract. Enquiries as to what a reasonable trustee ought to have foreseen or contemplated are not relevant in this context. This may not matter as much as in, for example, a tort action, because the spectre of virtually unlimited liability, such as could occur in a negligence action, for example if a cigarette end negligently thrown away causes a large ship to explode, is unlikely to arise. The value of the trust property and profits from its use provide a natural limit to liability without the need for additional remoteness rules, but trustees could find themselves in difficulties where, for example, the property unexpectedly increases in value. Nor, incidentally, can a trustee set off against the amount which he is obliged to restore to the trust funds the tax which would have been payable on that amount, had he not lost it through his breach (*Re Bell's Indenture* [1980] 1 WLR 1217).

Further, a trustee cannot set off a profit made in one transaction against a loss made in another. The reason is that any profits made out of the trust property belong to the beneficiaries, so the trustees have no claim against those profits to lessen their own liability for loss caused by a breach. A frequently quoted authority is the old case of *Dimes* v *Scott* (1828) 4 Russ 195.

The principle was not applied, however, by Brightman J in *Bartlett* v *Barclays Bank Trust Co. Ltd (No. 1)* [1980] Ch 515. In that case, the breach by the defendant bank lay in failure to exercise adequate supervision over the speculations undertaken by the directors of a company in which the trust owned almost all the shares. Loss had resulted from a disastrous development, but another development had produced a profit. Although acknowledging the general rule, Brightman J allowed that gain to be set off against the loss, remarking that it would be unjust to deprive the bank of an element of salvage in the disaster. A possible explanation, reconciling *Bartlett* with the general rule is that the loss and gain arose from the same policy of speculation in the *Bartlett* case, and it may be that, in the case where gains and losses arise in a single dealing or course of dealing, the trustees will be liable only to the extent that a net loss results.

11.3.2   Investments

Many of the cases concern losses arising from improper use by the trustees of their powers of investment, and some specific points should be noted:

(a)   If trustees make an unauthorised investment, they will be liable for any loss which is incurred when that investment is realised. There are, however, qualifications to this principle.

First, if the beneficiaries are all *sui juris* and collectively entitled to the entire trust property, they may adopt the unauthorised investment as part of the trust property. It is not clear whether, if they do this, they may nonetheless call upon the trustees to make good any loss which arises from that investment: *Re Lake* [1903] 1 KB 439 seems to suggest that they may, but this result appears contrary to principle. If the beneficiaries do not unanimously agree to adopt the investment, then the trustee's duty is to sell it and to make good any loss.

Secondly, the trustee is alternatively entitled to take over the investment for himself, subject to refunding the trust estate, the beneficiaries having a lien on the investment until the refund is made.

If an unauthorised investment brings in a greater income than an authorised one would have done, and this income has already been paid over to a beneficiary, the trustee cannot, it seems, require him to repay the excess above what he should have received, nor set off this excess against future income.

(b)   Where unauthorised investments are improperly retained, the measure of liability is the difference between the present value of the investment and the price it would have raised if sold at the proper time. For example, in *Fry* v *Fry* (1859) 28 LJ Ch 591 (see section 10.2.5) the trustees were liable for the difference between the offer of £900 and the sum eventually obtained.

(c)   If the trustees are directed by the trust instrument to make a specific investment, and either they make no investment at all, or else they invest the fund in something else, their liability is to supply the same amount of the specific investment as they could have acquired with the trust funds had they purchased it at the proper time. Account will, however, be taken of any payments which the trustees would have had to make regarding the investment if they had acquired it at the correct time.

Where the trustees are given a choice of investments but make no investment at all, they will only be liable to replace any deficit in the trust fund, with interest. This is simply because it cannot be assumed that any particular investment would have been chosen by the trustees if they had acted properly, and it is therefore impossible to base their liability upon the value of any particular investment.

(d) A trustee who uses trust money in his own business will be liable to hold any profit which he makes as a constructive trustee for the beneficiaries, or to account for the money with interest, whichever happens to be the greater. If he mixes trust money with his own, the beneficiaries may demand the return of the trust money with interest, or else claim a share in the profits proportionate to the amount of the trust money employed in the venture. Any loss must, of course, be borne by the trustee, and where he has become insolvent, the beneficiaries may have a proprietary claim for the return of the trust fund, in preference to his creditors (see section 11.4).

11.3.3 Interest

Normally, a trustee will be required to replace a loss with interest. Traditionally, the rate of interest was 4%, which was in line with the rate produced on old-style trustee securities, but this is now recognised as unrealistic, and the proper rate at present appears to be that allowed from time to time on the court's short-term investment account established under s. 6(1) of the Administration of Justice Act 1965 (*Bartlett* v *Barclays Bank Trust Co. Ltd (No. 1)* [1980] Ch 515).

A trustee may be liable for a higher rate, at the discretion of the court. If he has actually received more than the standard rate, he will be liable for what he has actually received. Similarly, if it can be shown that he ought to have received more than he did, he will be liable for what he should have received, for example, where a proper investment producing a higher rate has been wrongfully terminated. Traditionally, if the trustee was guilty of fraud or other active misconduct, the rate was raised from 4% to 5% on the presumption that this represented what he had actually received. On the same presumption, compound interest may be charged nowadays, and it seems that this will be a matter of course if the trustee was under a duty to accumulate. Despite the frequent reiteration that higher rates are charged merely as reflecting the actual gain made by the defaulting trustee and not by way of penalty, the extent of the trustee's misconduct may be a relevant factor in the court's exercise of its discretion (see *Wallersteiner* v *Moir* (No. 2) [1975] QB 373).

11.4 PROPRIETARY REMEDIES

The remedies so far considered have been personal remedies, the effect of which is to compel the payment of a sum of money by way of amends to the injured party. In certain limited circumstances, however, a plaintiff may be able to assert a right to some specific item of property, including a fund of money, which is in the hand of the defendant. He may, in other words, have a remedy which is proprietary and not merely personal.

There are certain advantages in a proprietary remedy. The property may have increased in value while in the defendant's hands, and the plaintiff will have the benefit of this increase if he can claim the property or its full value, and not merely compensatory damages. He will be entitled to any income which the property has produced since the moment when it came to the defendant, whereas a personal claim entitles him only to interest from the date of judgment. Further, it appears that a proprietary remedy may be available in some cases where a personal action against the defendant will not lie.

Most important, however, is the advantage that a proprietary remedy does not depend for its effectiveness upon the defendant having sufficient means to pay any compensation awarded to the plaintiff in a personal action. If the defendant is insolvent, a plaintiff entitled to monetary damages may have to be content with whatever dividend can be obtained in the defendant's bankruptcy, which will usually be considerably less than the full amount of the damages. If the plaintiff's right is proprietary, however, the property to which he is entitled will be treated as separate from the rest of the defendant's other assets, and will not therefore fall into the general fund available to be shared among the creditors.

Some of the methods of retaining legal or equitable property in goods have already been considered in chapter 2. For example, equitable property may be retained in situations analogous to loans, and in commercial sales of goods an attempt may be made by the seller to retain legal property in the goods until payment in full is received, thereby preserving the right as owners to recover the goods in the event of the purchaser becoming insolvent (the Romalpa clause).

The situations considered in this section differ to the extent that the original goods may have been sold, and the question may arise as to whether there is a proprietary remedy in the proceeds of sale, or, in the case of a fund, it may have become mixed with other money of the defendant. Such situations frequently arise where a breach of trust has taken place.

11.4.1 Tracing at common law

It is important to appreciate that a proprietary remedy is not the same as a 'real' remedy which allows the plaintiff to recover the actual physical thing or 'res' (Latin!) in question.

The common law developed an action for the recovery of a specific piece of land, but never extended this 'real' remedy to allow a plaintiff to recover a specific chattel. Although the common law acknowledged the plaintiff's ownership of the chattel, his action was a personal action in detinue, the remedy for which was damages. The defendant could therefore choose whether to return the plaintiff's chattel or pay him its full value as damages.

The Common Law Procedure Act 1854, s. 78, gave the court a discretion to order specific delivery of the chattel, and this power is retained by s. 3 of the Torts (Interference with Goods) Act 1977. But there is no absolute right to the return of the chattel. The importance of the proprietary claim lies rather in the fact that it entitles the plaintiff to the full value of the chattel, in preference to the claims of the defendant's other creditors.

The common law also concluded that the plaintiff's right should continue even if the defendant has exchanged the plaintiff's property for some other property, or sold it and purchased other property with the proceeds. So long as it was possible to 'trace' his original property — that is, to show that what the defendant now holds can be regarded as simply a substitute — his claim is unaffected.

An illustration is the old case of *Taylor* v *Plumer* (1815) 3 M & S 562. Sir Thomas Plumer had handed over money to a stockbroker with instructions to purchase Exchequer bonds, but the stockbroker instead purchased American investments and bullion, and attempted to abscond with these. He was caught before he could leave England, and the investments and bullion were seized by Plumer. The assignees of the stockbroker then brought an action to recover them from Sir Thomas, but failed. The investments and bullion were held to be Sir Thomas's own property. In effect, Plumer's money was traced into the investments and bullion for, according to Lord Ellenborough at p. 575, 'the product of or substitute for the original thing still follows the nature of the thing itself, as long as it can be ascertained to be such'.

The right of a plaintiff to claim the substitute is commonly called the 'remedy' of tracing, but the process of tracing the original property into its new form is not strictly a remedy at all, but rather a method by which the plaintiff establishes his claim to the actual remedy of restoration of the property or its value.

At common law, the possibility of tracing depends on the property continuing to exist in an identifiable form. Tracing is thus available where a straightforward exchange of the property has occurred, or where the property or its proceeds have been placed in a separate bank account (*Banque Belge pour L'Étranger* v *Hambrouck* [1921] 1 KB 321).

The orthodox view, however (but see Goode (1979) 95 LQR 360), is that if the property has been converted into money and this money mixed with other funds belonging to the defendant, it is no longer possible at common law to identify the subject-matter of the plaintiff's claim, and he is thereafter limited to his personal remedy in damages. Since this will often occur in the case where funds are misappropriated, the usefulness of tracing at common law is rather limited in breach of trust situations.

Further, since the common law does not recognise equitable interests in property, a beneficiary under a trust cannot follow trust property in the hands of a trustee, although he can in equity compel the trustee to trace the property at common law, where it has fallen into the hands of a third party.

11.4.2 Tracing in equity

The courts of equity have, however, themselves developed a method of tracing property which acknowledges and protects equitable interests. Equitable tracing also has the advantage that it applies where the defendant has mixed the trust money with his own. There are respects, however, where tracing in equity is less extensive than at common law.

In accord with ordinary equitable principles the right is lost if the property comes into the hands of a bona fide purchaser for value who had no notice of the plaintiff's right, whereas the common law recognises no such limitation.

Both common law and equitable rights can in some circumstances exist simultaneously, of course.

11.4.2.1   Advantages of equitable tracing

An important respect in which the right to trace in equity is more extensive than at common law is that tracing at common law does not extend to the case where the defendant has mixed the plaintiff's money, or money obtained by conversion, with money of his own. The equitable right is available not only in the common law situations where the plaintiff can identify his property *in specie*, or point to a fund representing its proceeds, but also where the defendant has created a mixed fund, and possibly even when this fund has itself been converted into other property.

Though the right is lost if the property comes into the hands of a bona fide purchaser for value who has no notice of the plaintiff's right, it will persist against a volunteer for as long as he retains the property, even if he has come by it innocently (i.e., without notice of the plaintiff's interest). The remedy granted by equity against a mixed fund or property acquired thereby is a charge for the value of the plaintiff's interest.

11.4.2.2   The working of the rules where funds are mixed

As against a trustee who is in breach of trust, who has mixed trust money with his own, the beneficiary is entitled to a first charge over a mixed fund or property purchased with it. The burden rests on the trustee to prove that some portion of the fund is his own, and the beneficiary is entitled to all the rest.

If on the other hand the trustee has mixed funds belonging to two or more trusts, or transferred trust funds to an innocent volunteer who has mixed them with his own, then the trusts in the former case, and the trust and the volunteer in the latter, will share *in pari passu* (i.e., in proportion to the amount each has contributed) in the mixed fund or any property purchased therewith.

If in addition the trustee's own property has also been mixed in such a fund, his claim will be governed by the rule that he must prove his entitlement to that portion which he claims as his own, after which the innocent parties will share *in pari passu* all parts to which the trustee cannot assert ownership.

11.4.2.3   Special rules about bank accounts: no third party involved

It is extremely likely that the mixing of funds will take place in a bank account. This produces an added complication if additions or withdrawals have been made since the time when the trust funds were paid in.

Again, different considerations apply depending on whether the plaintiff's claim is against a fiduciary or against an innocent third party (another trust or innocent volunteer).

Where the claim is against a trustee, equity relies upon the presumption that the trustee, in making withdrawals from the account, draws out his own money first and does not draw on the money subject to the trust until all his own money has been exhausted, no matter in what order the money was paid in. So what remains in the account is treated as trust money.

Thus, in *Re Hallett's Estate* (1880) 13 ChD 696, Hallett, a solicitor, was a trustee of his own marriage settlement. He had paid some of the money from that trust into his own bank account, into which he also paid money which had been entrusted to him for investment by a client. He made various payments in and out of the account, which at his death contained sufficient funds to meet the claims of the trust and his client, but not those of his personal creditors as well. The Court of Appeal held that both the trust and the client were entitled to a charge in priority to the general creditors, and that the various payments out of the account must be treated as payments of Hallett's own money. The basis of the principle is that where an act can be done rightly, the trustee is not allowed to say that he did it wrongfully.

The rule will not operate in derogation of the principle that the beneficiary is entitled to a first charge on a mixed fund. In *Re Oatway* [1903] 2 Ch 356 the trustee had withdrawn money from the mixed account and invested it in shares, leaving a balance which at that time was ample to meet the claims of the beneficiaries. Subsequently, however, he dissipated the balance further. The argument that he must be treated as withdrawing his own money first (so that his shares would be treated as his own property) was rejected. The beneficiaries' claim must be satisfied out of any identifiable part of the fund before the trustee could set up his own claim. They were entitled to the shares in priority to the general creditors.

However, there are limits to the rights of beneficiaries. Once it is clear that all money belonging to the trustee has been withdrawn, so that any further withdrawals must have been from trust money, they cannot claim that any subsequent payments in must be taken as intended to replace the trust money, unless the trustee shows an intention to make such repayment. In such a case, the right to trace will apply up to the lowest balance of the account in the period between the trust fund being paid into the account and the time when the remedy is sought. For example, if the trustee mixes £1,000 of his own money with £3,000 of trust money and later withdraws £2,000, the right to trace will not extend beyond the £2,000 which is thereby left in the account, even if the trustee later pays in further sums of his own.

In such a case, of course, the beneficiaries will have a personal claim against the trustee for any outstanding sum.

Another limit on the beneficiaries' right to trace is that there may not be any principle of proportionate entitlement. Suppose, for example, the trustee has used the mixed fund to purchase property which has increased in value. Can the beneficiary claim any part of the increase? It appears not on the basis of *Re Hallett's Estate* and *Sinclair v Brougham* [1914] AC 398, where it was assumed that the beneficiary's remedy was limited to a charge upon the property for the amount of trust money expended in its purchase. This is a surprising result given the strict rule against profits by trustees, and some doubt has recently been cast on it (though only *obiter* in a first-instance decision).

The discussion took place in *Re Tilley's WT* [1967] Ch 1179, where a sole trustee who was also the life tenant had mixed a small amount of trust money in her own bank account before embarking on a series of property speculations which were so successful that upon her death her estate was worth £94,000. The beneficiaries entitled in remainder claimed a share of this wealth in the proportion which the trust money in the account bore to the balance of the account at that time. Ungoed-Thomas J held them entitled only to the return of the trust money with interest.

His decision was based on a finding of fact, however, that Mrs Tilley had not invested the trust money in property but merely used it to reduce her overdraft. If a trustee has in fact laid out trust money towards a purchase, Ungoed-Thomas J thought that the beneficiaries would then be entitled to the property and any profit to the extent that it had been paid for with trust money.

The reasoning is that if the trustee draws on a mixed fund to purchase property but leaves enough in the account to cover the trust funds, the rule in *Re Hallett's Estate* requires that the purchase be treated as made entirely with his own money, in which case, should no further dissipations to the mixed fund occur, the property, and any profit, belong to him. But should he then go further and dissipate the remaining balance, the beneficiaries will have a charge on the property (*Re Oatway*) and this, according to Ungoed-Thomas J, may be for the proportionate part of the increased value, and not merely for the original amount of the trust fund.

The solution is consistent with the rule applicable to unauthorised investment, where, as we saw in section 11.3.2 the beneficiaries may elect to adopt the investment. Its effect would be to allow the beneficiaries the choice of a charge for an amount of the trust money, which will be to their advantage where the funds are depleted, or a share in the property where its value has risen.

11.4.2.4 Bank accounts: third party involved

Where the rival claims to the mixed fund arise between two or more trusts, or between the beneficiaries under a trust and an innocent volunteer, there is no obviously just solution, so the rule developed in *Clayton's case* (1817) 1 Mer 572 is applied. This rule, which only appears in the context of a current bank account, enshrines the principle of 'first in, first out'. The first payment in is appropriated to satisfy the earliest debt.

The basis of the rule is said to be the presumed intention of the person operating the account. A preferable solution, in the opinion of the authors of the Report of the Review Committee on Insolvency Law and Practice (Cork Report 1982, Cmnd 8558), paras 1076–80, might be to divide the mixed fund rateably (i.e., *in pari passu*). This solution has not been brought to fruition, however, by the Insolvency Act 1985.

11.4.2.5 Position of volunteers

The right to trace is available not only where the mixing was done by a trustee, but also where it has been done by an innocent volunteer.

In *Re Diplock* [1948] Ch 465 the testator, Caleb Diplock, gave the residue of his property 'for such charitable institutions or other charitable or benevolent object or objects in England' as his executors should, in their absolute discretion, select. In the belief that this created a valid charitable trust, the executors distributed some £203,000 among 139 different charities. Then the next of kin challenged its validity, and as we saw in chapter 8, in *Chichester Diocesan Fund & Board of Finance* v *Simpson* [1944] AC 341, the House of Lords held the bequest void as not being exclusively for charitable purposes. The next of kin, having exhausted their remedy against the executors, claimed to recover money from the various charities. They succeeded both in a claim *in personam* (i.e., personal claim), which is not relevant to this section, and in a claim in rem (i.e., proprietary claim) which is. The personal claim was later confirmed, incidentally, on appeal to the House of Lords in *Ministry of Health* v *Simpson* [1951] AC 251.

On the proprietary claim, the Court of Appeal held that the right to trace into a mixed fund is not limited to cases where the defendant is the person who had mixed the funds. Nor does there need to be a fiduciary relationship existing as between the parties to the action (the relevance of this point will become clear in section 11.4.2.6). The right to trace is available against an innocent volunteer. This is an application of the bona fide purchaser rule discussed in section 1.4.6: a volunteer is not a purchaser, and provides no value.

There are limits to the liability of the volunteer, however. He is not treated as though he himself stood in a fiduciary relationship to the plaintiff. His duty of conscience is regarded as akin to that of a person having an equitable interest in a mixed fund towards the other equitable owners, and he is therefore allowed to claim rateably on the principles discussed earlier.

Further, the situation of the innocent volunteer who has unwittingly blended the property of another with his own is not quite the same as that of a donee of property, who is in a position simply to return the property to its rightful owner.

It seems that the volunteer is not liable to the full extent if any property purchased with the mixed fund has decreased in value, because otherwise he would be compelled to pay out of his own pocket for the mistake of the trustee who transferred the property to him in breach of trust. Nor, for the same reason, is he liable to the extent that he has spent the money on irreversible alterations to his own property, or to pay off his debts (the latter case may also be an instance in which the property has 'vanished' — see section 11.4.3). Nor is it obvious, if he purchases property with the mixed fund which increases in value, that justice requires him to share any increase, unless some allowance is made for his effort (see Hodkinson [1983] Conv 135). So, rightly or wrongly, the Court of Appeal in *Re Diplock* understood *Sinclair* v *Brougham* [1914] AC 398 as raising the position of the innocent volunteer above that of the ordinary donee of property, and on balance this result seems correct.

11.4.2.6   Situations where tracing is only possible at common law

Given that the right to trace in equity is so extensive, it may be wondered why common law tracing is still used at all. The reason is that sometimes the tracing action in equity is unavailable.

Most importantly, unlike tracing at common law, tracing in equity requires that at some stage, there must have existed a fiduciary relationship of some sort which was sufficient to give rise to an equitable proprietary right in the plaintiff. The clearest case is that of the relationship of trustee and beneficiary, so that in breach-of-trust cases there is no problem. As we saw in section 9.5, agents and bailees (and others) may also occupy a fiduciary position. A recent decision, extending the notion of a fiduciary relationship, is *Chase Manhattan Bank NA* v *Israel–British Bank (London) Ltd* [1981] Ch 105.

It is not necessary that the fiduciary relationship should precede the transaction by which the property falls into the defendant's hands. Nor need it exist between the parties to the action, so long as it originally existed. The usual authority is the important case of *Sinclair* v *Brougham* [1914] AC 398, but it also follows from *Re Diplock* [1948] Ch 465, considered above, where an action was successful against a volunteer.

If there has never been any fiduciary relationship at all, the plaintiff has no right to trace in equity. It is not enough to show that the property has somehow got into the hands of someone who is not entitled to it: in this respect, the common law right to trace is slightly wider, since no fiduciary relationship need be shown at law.

Further, even where a fiduciary relationship exists, the tracing action only protects the plaintiff's equitable property rights. In *Lister & Co.* v *Stubbs* (1890)

45 ChD 1 the defendant was a purchasing agent (i.e., a fiduciary) of the plaintiff company, and had been taking bribes secretly from a firm from whom the company bought supplies. This was a clear breach of fiduciary duty, and equally clearly the defendant would have been liable to account for all his profits in a personal action, as in the cases considered in section 9.5.

The plaintiff company was able to recover in a tracing action the part of the commissions that was still in the form of money at the time of the action, but failed to recover the part of the illicit gain that the defendant had invested in land. The Court of Appeal held that the money so invested had never been money belonging to the plaintiff company; the defendant was merely a debtor to the plaintiff for that sum. In other words, a personal but not a proprietary action lay.

11.4.2.7 Criticisms, and criticisms of criticisms

The requirement of a fiduciary relationship for a tracing action in equity leads to the possibility that a mere equitable owner may have a better action than someone who is both legal and equitable owner of property. This seems strange when one remembers that both actions can exist at the same time, but whereas a trustee owes a fiduciary duty to a beneficiary, the absolute owner owes no such duties (as legal owner) to himself (as equitable owner). Thus a beneficiary can always trace in equity — someone who is both legal and equitable owner can only do so if he can find an additional fiduciary relationship, and situations where this could occur in practice are limited.

This has provoked criticism, and it is indeed a result that is difficult to justify. The usual solution canvassed is to extend the equitable remedy, on analogy with a theory of what in other jurisdictions, e.g., the United States, is known as 'unjust enrichment', that is, a general right to recover property which has without qualification fallen into the hands of another. There also seems to be an assumption that tracing actions are a good thing.

On unjust enrichment theories there has already been comment in chapter 6. No such theory operates in English law. To eliminate the requirement of a fiduciary relationship would be to create a remedy quite different from the equitable right to trace; in effect, a new law of restitution. I have suggested already that this would be undesirable.

It is also questionable whether tracing remedies should in principle be extended. Bear in mind that they are additional to personal remedies — to lose in a tracing action may not be to lose altogether. In reality, these actions are attempts either to claim priority over the general creditors when the guilty party has become insolvent, or to find someone else who can be made to pay up. Others therefore have to pay for successful attempts, and as we have seen these others are often innocent.

It may be, therefore, that retention of the anomaly is a better solution than the alternative usually proposed.

11.4.3   Absolute limits to tracing

Finally, it should be pointed out that the right to trace will be lost in certain eventualities. Tracing will not be available if the property has ceased to be identifiable, as where it has been dissipated: the personal action remains unaffected. As noted earlier, if the property comes into the hands of a bona fide purchaser for value without notice, the beneficiaries cannot proceed against the property, and must pursue their remedy against the proceeds or against the trustee personally. And in *Re Diplock* [1948] Ch 465 it was held that the remedy of a charge upon the property will not be granted where the result would be inequitable, as where the volunteer has spent the money on alterations or improvements on his land and the imposition of a charge enforceable by sale would cause undue hardship — not to mention the practical difficulties arising where the land is, e.g., a hospital.

12

Variation of Trusts

12.1 INHERENT EQUITABLE JURISDICTION

As a general rule, as we have seen, trustees are bound to carry out the settlor's wishes, and any deviation from the terms of the trust will amount to a breach of trust. Nonetheless, circumstances may arise in which an extension of the trustees' powers, or even a substantial alteration in the beneficial interests of the trust, would be desirable in the interests of efficient administration, or for the sake of preserving the value of the beneficiaries' entitlements.

The main reason for wishing to vary trusts is to reduce liability to taxation, and that is what this chapter is really about. Yet although equity permits trustees discretion, as we have seen, in many aspects of performing the trust, it does not generally allow them to recast its terms. Until recent statutory reforms, therefore, powers to vary have been extremely limited, especially where tax planning is the motive.

There are nevertheless circumstances apart from those provided for by statute where variation is possible.

12.1.1 Express powers to vary

Obviously the trust instrument itself may have been drafted so as to confer upon the trustees powers far wider than those contemplated by the general law. Modern trust instruments generally contrive to allow the trustees considerable discretionary powers, and not uncommonly provide for variation of the beneficial interests themselves, by means of suitably drafted powers of appointment. The terms of such powers must, of course, be strictly observed, but it is often possible through careful drafting to obviate the need for recourse to more complex variation procedures. Reliance upon express powers contained in the trust instrument, needless to say, creates no exception to the duty not to deviate from the terms of the trust, for such powers are themselves among the terms of the trust.

12.1.2 *Saunders v Vautier*

In the absence of express powers, it may be possible to effect a variation in the trust by taking advantage of the rule in *Saunders* v *Vautier* (1841) 10 LJ Ch 354. Collectively, the beneficiaries, so long as they are all adult, *sui juris* and between them entitled to the entirety of the trust property, can bring the trust to an end and resettle the property on any terms they wish. Thus, in a simple settlement of property upon a life interest for X with remainder for Y, X and Y may agree to end the trust and divide the capital between them immediately. More complex settlements may require more sophisticated measures, involving perhaps the actuarial valuation of future entitlements, and possibly the need for insurance against any risk of loss, but the principles are basically the same.

They can also collectively consent to any act by the trustees which has the effect of varying the terms of the trust, without going through the process of dissolving the trust and resettling the property, which may involve a number of separate conveyances, all attracting stamp duty. It is very important, however, to appreciate the limits of the *Saunders* v *Vautier* doctrine. First, it depends on the beneficiaries all being collectively entitled. Thus, donees under a power cannot use it, and though beneficiaries under a discretionary trust actually can, they will not be able to unless the entire class of objects is ascertainable. Secondly, it turns upon all the beneficiaries being able to consent to dissolve the trust, or to what would otherwise be a breach of trust by the trustees. If some of the beneficiaries are infants, or if the settlement creates any interests in favour of persons who are not yet born or ascertained, variation of the trust upon this basis will not be possible. This is a serious limitation when dealing with family settlements of the usual type, which almost invariably give interests to non *sui juris* persons. As will appear below, this is the difficulty tackled by the Variation of Trusts Act 1958.

Thirdly, unless the trustees also agree, the beneficiaries cannot vary an existing trust, and keep it on foot, instead of dissolving it and resettling the property. *Re Brockbank* [1948] Ch 206 has already been discussed in section 9.2.4.4, and although the *ratio* of the case is confined to the appointment of new trustees under s. 36 of the Trustee Act 1925, there are remarks by Vaisey J of a much wider scope:

> It seems to me that the beneficiaries must choose between two alternatives: either they must keep the trusts of the will on foot, in which case those trusts must continue to be executed by trustees . . . not . . . arbitrarily selected by themselves; or they must, by mutual agreement, extinguish and put an end to the trusts.

Walton J expressed similar views in *Stephenson* v *Barclays Bank Ltd* [1975] 1 WLR 88. One reason may be that otherwise the beneficiaries could force upon the trustees duties quite different to those they had originally accepted.

12.1.3 Limited inherent jurisdiction of courts to vary trusts

The problem arises with persons unable to give consent, especially children and unborn persons. As will shortly be explained, the Variation of Trusts Act 1958 confers upon the court a discretion to give its approval to a proposed variation on behalf of such persons, if the court is satisfied that such a variation would be for their benefit. Before considering the effect of that Act and other statutory provisions, however, it is necessary to outline the extent to which the courts have traditionally been willing to permit a variation of trust under their inherent jurisdiction, where not all beneficiaries are adult and *sui juris*.

It has long been recognised that the court may, in the case of necessity, permit the trustees to take measures not authorised by the trust instrument. In *Chapman* v *Chapman* [1954] AC 429, the House of Lords indicated that this inherent jurisdiction is narrow, encompassing for the most part only emergency and salvage. Originally, this seems to have been confined to cases where some act of salvage was urgently required, such as the mortgage of an infant's property in order to raise money for vital repairs. Gradually, it was widened to cover other contingencies not foreseen and provided for by the settlor, but the House of Lords reaffirmed in *Chapman* v *Chapman*, unanimously approving the formulation of Romer LJ in *Re New* [1901] 2 Ch 534, that some element of emergency still needs to be shown.

Another limited situation which survived *Chapman* was where the court approved a compromise of some dispute regarding the beneficial entitlements on behalf of infant or future beneficiaries. Arguably, this is not a case of genuine variation of the trust, since by definition its terms are not clear: hence the dispute. The courts, however, had showed a willingness to extend the term 'compromise' to cover situations where no real dispute had arisen, and approval was sometimes granted to what were, in reality, mere variations worked out between the beneficiaries. This broad conception of the inherent jurisdiction was firmly disapproved by the House of Lords in *Chapman* v *Chapman*, and held to be confined to instances where a genuine element of dispute exists.

Thus, in *Re Powell-Cotton's Resettlement* [1956] 1 All ER 60, the Court of Appeal decided that there were no disputed rights where an investment clause was ambiguous and it would have been advantageous to the beneficiaries to replace it with a new clause. In *Mason* v *Farbrother* [1983] 2 All ER 1078, genuine points of difference were found to have arisen where two contending interpretations of an investment clause had widely different implications for the permitted range of investments. The court, however, was reluctant to approve the substitution of a new clause under its inherent jurisdiction, preferring to rely upon s. 57 of the Trustee Act 1925 (see section 12.2.3). In *Allen* v *Distillers Co. (Biochemicals) Ltd* [1974] QB 384, the court was asked to approve a settlement of the claims of the child victims of the drug thalidomide, and the question arose as to whether the court could postpone the vesting of capital in the children to an age greater than 18. Eveleigh J, on the basis of the rule in *Saunders* v *Vautier*, held there was no inherent jurisdiction to order such a postponement, but found it to be authorised by the terms of the settlement itself.

Clearly, therefore, the inherent equitable jurisdiction is of limited value to those whose main motive for variation is to reduce liability for taxation.

12.2 STATUTORY POWERS TO VARY TRUSTS

12.2.1 Matrimonial Causes Act 1973

The narrowness of the court's inherent jurisdiction to give approval to variations in the terms of the trust is, however, offset by several statutory provisions. A particularly useful and important addition to the jurisdiction was added by the Matrimonial Causes Act 1973, which by ss. 23 and 24 gives a wide power to make orders affecting the property of parties to matrimonial proceedings, so as to avoid the unfairness which sometimes arose where the property of a married couple, in particular the matrimonial home, came under the rules governing resulting trusts (see section 5.5). The court may order provision for either spouse to be made by payments in cash, by transfers of property, or by the creation of a settlement for the benefit of a spouse and children.

More important in the context of variation, ss. 24(1)(c) and (d) allow for variation of an ante or post-nuptial settlement, including settlements made by will or codicil, and also permit the making of an order extinguishing or reducing the interest of either of the spouses under such a settlement. The term 'settlement' has been widely interpreted to include any provision (other than outright gifts) made for the benefit of the parties to a marriage, whether by themselves or by a third party, and the acquisition of a matrimonial home has been held to be a settlement (*Ulrich* v *Ulrich* [1968] 1 WLR 180). Further, the court has the power to vary or discharge any order for a settlement or variation under s. 24(1) made on or after a decree of judicial separation, if the separation order is rescinded or the marriage subsequently dissolved.

12.2.2 Mental Health Act 1983

The power given by s. 96(1)(d) of the Mental Health Act 1983 to the Court of Protection to make a settlement of a patient's property also allows the judge to vary the settlement as he thinks fit if it transpires that some material fact was not disclosed when the settlement was made, or if substantial changes in circumstances arise. See, in general, section 3.6.

12.2.3 General powers in the 1925 legislation

The above provisions are designed to meet rather special types of situation. More general powers may be made available to trustees by virtue of provisions contained in the Trustee Act and the Settled Land Act of 1925. Section 57(1) of the Trustee Act 1925 in effect widens the inherent jurisdiction with regard to 'emergency' by making the jurisdiction available in cases where it is 'expedient'. The section operates as though its provisions were to be read into every settlement, but it is clearly limited to matters falling within the management or administration of the trust property, and does not permit the alteration of beneficial interests under the trust.

Applications under the section are usually heard in chambers and so are not generally reported, but the few reported cases show that it has been used to authorise a sale of settled chattels, to partition or sell land where necessary consents had been refused, to purchase a residence for the tenant for life, and to sell prematurely a reversionary interest.

Settlements of land do not fall within s. 57(1) of the Trustee Act 1925, but they may be varied by recourse to s. 64(1) of the Settled Land Act 1925, which allows the court to make an order authorising the tenant for life to effect any transaction affecting or concerning the settled land or any part of it, if the court is of the opinion that the transaction would be for the benefit of the settled land or any part of it, or of the persons interested under the settlement. The transaction must be one which could have been effected by an absolute owner. The section is not confined to cases of management or administration alone, although it includes such purposes, and allows alteration of the beneficial interests with a view to reducing tax liability. In the days of estate duty, the especial vulnerability of the strict settlement to onerous charges might be mitigated by rearrangement of the beneficial interests under this section.

The Settled Land and Trustee Acts (Court's General Powers) Act 1943, as amended by the Emergency Laws (Miscellaneous Provisions) Act 1953, permanently extends the court's jurisdiction to authorise the expense of any action taken in the management of settled land or land held on trust for sale in the context of ss. 57 and 64, above, to be treated as a capital outgoing where the action is beneficial and the income insufficient to bear the expense.

The inherent jurisdiction to make provision for infants is somewhat extended by s. 53 of the Trustee Act 1925, which allows the court to authorise dealings with the infant's property with a view to application of the capital or income for the infant's maintenance, education or benefit. 'Benefit' has been interpreted to cover dealings having the effect of reducing estate duty for the benefit of the infant (*Re Meux* [1958] Ch 154).

In that case, the proceeds of sale of property were to be resettled upon the infant, and so could be regarded as an 'application' for the infant's benefit. However, in *Re Hayworth's Contingent Reversionary Interest* [1956] Ch 364, a proposal to sell an infant's contingent reversionary interest to the life tenant for cash, thus ending the trusts, was thought not to be for the 'benefit' of the infant. Other types of dealing approved under the section have included the barring of

entails to exclude remote beneficiaries (*Re Gower's Settlement* [1934] Ch 365) or
to simplify a proposed application to the court for approval of a further variation
under the Variation of Trusts Act 1958 (*Re Bristol's Settled Estates* [1964] 3 All
ER 939).

12.2.4 Variation of Trusts Act 1958

The decision of the House of Lords in *Chapman* v *Chapman* [1954] AC 429
curtailed, as explained above, the broad approach previously developed by the
courts in the exercise of the inherent jurisdiction to approve compromises or
'disputes', and the Law Reform Committee was asked to consider the question of
the court's powers to sanction variations (see Law Reform Committee, Sixth
Report (Court's Power to Sanction Variations of Trusts) Cmnd 310). The
Variation of Trusts Act 1958 was based on these recommendations, and provides
a new statutory jurisdiction independent of the Trustee or Settled Land Acts.

Under s. 1(1) of the Act, the court has discretion to approve, on behalf of four
categories of person, any arrangement varying or revoking all or any of the
trusts, or enlarging the trustees' powers of management and administration over
the property subject to the trusts. Proposals to vary the beneficial interests under
a trust may thus be approved, provided that the court is satisfied that such
variation will be for the benefit of the persons on whose behalf approval is given.

In deciding whether to approve a proposed settlement, the court will consider
the arrangement as a whole, since it is the arrangement which has to be approved,
and not just those aspects of it which happen to affect a person on whose behalf
the court is being asked to consent.

12.2.4.1 Use of the 1958 Act
Where an extension of the trustee's powers of management is sought, the
jurisdiction of the Variation of Trusts Act 1958 is invoked in preference to s. 57
of the Trustee Act 1925 wherever possible. The courts have shown themselves
willing to approve the insertion of powers of advancement or a period of
accumulation, or to terminate an accumulation, among other matters.

So far as investment is concerned, the courts are now prepared to recognise
that the powers conferred by the Trustee Investments Act 1961 are becoming
outdated, and that the effects of inflation and the character of the trust may
amount to special circumstances in which it would be proper to give approval
under the 1958 Act (see *Trustees of the British Museum* v *Attorney-General* [1984]
1 WLR 418).

The main application of the Variation of Trusts Act 1958 has been to vary the
beneficial interests for tax-saving purposes, and this has been assumed to be its
natural sphere of operation. Some would argue that those who, like infants and
the unborn, cannot give a valid consent to schemes which would be for their
benefit, should not be deprived of the advantages which their adult counterparts

could obtain on *Saunders* v *Vautier* principles; nor should their incapacity prevent the opportunity of gain to the trust as a whole.

As will appear in section 13.5, however, the extent to which worthwhile tax savings will continue to be available through reorganisation of the beneficial interests has been reduced, but not entirely negated, by the replacement of estate duty by capital transfer tax (inheritance tax). On the other hand, as appears in section 13.5.5, there is still scope for the use of the 1958 Act to reduce liability to CTT (inheritance tax), and indeed the volume of applications under the Act may actually increase in future years.

12.2.4.2 *Persons on whose behalf the court may give its approval*

The way in which the Variation of Trusts Act 1958 works is to allow the court to give consent on behalf of non *sui juris* beneficiaries, but the principles underlying the rule in *Saunders* v *Vautier* were preserved by the Act, inasmuch as the court will not provide a consent which ought properly to be sought from an ascertainable adult, *sui juris* beneficiary.

The categories of person on whose behalf consent may be given are set out in s. 1. They include infants and other people who are not capable of assenting by reason of incapacity (e.g., those who used to be called lunatics) and unborn persons, so long as the proposed arrangement would be for their benefit. Beneficiaries under protective discretionary trusts are also included: in the last case the statute does not expressly require that a benefit be shown.

The application should be made by a beneficiary, preferably by the person currently receiving the income, but the settlor may also apply, and as a last resort the trustees may apply if no one else will apply and the variation is in the interests of the beneficiaries. Otherwise, it is undesirable for trustees to apply, as their position as applicant may conflict with their duty impartially to guard the interests of the beneficiaries. The settlor, if living, and all the beneficiaries, including minors, should be made parties, special attention being paid to ensure proper representation for minors and the unborn.

12.2.4.3 *What is benefit?*

The Variation of Trusts Act 1958 requires that the court must, in general, be satisfied that the arrangement will be for the benefit of the persons for whom it is consenting, considered as individuals and not merely as members of a class (*Re Cohen's ST* [1965] 1 WLR 1229). The requirement does not extend expressly to a variation proposed on behalf of a beneficiary under a discretionary protective trust, but the court has an unfettered discretion as to the exercise of its powers under the Act, and in *Re Steed's WT* [1960] Ch 407 (considered below) the Court of Appeal refused its consent in even such a case, where it thought no benefit was shown.

12.2.4.3.1 *Nature of benefit* It is not possible to state clear definitions of what

the courts will regard as benefit, except that it will adopt the test of what a reasonable *sui juris* adult beneficiary would have done in the circumstances. No rigid rules seem to apply, however.

Financial benefit is clearly included, and most tax-saving schemes will satisfy the requirement, since such saving preserves the total quantum of property available for distribution among the beneficiaries.

In assessing financial benefit, the court may have to balance short-term against long-term factors, and take account of the character of the persons on whose behalf approval is sought. Thus, the court may approve a proposal which is to the financial disadvantage of a beneficiary in the short term if long-term advantages may result. In *Re Towler's ST* [1964] Ch 158, Wilberforce J was prepared to postpone the vesting of capital to which a beneficiary was soon to become entitled, upon evidence that she was likely to deal with it imprudently. In *Re Steed's WT* [1960] Ch 407, the proposed scheme was for the elimination of the protective element in a trust relating to land. The principal beneficiary, who was a life tenant (but not *sui juris* because of the protective element), wanted a variation such that the trustees held the property on trust for herself absolutely. Clearly this was in theory to her financial advantage, but evidence suggested that advantage would in fact be taken of the life tenant's good nature by the very persons against whose importuning the settlor had meant to protect her, and the Court of Appeal refused its consent. As noted above, there is no express statutory requirement of benefit in such a case.

But financial benefit alone, even if clear, may not be sufficient. In *Re Weston's Settlements* [1969] 1 Ch 223, the Court of Appeal refused to approve a scheme which would have removed the trusts to a tax haven (Jersey) on the ground that the moral and social benefits of an English upbringing were not outweighed by the tax savings to be enjoyed by the infant beneficiaries (the court will not always refuse approval to the removal of a trust from the jurisdiction: see *Re Windeatt's WT* [1969] 1 WLR 692).

Another possibility is that some beneficiaries will benefit at the expense of others. An example is *Re Remnant's ST* [1970] Ch 560, where Pennycuick J approved the deletion of a forfeiture clause in respect of children who became Roman Catholics. Some of the children were Protestant and others Roman Catholic, but the court deleted the clause on policy grounds, as being liable to cause serious dissensions within the family, although this was clearly to the disadvantage of the Protestant children. The settlor's intentions were also not considered conclusive (indeed, they were overridden).

The courts may go further and approve schemes where there is only a positive disadvantage in material terms. In *Re CL* [1969] 1 Ch 587, the Court of Protection held that there was a benefit to an elderly mental patient in giving up, in return for no consideration, her life interests for the benefit of adopted daughters. The lady's needs were otherwise amply provided for, and the court, in approving the arrangement, was acting as she herself would have done, had she been able to appreciate her family responsibilities.

These cases are instructive with regard to the courts' understanding of what constitutes a 'benefit', but they should not be regarded as typical. Assuming that a proposed arrangement is otherwise unobjectionable, it will be rare for the court to look beyond the financial advantages contained therein.

12.2.4.3.2 Risks Sometimes, a proposed arrangement may involve some element of risk to the beneficiary for whom the court is asked to consent. Similar factors apply to those above. Thus an element of risk will not prevent the court from approving the arrangement, if the risk is one which an adult beneficiary would be prepared to take. Such a test was applied by Danckwerts J in *Re Cohen's WT* [1959] 1 WLR 865 (*not* to be confused with *Re Cohen's ST* — see section 12.2.4.3.3) where the beneficiary was an infant. Another example is *Re Robinson's ST* [1976] 1 WLR 806. The plan was to divide up a fund held on a life interest in favour of a lady of 55, with provision for the fund to be divided upon her death among her three children, one of whom was an infant at the time of the application. The dividend would give each child a share which was less than he or she would have received had the mother died immediately. It was calculated, however, that, given the mother's life expectancy, the deficiency would be made up. Templeman J took the view that the court should require evidence that the infant would at least not be materially worse off as a result of the variation: a 'broad' view might be taken, but not a 'galloping, gambling view'. The arrangement was approved subject to a policy of insurance to protect the infant's interests.

12.2.4.3.3 Chances of being born at a given time disregarded A problem can arise in the case of unborn persons, however. In *Re Cohen's ST* [1965] 1 WLR 1229, the life tenant wished to substitute a specified date (30 June 1973) for the vesting of her grandchildren's interests, rather than her own death, with a view to saving estate duty. It was unlikely that the lady would live beyond 30 June 1973. The alteration might have affected the number of grandchildren who might have become entitled. Assuming, as was likely, she died before that date, any grandchild who might be born between her death and 30 June 1973 would clearly benefit (because under the unvaried scheme such a person would receive nothing, whereas he or she would share under the varied scheme). But Stamp J refused to take this possibility into account.

My mind recoils at the idea of the unborn having prior to his birth such an identity as to enable the court to ascribe to him any such chance, or to enable one to say that he can more or less easily satisfy a condition of coming into existence during some particular period.

So an unborn person's chances of being born at a particular time are not taken into account. Chances are only ascribed to persons once they have become legal entities, even though that time may be still in the future.

On the other hand in *Re Holt's Settlement* [1969] 1 Ch 100, if a child was born next year, and his mother died very soon afterwards, that child could not possibly benefit. *Re Cohen's ST* [1965] 1 WLR 1229 was distinguished, however, because here two chances had to occur: that of the unborn person being born next year, and secondly, that child having been born (and thus become a legal entity), his or her mother dying shortly afterwards. The first chance was disregarded on *Cohen* principles, but not the second. Both were independently unlikely possibilities, so approval for the scheme was given.

12.2.4.4   Variation or resettlement?

 According to Megarry J in *Re Ball's Settlement* [1968] 1 WLR 899, the courts will not approve a proposal for a total resettlement which alters completely the substratum of the trust. This is a question of substance not form.

12.2.4.5   Juristic basis of variation

The precise effect of the court giving its approval to an arrangement is not entirely clear. Does it merely provide consent or does the order of the court actually vary the trusts?

In *Re Holmden's ST* [1968] AC 685, Lord Reid stated that the arrangement must be regarded as one made by the beneficiaries themselves, the court acting merely on behalf of those beneficiaries who are unable to give their own consent and approval. On this view of the matter, it seems that the adult beneficiaries at least ought to give their consents in writing so as to comply with s. 53(1)(c) of the Law of Property Act 1925.

There are two points to note about these remarks, however:

(a)   The remarks do not form part of the *ratio* of the case, since this issue did not in fact arise.

(b)   We saw in section 12.1.2 that even where all beneficiaries are *sui juris* and consenting they may not be able to vary the trusts in all circumstances. This would not necessarily be a problem if the jurisdiction under the Act was regarded as being in the form of a revocation and resettlement, rather than a variation.

In fact, however, variations are seldom in writing. In *Re Viscount Hambledon's ST* [1960] 1 WLR 82, it had been stated that the court's approval was effective for all purposes to vary the trusts, and this has been relied upon in countless subsequent instances. The problem was posed directly in *Re Holt's Settlement* [1969] 1 Ch 100, considered in section 12.2.4.3.3, where Megarry J, aware that possibly thousands of variations had been acted upon without writing conforming with s. 53(1)(c), accepted, though without enthusiasm, two grounds put forward by counsel in favour of the view that no writing was necessary.

First, it might be said that in conferring express power upon the court to make an order, Parliament had impliedly created an exception to s. 53. Secondly and alternatively, the arrangement might be regarded as one in which the beneficial interests passed to their respective purchasers upon the making of the agreement, that agreement itself being specifically enforceable. The original interests under the (unvaried) trusts would thus be held, from the moment of the agreement, upon constructive trusts identical to the new (varied) trusts and, as constructive trusts, would be exempt from writing under s. 53(2). Whether or not these reasons are regarded as adequate, the assumption that no writing is required has continued to prevail.

Inevitably, of course, the arrangement will be contained in some documentary form, even if insufficient for the purposes of s. 53. The order of the court may itself be subject to stamp duty.

13

Trusts and Taxation

13.1 INTRODUCTION

In the preceding chapters, reference has frequently been made to the importance of tax considerations in the creation and administration of trusts. It is impossible here to offer a detailed account of the tax structure in the United Kingdom, and since changes occur almost annually, little purpose is served by attempting too much in a book of this nature.

A broad indication of the ways in which taxation impinges upon trusts at the present time will therefore be given, though it should be noted that charities enjoy certain advantages (see above, section 8.2.1). For detailed treatement, the reader is referred to specialist works such as A.R. Mellows, *Taxation for Executors and Trustees*, 5th ed. (London: Butterworths, 1981) or *Sumption and Lawton's Tax and Tax Planning*, 10th ed., by A. Sumption and G. Clarke (London: Oyez Longman, 1982).

13.1.1 Tension between settlors and Parliament

The advantages of trusts in tax planning have been appreciated by settlors since the earliest practices of putting land into uses to avoid feudal dues (see chapter 1). They have also been appreciated by successive governments in the 20th century, who have attacked trusts vigorously through a succession of legislative provisions.

The most significant recent blow was the introduction of capital transfer tax (CTT), which struck at gifts made during the settlor's lifetime as well as at his death. The tax was part of a strategy which was to have included also a wealth tax, although this has not as yet materialised. In its inception, it produced a major disincentive to the creation of *inter vivos* trusts, since the settlor himself became immediately liable to tax, but it became recognised that certain types of family trust, such as accumulation and maintenance settlements, could still offer advantages if properly planned and kept within relatively modest bounds. There was also some amelioration of the initial rigours of the tax. Its main impact (no doubt intended) was a reduction in opportunity for tax saving, and some modification of tax planning. The conventional wisdom of aiming to spread taxable income and wealth still held, however, inasmuch as liability remained greatest among the highest concentrations of income and capital funds. In any event, many of the rigours of capital transfer tax have been reduced by its replacement in 1986 by inheritance tax (see 13.5.6).

13.1.2 Taxes which affect trusts

Apart from incidental liabilities affecting particular forms of trust property, such as rates, settlors and trustees are chiefly affected by income tax, capital gains tax (CGT) and CTT (inheritance tax). Another tax which affects many *inter vivos* settlements is stamp duty, and since this has often been referred to in earlier chapters, a short description is given here.

13.2 STAMP DUTY

Stamp duty derives from the Stamp Act 1891 and is a tax payable only upon certain classes of document, including conveyance or transfers operating as voluntary dispositions, including settlements which are voluntary or made for less than full consideration.

Duty is assessed according to the value of the property transferred (*ad valorem*) and may constitute a significant additional cost in the creation of a trust of valuable property (the rate is currently 1%, or ½% on shares from 1986, having been reduced from 2% by the Finance Act 1984). It only applies to transfers exceeding £30,000 (except shares), but on transactions over that amount the whole transfer value (i.e., not just the excess over £30,000) is stampable. This is one reason, incidentally, why private houses are never sold for an amount just over £30,000.

No stamp duty is payable on a will or grant of representation, so testamentary trusts escape this tax. Declarations of trust upon marriage are specifically exempt. Since only documents are stampable, duty can also be avoided where it is possible to create the trust by oral declaration alone. As was shown in section 3.5, however, settlors have had little success in avoiding duty by this means. Although a trust of personalty can be declared orally, the transfer to the trustees of such property as land or shares will involve stampable transfers. In any event, trustees may well refuse to act upon undocumented verbal declarations. The possibility of using audio or video recordings remains untested.

Duty may become payable not only at the beginning but also during the continuance of the trust, as where the trustees switch the investments. Duty will be paid upon each purchase of shares, but as this duty ranks as part of their acquisition costs for CGT purposes, some of it can be effectively reclaimed on resale. Other occasions requiring a stamped document will be the appointment or retirement of trustees, and the transfer of assets from old to new trustees. Documents affecting only bare legal title without altering beneficial entitlement carry only a fixed duty of 50p, however, and only this rate will be payable on such transactions. The termination of a trust upon which beneficiaries become absolutely entitled will be similarly free from the *ad valorem* duty, as only the bare legal title is transferred, but where the termination is by way of a rearrangement of the beneficial interests, the document altering the interests will be stampable.

The duty must be paid within 30 days of the execution of the document by presenting it at a stamping office of the Inland Revenue, where the stamp showing the amount of duty paid is impressed on the document. A fixed penalty plus interest on the unpaid duty is charged on documents stamped out of time, but the real sanction for failure to stamp a stampable document is that it will not be admitted to evidence in any legal proceedings or accepted for registration by any registrar. Trustees must therefore ensure that all stampable trust documents bear the correct stamp.

13.3 INCOME TAX

A trust is liable to pay income tax rather as if it were a person, except of course that it cannot claim the personal allowances available to individuals. The trustees must deduct and account for the tax due on investments, such as land or any trade carried on by the trust, but usually need take no action in relation to income from Stock Exchange investments, as this is generally paid with tax already deducted. If the income is then paid over to a beneficiary, he will be responsible for paying any greater amount or making a claim for any refund which may be due in the light of his own personal tax liability.

Trusts pay income tax at the basic rate, currently 29%, regardless of the size of the fund. There are important exceptions, however. Trusts where there is no interest in possession, of which the most important are discretionary trusts and trusts for accumulation, are liable to the additional rate of 15%. These types of trust call for special comment: see section 13.6.

Where one of the aims of the settlement is to reduce the income tax liability of the settlor by spreading his wealth, it is important to ensure that he divests himself of his entire interest. The strategy of fiscal legislation has been to presume the income of a trust to be that of a settlor, and even a tenuous connection with the trust may result in its income being deemed to be that of the settlor.

If trustees have a discretion as to who shall receive income, children and others with no significant personal income are an obvious choice, since their liability to tax will be minimal. Some children's settlements are set up mainly to reduce the tax liability of high-earning settlors. But there are traps: should the trustees make income payments to or for the benefit of an unmarried infant child of the settlor, the income will be treated as that of the settlor, so increasing his personal liability. The usual solution is the 'granny trust', where grandchildren, rather than children, benefit.

Other traps for the unwary or badly advised settlor include connections with the trust arising through settlement of the shares of the family company, and the retention of any option over the trust assets, as in *Vandervell* v *IRC* [1967] 2 AC 291 (see section 3.5).

Income tax considerations may therefore exert a significant effect upon the way in which trustees exercise their discretions, both in regard to any power to select the objects of income distribution and in the policy of the trust dealings with any family business.

13.4 CAPITAL GAINS TAX

CGT was introduced by the Finance Act 1965, and is presently charged at 30%. As its name implies, this tax is charged upon the increase in value of an asset between the date when it was acquired and the date of its disposal. It applies not only to the sale of assets but also to gifts, which includes settlements. The tax affects only assets of value, and not cash payments.

There are a number of exemptions which at present include an annual exemption for gains to a trust up to half of that permitted to an individual, dated gilt-edged securities when held for at least one year, and a chattel worth less than £3,000. Most of the types of property commonly held by trustees are affected by the tax, however, and the possibilities for avoidance are limited.

Upon creating the trust, the settlor is deemed to be making a disposal of the entire settled property at its market value, and may therefore be liable to CGT upon that disposal. Some amelioration can be obtained by careful consideration of the precise nature of the property to be settled, for example, by selling loss-making assets prior to the settlement in order to create an allowable loss to carry forward to set against chargeable gains and then settling the cash proceeds free of CGT.

It has also been possible since 1980 to reduce liability by virtue of holding over (the relevant provisions now are contained in s. 78 of the Finance Act 1981 and s. 82 of the Finance Act 1982). These provisions apply essentially to gifts, and therefore trusts, such that, if both donor and donee agree, the donor's capital gain can be held over so that the donee is treated as acquiring the property at the value it had when the donor originally acquired it. This means that the donor need pay no CGT but, of course, the donee will be liable to pay more when he in turn disposes of the property.

The usual reason for holding over is that unlike a sale no cash will be obtained for a gift and thus any CGT payable will have to come out of the remainder of the donor's assets. Holding over allows payment to be postponed until there is an ultimate sale of the property. The provisions will also be advantageous if the donee has allowable losses to set against CGT but the donor does not, or the donee can bring himself within the annual exemption whereas the donor cannot (because he has other gains).

During the continuance of the settlement the trustees will be responsible for CGT on any particular assets which they realise in the course of administering the trust, and this will affect any gain realised in the course of changing investments. There are also certain occasions on which a disposal is deemed to have been made so that liability to CGT arises.

Until the Finance Act 1971 a disposal was deemed to occur on the death of a life tenant but this has now been changed. This is now one circumstance in which there is no liability to CGT.

A charge to CGT will still arise if a life interest terminates otherwise than by the death of the life tenant, however, and here the trustees are treated as having disposed of the property and immediately reacquired it. They must account for tax on any gain since the fund was acquired but, of course, the notional reacquisition will be at the new, higher value, so reducing the gap for the next occasion upon which a charge to CGT arises.

CGT is charged whenever a person becomes absolutely entitled as against the trustees, and this includes the case where a beneficiary becomes absolutely entitled upon fulfilling a condition, for example, reaching his majority, or when an advancement is made to him. The trustees are deemed to have disposed of the whole fund and must account for tax on any gains over the base value of the assets of the fund. Such matters may have to be borne in mind where any variation of the interests under a trust is contemplated.

Once all the beneficiaries have become absolutely entitled as against the trustees, so that the trustees are bare trustees, an actual transfer of assets to the beneficiary is not a chargeable disposal. If the trustees have to realise assets for this purpose, the beneficiary and not the trust is chargeable for any gain and can take advantage of the more generous exemptions for small gains available to individuals.

Discretionary trusts are slightly worse hit by CGT than other types of trust for as well as the liability which arises at the outset, and where assets are realised during the continuance of the trust, there will almost inevitably be liability to CGT on termination as by definition this cannot be due to the death of a life tenant.

13.5 INHERITANCE (CAPITAL TRANSFER) TAX

13.5.1 History of the tax

Though the history of capital transfer tax is obviously of no interest today for tax planners, it is necessary to describe it briefly to explain many of the cases where the trusts were constituted before 1975. CTT is renamed inheritance tax from 1986.

Originally intended as part of a major restructuring of taxation, CTT was brought into operation by the Finance Act 1975, with retroactive effect from

26 March 1974. One of its purposes was to replace estate duty, which was the only tax on private capital then in existence and was originally payable only on property passing upon a death.

As an inevitable consequence, therefore, it could be avoided by giving away one's property before death. In an attempt to prevent circumvention, the legislature countered by extending the ambit of the tax to gifts made within a certain period prior to death, which by 1968 was seven years.

In fact, however, the tax was frequently avoided, not only upon the death of the donor, but also upon the death of the recipients, by the creation *inter vivos* of a discretionary trust while the settlor still retained comparative youth and good health. A discretionary trust was necessary, since it had long been held that estate duty was payable on the entire fund on the death of a life tenant or holder of some other limited interest. Discretionary beneficiaries own no part of the fund, however, and so escaped.

The Finance Act 1969 attempted to catch these trusts by imposing a charge upon the death of any beneficiary who had received payments of *income* during the previous seven years. The tax planner's reply was to empower trustees to make payments of *capital*. In short, estate duty was little more than a voluntary tax, and its replacement no surprise.

The effect of the 1986 Finance Bill is that for out-and-out gifts the position reverts to one similar to that which obtained before 1974. Discretionary trusts in general are not directly affected, though the new Bill may render them largely redundant.

13.5.2   Inheritance (capital transfer) tax

Inheritance tax is a most complicated tax which operates upon capital transfers whether on death or *inter vivos* (so as to catch estate duty avoiders) and it is designed to tax family capital at least once a generation. Only its effect upon trusts is considered here, but it should be appreciated that the tax is imposed upon 'transfers of value' made after 26 March 1974. The position for trusts is generally unaffected by the Finance Bill 1986 (see section 13.5.6).

A transfer of value occurs where a person makes a disposition which reduces the value of his estate, and the tax is calculated on the amount by which that estate is diminished. It is levied on two scales, the first applicable to transfers on death and within three years of death, and the second to all others. The rate of this second category is at present half that of the first. Further, the rates which will apply to any particular gift are calculated by reference to the total of gifts made during the previous 7 years (reduced from 10 in 1986), so that the more the settlor gives away, the harder the tax bites.

There is therefore some disincentive to settle property even in one's lifetime (though because of the differential rates, this is still preferable to a settlement on death), and any settlement requires careful planning in the light of the settlor's personal history of giving. The tax has by no means killed off the trust as a tax-saving device, however.

In the first place, many people today enjoy high income but little capital and, as we saw in section 13.3, saving of income tax can still be accomplished by, e.g. the 'granny trust'. Secondly, even where large amounts of capital are involved, the avoidance of the higher rates payable on death may be worth the immediate outlay. Also, there are lower threshold limits on amounts transferred, below which no inheritance tax is payable on either scale, so that if A settles some of his estate now and survives for 7 years, both the *inter vivos* transfer and that on death may be below the minimum threshold. On the other hand, had the entire settlement been delayed until death, the amount might have been sufficient to attract inheritance tax liability. There are also certain limited exemptions to liability to inheritance tax.

The effect of the tax upon a trust depends upon whether or not there is an interest in possession under the settlement. Discretionary trusts were originally hard hit but this has been partially ameliorated.

13.5.3   Settlements where there is an interest in possession

The basic principle is that where a beneficiary has an interest in possession, he is regarded as owning the entirety of the settled property absolutely, and not merely the value of his own interest therein (usually a life interest).

This principle is necessary because when a life tenant dies his interest totally disappears. It therefore no longer has any taxable value, and were the life tenant not taxed on the value of the entire settled estate there would be nothing to tax him on. No tax would ever be paid on settled estates and funds were that so. In fact, however, the principle leads to potentially grievous tax consequences.

For example, when a life tenant in possession dies, he is treated as having made a transfer of the entire value of the settled property immediately before his death, and the rate of tax payable is calculated on the basis of his personal history of giving. If, on the other hand, he sells his interest during his lifetime, the price he will be able to obtain for his limited interest will naturally be less than the full value of the entire settled fund. This then is treated as if he had made a gift of the remainder of the fund. Prior to the sale, he was regarded as owning the whole fund; after the sale, he owns only the price which he received for his interest. Therefore, he is treated as having given away the rest of the fund, and tax will be charged on the value of the imaginary 'gift'. The same seems to apply where he gives his interest away or it comes to an end under the terms of the original settlement.

On the other hand, it also follows that, if the limited interest terminates due to the beneficiary becoming absolutely entitled to the settled property, there will be no charge to tax, since he was already the notional owner.

The principle also has a converse, which is that the reversioner is treated as owning nothing. Thus if X settles property on his wife for life, remainder to his daughter, the daughter is free to transfer her reversionary interest, to her own children, for example, during the lifetime of the wife, with no inheritance tax consequences because at that time she is treated as owning nothing.

There is also an exception to the principle. Thus, generally, no charge to tax arises if an interest in possession comes to an end and reverts to the settlor or his or her spouse or widow or widower (e.g., in 'granny trusts', there is usually a provision for the property to result to the settlor if any of the children dies).

Although the tax is calculated by reference to the personal history of the beneficiary, the tax is payable out of the trust property itself and responsibility for payment rests with the trustees.

13.5.4   Settlements where there is no interest in possession

The provisions applicable to discretionary trusts have been somewhat modified by the Finance Act 1982. Broadly, two situations must be considered.

First, there is an 'exit' charge imposed on any part of the funds which cease to be settled (i.e., are paid out), and this applies where a payment of capital is made to a beneficiary (unless this payment can be treated as income for income tax purposes in the hands of the beneficiary) and also where the trustees convert the settlement into one having an interest in possession or into a settlement for accumulation and maintenance.

Secondly, to meet the possibility that trustees will delay distributing the capital until the last moment permissible under the perpetuity rules, thereby avoiding the 'exit charge' for as long as possible, tax is charged once every 10 years anyway (called the periodic or decennial charge).

Different rates apply to the two kinds of charge, both being based on the lower 'lifetime' rate. The rules for calculating the tax incorporate the personal history of the settlor and the trust itself, and are extremely complex.

13.5.5   Capital Transfer Tax Act 1984, section 142

The introduction of CTT left many trusts created with estate duty in mind stranded by the new provisions, and a period of grace for trustees to alter disadvantageous settlements was permitted (e.g., to vary the trusts under the Variation of Trusts Act 1958, discussed in chapter 12). This has now passed, but it is likely that for some time to come those entitled under a testamentary trust will wish to take advantage of the provision introduced by the Finance Act 1978, s. 68, and now re-enacted in s. 142 of the 1984 Act, permitting beneficiaries under a will or intestacy to vary in writing the provisions of the will, or disclaim or transfer a legacy. An individual can act to improve his tax position, or the beneficiaries can collectively rewrite the will. Such variations attract neither inheritance tax nor CGT and take effect as if made by the deceased. Where the original will contains trusts which are disadvantageous from a tax standpoint, these provisions may prove valuable. The variation must be carried out within two years of the death of the testator and may require the sanction of the court under the Variation of Trusts Act 1958. Trustees should therefore be prepared to act promptly.

There are also other similar reliefs provided by ss. 143 and 144 of the Capital Transfer Tax Act 1984.

13.5.6   1986 Budget

The Finance Bill 1986, based on the 1986 Budget proposals, radically affects CTT. In many ways, the position reverts to that which obtained before 1974.

The most important change is the abolition of CTT on out-and-out lifetime gifts to individuals. But no retention of benefit will be allowed by the donor, so the advantages will not normally affect discretionary trusts. In many such trusts the settlor retains a discretionary beneficial interest, and this will be regarded as a retention of benefit (it has not been up to now). These will be subject to what is notionally a new tax, as CTT is being renamed inheritance tax..

Another change is the reduction in the cumulation period from ten years to seven. In effect, therefore, as before 1974, out-and-out gifts (with no benefit reserved to the donor) will be exempt from tax if made seven years or more before death. There will be a sliding scale on gifts from three to seven years before death (in four equal 20% steps), and the full amount will be payable on gifts up to three years before death.

Further, transfers to accumulation and maintenance trusts, described in the next section, will be regarded as an out-and-out transfer, so similarly transfers into such trusts more than seven years before death of the donor will escape tax liability. The same will apply to bare trusts.

13.6   SPECIAL CONSIDERATIONS: DISCRETIONARY TRUSTS AND TRUSTS FOR ACCUMULATION AND MAINTENANCE

Although discretionary trusts suffered badly from the introduction of CTT, it is still possible to have the advantages of this kind of trust so long as they are kept to a modest size. Even with the additional rate of 15% it may still be cheaper to accumulate income in a trust than in the hands of a settlor, and the trustees can select the beneficiaries with regard to their personal income tax liability. Where the property available for settlement consists of a family business, it may be possible to arrange matters so that profits pay income tax rather than corporation tax, or to obtain earned income relief for beneficiaries engaged in managing the business. For the majority of settlors, however, discretionary trusts are unattractive today.

Protective trusts, on the other hand, are less harshly treated by CTT (inheritance tax), inasmuch as there will be no charge to CTT (inheritance tax) where the protected life interest is terminated by forfeiture and not by death. The life interest is treated as continuing during the discretionary trusts which thus arise. The desirability of this type of trust will depend on the circumstances of the individual case.

Accumulation and maintenance settlements (infant settlements) continue to be popular. The settlor may reduce his own income tax liability, so long as the income is accumulated and not paid to his unmarried infant child. For this reason, as we have seen, such settlements are often made for the benefit of grandchildren. Inheritance tax will not be payable so long as the transfer into trust is made at least 7 years before the death of the settlor.

The favourable treatment accorded to these trusts is premised on the view that they are made to benefit minors so that although in principle accumulations can be made for older people, the tax privileges are fully available only where the beneficiaries will be entitled by the age of 25 at the latest. The trust will cease to qualify 25 years after its creation, unless all the beneficiaries are the grandchildren of a common grandparent, after which tax will become chargeable.

Index